MAIN-COURSE
SOUPS
& STEWS

Also by Dorothy Ivens

Glorious Stew
Pâtés & Other Marvelous Meat Loaves
Casseroles
Beautiful Soup
Great Dinners with Less Meat

MAIN-COURSE SOUPS & STEWS

Dorothy Ivens

1817

HARPER & ROW, PUBLISHERS, New York

Cambridge, Philadelphia, San Francisco, London

Mexico City, São Paulo, Sydney

Grateful acknowledgment is made for permission to reprint:

Recipes for "Five Fragrances Beef," "Jade-Green Broccoli," "Pickled Sweet and Sour Vegetables," and "Stewed Shin Beef, Peking Style" from *Jim Lee's Chinese Cookbook* by Jim Lee. Copyright © 1968 by Jim Lee. By permission of Harper & Row, Publishers, Inc.

Adapted recipe for "Abbacchio alla Ciociara" from *The Pleasures of Italian Cooking* by Romeo Salta. Copyright © Romeo Salta 1962. Reprinted by permission of Macmillan Publishing Company.

FIRST EDITION

Designer: C. Linda Dingler

Library of Congress Cataloging in Publication Data

Ivens, Dorothy.
  Main-course soups & stews.

  Includes index.
  1. Soups. 2. Stews. I. Title. II. Title: Main-course soups and stews.
TX757.I84 1983   641.8'13   83–47536
ISBN 0–06–015131–5

83 84 85 86 87 10 9 8 7 6 5 4 3 2 1

for Kate and John

CONTENTS

II. FISH AND SEAFOOD SOUPS AND STEWS

5. Chowders and Gumbos

6. Soup-Stews

III. STEWS

7. Beef

12. Vegetable

Suggested Accompaniments

For page numbers, consult index starting on page 329.

Appetizers, Sauces and Dips

Chinese Pickles
Curry Condiments
Deviled Eggs
Dip for Corn Chips
Hors d'Oeuvre Variés
Hummus
Pâté de Foie de Volaille
Pierre Franey's Harissa
Seviche
Sour Cream and Dill Dip
Sour Cream and Horseradish
   Sauce
Tapas

Soups

Avgolemono Soup
Orange Soup (also see
   desserts)

Vegetable Dishes

Chinese Broccoli
Chinese Green Beans
Garbanzo Bean Casserole
Ginger Corn
Lemon Rice
Purée of Broccoli
Ratatouille
Risotto alla Milanese
Sweet-Sour Cucumbers

Salads

Orange, Cucumber, and
   Scallion Salad
Salade Savoyarde
Suggestions for Salads with
   Fruit (not dessert)
Cucumber and Yogurt Salad

Breads

Bruschetta
Popovers
Spinach and Cheese Puffs

Desserts

Avocado Dessert
Baked Apples
Caramel Custard
Chocolate Almond Mousse
Chocolate Mousse
Frozen Banana Dessert
Fruit Crisp
Gingerbread
Lemon Granita
Lemon Mousse
Lemon-Walnut Cake
Lime Snow
Melon, Pear, and Cucumber
  Mélange
Orange Cake
Orange Rice
Orange Soup (as dessert or
  soup dish)
Peach Ice Cream
Pears in Madeira
Pears in Red Wine
Sangría
Triple Sec Pears
Zabaglione

Preface

When thinking back over some of our most memorable meals, we all recall certain dishes that were so gratifying, so fragrant and pleasing that their recollection sends us right to our cookbook shelf in search of a recipe that promises to duplicate that pleasurable experience. Meals that feature hearty soups or stews never fail to come to mind when I conjure up those magical occasions, and it was with this longing in mind that I set out to write this cookbook.

Travelers in particular are bound to recall many a steaming bowl from coastal places, where fruits of the sea are made into soups far too fabulous to be anything but a main course. Inland, too, soups remind one of happy times—hearty and warming meals by the hearth in the winter, fresh and light with garden vegetables in the summer. This country also has its share of famous main-course soups to match the bouillabaisses and minestrones of Europe; from the cioppinos of the West Coast to the gumbos of the South, our soups have long been a reflection of our varied cuisines.

When it comes to fish and seafood, soups and stews are so hard to tell apart I often call them soup-stews. These are splendid dishes, glamorous and elegant, if you want to present them that way, or just plain delicious for the family for whom nothing is too good.

Gumbos are the perfect example of a soup that is a meal in itself. A product of French, Spanish, and Indian cuisines, this pride of Louisiana kitchens gets its name from the African word for okra—*quingômbo,* although not all gumbos have okra in them. Okra acts as a thickener, and if okra is not used, the soup is subtly thickened with filé, which is powdered sassafras, an ancient Choctaw Indian touch. Okra is cooked with the soup, filé is stirred in after the cooking, just before serving.

The last section of the book is devoted to stews—the French daubes, the Texan short ribs, the Hungarian oxtail, the blanquettes and navarins, the Irish stews and Portuguese stews; the good sausage-based stews, Italian and Spanish; the chicken curries and fricassees; Brunswick stew from the south; even duck and rabbit stews and ratatouille and all the other good vegetable stews. Served with wine and country bread, they are good the first day and better the second, and they give body to the repertoire of cooks everywhere.

Main-Course Soups and Stews expands upon the marvelous theme that I explored in my first cookbook, *Glorious Stew.* It encompasses a wide variety of international recipes: some are old favorites that I've adapted from *Glorious Stew;* others are new and original. Almost all reflect a trend toward greater use of vegetables and less reliance on red meats for both health and financial reasons.

The beginning chapter details the ingredients, equipment, and techniques that will make soup and stew making second nature. As with the move from meats to less expensive ingredients, my recipes are inclined toward ingredients that are easy to obtain and leftovers that are a blessing to put to use.

In addition to the soups and stews, you'll find recipes for suggested accompaniments, from salads, appetizers, and dips to quick desserts, as well as wines to partner each meal. The suggestions are meant not only to help with the everlasting problem of what else to serve, once the main course is established, but also to give you a sense of the dish—whether something moist or dry is needed with it; whether or not a salad is required; what would be the most suitable starchy accompaniment, if any; and what to drink with it. At least two wines are suggested to complement the dish; sometimes tea is the thing—or beer.

Serving meals in courses conjures up visions of elegant preparation, servants in white gloves ladling soup into wide, shallow bowls, followed by a sherbet to clear the palate. But a course can be as simple as a green vegetable or salad served alone, a pasta dish to stretch a lighter course, or a tray of cheeses at the end of the meal. This book will help you design meals and learn how to orchestrate them around satisfying soups and stews.

I have tried to suggest simple accompaniments, so the focus is on the soup or stew. That is where most of the effort should go; the rest is the chorus line, essential but subsidiary. The suggestions given also take into account the need to have everything ready at the same time. Some can be store-bought, others are easy to make and can be made ahead or their cooking is coordinated with the rest of the meal. Some old favorites are back in style with a new twist; some, once too difficult, are now made easy with a food processor. (See suggested accompaniments after the contents.)

Quick these meals are not, but if the preparations are approached with a spirit of adventure and with the assurance that the end result will be a splendid happy feast for the family or the most awesome company, it will all be worthwhile.

In conclusion I would like to thank some people and places for help, encouragement, inspiration, advice, testing, tasting, and just being there: Kate Tremper, John Massee, Holly and Jack Massee, Penny Miller, Angelica and Jack Hirshot, the Periscope Restaurant in Santa Fe, the Blue Mill Restaurant in New York, Barry Soprano, Gail Bird, Mary Gandall, Manuel Oliveira, and my husband, Bill Massee, who qualifies for thanking in all departments.

✻ This ornament throughout indicates the point to which a recipe can be prepared ahead. At this time the dish can be refrigerated or frozen for later serving. Be sure to read the instructions for storing and reheating on page 41.

1

Equipment, Ingredients, and Technique

EQUIPMENT

Scales

Scales are essential for weighing meat after trimming fat and bones from it. They are also indispensable when you only need *part* of a large package of stewing meat or part of a whole fish for soup or stew. When you buy a large chunk of meat on sale, top or bottom round or cross rib of beef, rolled neck of lamb, or loin end of pork, for instance—all of which make splendid pot roasts—you might want to cut off 2 or 3 pounds for soup or stew.

When you have a scale, you will wonder how you ever got along without it.

Cooking and Serving Vessels

For cooking soups, a 3-quart and a 4-quart heavy aluminum pot or kettle, or better still, enameled ironware, are the most useful. Lids are essential. Larger pots are needed when a recipe calls for a vegetable like cabbage or spinach, which is bulky until cooked, and for stock made with plenty of bones. Thin aluminum spaghetti pots are fine for this.

For cooking fish and seafood chowders and stews, wide, shallow saucepans or flameproof casseroles equipped with lids are better than big, deep kettles.

A tureen is not essential for serving but it is nice if you plan to serve the soup as the main item in a buffet, or more formally at the table. The bright enameled-ironware casseroles used for cooking the soups can double as tureens and have the advantage of going from stove to table. They might need a little cleaning on the outside, and on the inside from the top down to the contents, before serving. A heated ceramic or glass salad bowl can serve as a tureen in a pinch, and a Dutch oven gives a homey touch.

It is nice to have a variety of soup bowls, deep and shallow, plain and fancy, even mugs. Those wide, old-fashioned soup plates, the kind with a flat rim, are almost essential for soups like chowders and borscht, for example, that have large pieces of fish or meat in them. The pleasures of soup making might turn you into a collector of soup bowls. . . .

For cooking stews, I find a 2½-quart and a 3-quart enameled iron casserole most convenient. Larger pots are needed when the meat is bony and therefore bulky, and, as with soups, when the vegetables, such as cabbage, are bulky before cooking—and when a recipe is to be increased. At least one large, heavy skillet is needed for browning meat or chicken; an extra one comes in handy if there is a large quantity of meat to brown.

Some stews are better served in baking dishes or deep platters rather than the pot used for cooking. In some recipes the meat of the stew is kept warm in a deep platter or baking dish in the oven, while the sauce is coped with on top of the stove, and then poured over the stew. Pottery and earthenware casseroles are good for this. They cannot be used over direct flame, but for warming and serving, they are efficient and beautiful.

Blender and Food Processor

Almost standard now in many homes, these two appliances make many processes easy but are not essential, except perhaps for some desserts. Soups can be puréed, partially or completely, through a sieve or a food mill. Large quantities of onions or celery chopped in the food processor are apt to end up either in large chunks or too fine and watery. I like to do the chopping with a good sharp knife. It is an easily acquired skill—and impresses kibitzers enormously.

INGREDIENTS

Stock or Broth

The recipes that follow are for basic chicken and beef stocks, to use whenever stock or broth is called for. Throughout the book a few other recipes for stock appear, mostly fish. They are designed with ingredients and quantities appropriate for the soup or stew in which they are used.

Making stock from scratch not only gives one a good feeling but results in a good-tasting stock. However, don't expect to save money by making stock, particularly beef stock, because of the high cost of meaty bones. Chicken stock can be more rewarding financially if you save and freeze all the giblets that come with chickens and make stock when 2 or 3 pounds have been accumulated.

When recipes include instructions for homemade stock, canned beef or chicken broth may be used. Canned broths are salted, and if you use them in place of water, check the taste before adding salt. Dilute if called for on the can. Consommé is not recommended because it is too sweet. Powdered stock and bouillon cubes can be used, but they have a taste that can get too familiar, and the salt content can make the soup or stew too salty.

Broth cans come in an irritating variety of sizes. It is a good idea to have several cans on hand—leftover broth can be frozen. Sometimes, when I find I am only short a couple of ounces, I make up the difference with water rather than open another can and adjust the seasoning accordingly. It helps too if you have some old but still good vegetables to throw in.

The following recipe is a guide; the proportions can vary but giblets are important for the chickeny taste.

CHICKEN STOCK

2 pounds chicken backs and necks (raw)
1 pound gizzards (giblets without liver or neck)
2 medium carrots, scrubbed and halved
2 medium onions, peeled and quartered
2 stalks celery and celery tops, broken up

6 sprigs parsley
4 quarts water
1 bay leaf
1 teaspoon thyme
2 teaspoons salt
2 teaspoons crushed black peppercorns

Two large pots are needed for this, one to cook the stock in and the other to strain it into.

Place the chicken parts, gizzards, carrots, onions, celery, and parsley in one of the large pots with the water. Bring to a gentle boil and cook for 10–15 minutes, skimming off foam as it appears. When foam no longer rises, add the remaining ingredients. Simmer, partially covered, for 2–3 hours, or until gizzards are really tender.

Set a large sieve, or a colander lined with dampened cheesecloth, over the other large pot. Ladle the stock and solids into the sieve. Discard the solids and skim the fat from the stock, or refrigerate until fat hardens for easy removal. To prevent souring, refrigerate stock uncovered, or bring to room temperature first, then cover and refrigerate.

Measure the stock; if it is less than 2 quarts, add water. If it is more, cook down to 2 quarts. Add salt to taste.

The stock can be refrigerated for 1 or 2 days; for longer refrigeration, boil it up every 2 days. Stock can be frozen after cooling. Freeze in 2-cup containers for convenience. *Makes about 2 quarts*

BEEF STOCK

3–4 pounds meaty soup bones, cracked
About 5 quarts water
3 medium onions, peeled and halved
2 medium carrots, scrubbed and halved
2 stalks celery and celery tops, broken up

6 sprigs parsley
1 teaspoon thyme
1 bay leaf
1 tablespoon salt
1 teaspoon cracked black peppercorns

Two pots are needed, one to cook the stock in, the other to strain it into.

Put the bones into a large pot with the water. Bring to a boil and boil gently for 10–15 minutes, skimming off foam as it appears. When foam no longer forms, add the remaining ingredients. Simmer, partially covered, for 4–5 hours.

Set a large sieve or a colander lined with dampened cheesecloth over the other pot and ladle the stock and solids into it. Discard the solids and skim fat from the top of the liquid, or refrigerate until fat hardens on top for easy removal. To avoid souring, refrigerate stock uncovered, or bring to room temperature first.

Measure stock; if less than 2 quarts, add water. If it is more, cook down to about 2 quarts. Stock can be kept for a week or two in the refrigerator if it is taken out and boiled up every 2 days. Freeze, after cooling, in 2-cup containers for convenience.   *Makes about 2 quarts*

Meat

Stews and hearty main-course soups are an important part of my family and entertaining meal planning, so I buy meats for stews and soups when on sale and freeze them. It can be a rolled boneless neck of veal, a rolled boneless shoulder of pork, top or bottom round of beef, chuck steak, or that mixture of lamb pieces which includes chops and stewing meat. Sometimes it is packaged stewing meat—beef or veal. Packaged lamb for stew is usually neck, with bone, a very good choice for stew or soup, bones and all.

The bony cuts—short ribs, pork barbecue ribs, lamb neck, oxtails—all make wonderful stews and main-course soups. Buy about 1/3 more weight to allow for bones. Supermarket butchers used to be able to help you with special cuts for stewing, but now they rarely receive the whole side of the animal to cut up. You need to go to a real butcher. Here's a quick survey course on stew meats and fish.

Beef

The following paragraphs, which readers of my first book, *Glorious Stew*, will recognize, tell you what you need to know about stewing beef.

Cuts of beef for stewing can be confusing because they vary in appearance and name, not only from one part of the country to another, but even from store to store. New names are constantly being invented for cuts of meat, particularly beef. It can help if you know a little about the animal and what to ask for, no matter what the regional, fashionable, or just plain gimmicky local name is. Don't let the butcher talk you out of a cheaper cut if that is what you want; the cheaper cut will probably be a better one for stew.

Except for rump and round, which will be dealt with later, stewing beef comes mostly from the forequarter. The most familiar and most universal cut for stew is *chuck*. But there are chuck roasts, chuck steaks, chuck fillet steaks, and packages labeled simply "Stewing Beef, Chuck." If you buy chuck fillet steaks thick enough and cut them up yourself, you will have good stewing meat, although there is some waste unless you use the bones for stock. Regular chuck steaks or chuck roasts may have some less tender parts, as will the so-called stewing chuck. The best and cheapest in the end is boneless *middle chuck,* which is merchandised as "Chuck Fillet." But to get this, without some bits of neck or blade, which can be stringy, you have to have a good butcher you can trust. It helps to know that what you want is the real middle chuck and to ask for it with authority. Even good supermarket butchers will give you what you want, but you may have to order it ahead.

The end pieces from sirloin and porterhouse steaks are marvelous for stew. Instead of having them ground, freeze them and save them for stew.

Boned shoulder, often called *cross ribs*, is another good cut for stew. *Shank* and *shin* are inexpensive cuts which can be bought boned or unboned. There are a variety of textures in the pieces and they require long slow cooking in plenty of liquid.

Slabs of meat from over the ribs, the thin strips from the ends of the ribs of a rib roast, are excellent for stewing, and are called *top rib*, or *top of rib*. Also good are strips from the breast. Going toward the back of the animal from the shank, and getting progressively fatter, there is *brisket*, followed by *short plate*. The first cuts of brisket nearest the shank are excellent, but again, you need a good butcher to be sure you are getting what you ask for.

Flanken is a favorite stewing cut for many European cooks when it is well marbled with fat, and grainy; it comes from the first cuts under the shoulder and on the first ribs. Second cuts are called *short ribs*—good, too, but bonier.

Two cuts very good for stew, but not ordinarily sold as such in regular butcher shops or supermarkets, are *corner pieces* and *deckle*. They are "restaurant cuts," usually sold only wholesale. Corner pieces, often used for restaurant browned stews, are the first cuts from the short plate, nearest the brisket. *Deckle* is an overall term for the thin strips of meat over the ribs and the thinner ones from under the ribs, very good for boiled beef, if you can get it.

Rump and *round*, from the hindquarter, are sometimes used for stew, but they lack the marbling of fat, and tend to be dry. However, in slices or in small cubes, and cooked in plenty of liquid, they have a firm texture that many people enjoy.

Lamb

Boned shoulder is the best cut for boneless lamb stew or soup. Neck, bones and all, is marvelous for taste and texture. Thick shoulder chops can be deboned with a sharp knife and cut up or chopped with a cleaver to use the bones too.

Veal

Boned shoulder or neck is good, except when slices from the leg are called for. The neck sometimes comes in the form of a rolled roast; buy it and cut it up. Packages labelled "Stewing Veal" may have pieces of varying texture, which shouldn't matter.

Pork

Again use boned shoulder, but rib end and loin end are good, too. Fresh ham can be used, but it comes in a large piece. Cut some off for stew, leave the rest for roasting, and possibly freeze both for later use. Scales are handy for this operation, so you can tell how much you have of each.

Sausages

The uncooked sausages suggested in these recipes can be regular "breakfast," or Italian, hot or sweet. I prefer the hot version usually because of the stronger taste. Anise, or fennel, a slightly licorice flavor, is characteristic of the hot sausages and used in combination with the sweet sausage give a pungent, zesty taste.

Cooked sausages add a wonderful distinctive flavor to soups and stews. Usually added to heat through, they are sometimes lightly sautéed first to render their fat. Some of the sausages are:

Polish, or Kielbasa: large, garlicky
Danish salami: like Polish, slightly milder
Genoa salami: quite fat, garlicky, and studded with peppercorns
Pepperoni: small, dry salami
Thuringer, or summer sausage: milder than some, salty, and tasting of coriander

Chorizos, Spanish and Portuguese: small, dry, hard, with pimiento, garlic, and paprika

Linguiça, a slim Portuguese sausage: plenty of garlic and paprika

The small sausages just need to be sliced. Larger ones may need to be sliced and quartered into pleasant bite sizes. Julienne strips, about 2 inches long, are good in some cases and are decorative as well as adding flavor.

Fish and Seafood

Often the cheaper fish is best for chowders and stews. It is firmer and holds up longer in the cooking, thereby assimilating more flavor from the cooking sauce. Monkfish, tile, and blackfish are some that appear, but unless a lighter fish is called for, ask the fish merchant for something inexpensive and suitable.

It is most important that the fish and seafood be impeccably fresh, without the slightest "fishy" odor. Personally, I have not had much luck with frozen fish, but if you have a good brand or good source, by all means use it.

THE SOUP WAY OF LIFE

When our daughter was married and moved far away, we sent the newly-weds off with stemmed wine glasses, an enameled iron casserole, a popover pan, and a few pages on soupmaking. They had asked for the soup material because they both liked soup and rightly assumed that hearty soups would be an important item to help them eat well on a very small student budget.

Slightly revised, the material follows, for those who would like to make soups from scratch, and be ready with basics when they want to use a recipe.

Once you are in the soup-making state of mind, you will save all kinds of things. Leftover vegetables and slightly tired fresh vegetables will be fine if the soup is puréed, for instance. Rather than freezing individually some of the elements you plan to use in soup, you might take a few minutes to make a soup base with them and freeze that, so you are a step ahead when you are ready to make a soup.

Hot sauces like Rouille or Pistou can be frozen, ready to pep up a soup on short notice. Make a cup or so of Pistou, for instance, when fresh basil is around, and freeze in small quantities, using foil or plastic wrap.

Canned goods to have on hand for soup making

Beef and chicken broth
Tomato juice, purée, paste, and whole tomatoes
Kidney, garbanzo, and black beans
Pimientos
Anchovies
Green chilies

Leftovers to save for soup

Any leftovers in cans should be transferred to plastic containers—a twist of foil or plastic in the case of anchovies, tomato paste, or pimientos—and frozen
Vegetable cooking water (freeze)
Leftover vegetables (can be frozen, but better if not)
Noodles, rice, pasta, kasha, beans (freeze)
Cream sauce, spaghetti sauce, gravy (freeze)

Good additions to soup

Tiny pasta—miniature versions of larger shapes:
Anellini . . . rings
Conchigliette-piccole . . . shells
Farfalline . . . butterflies or bows
Maruzzine . . . seashells
Pennine or pennette . . . quill pens
Stellini . . . little stars
Tubettini . . . tubes
Orzo . . . small pasta resembling barley or rice
Little elbows and, of course, alphabets

Regular long pasta, spaghetti, linguine, et cetera, can be used too: just break it up. Use the package directions for a guide to cooking time. Remember a little goes a long way—use ¼ to ⅓ of a cup for 6 cups of soup; 1 to 1½ cups of broken up thin pasta is about enough for 6 cups of soup.

Dried beans of all kinds; split peas, yellow and green; rice, white and brown. Again, a little goes a long way, check recipes using these for guidance as to quantity

Fresh food: potatoes, carrots, celery, onions, parsley, lemon

Some soup notes

Before freezing leftover vegetable water, stock, broth, or tomato product, cook some finely chopped onion, celery, and carrot in 1–2 tablespoons of butter until they soften, then add the liquid and salt and pepper. Freeze the mixture and you will have a soup starter. Use ⅓ to ½ cup of each vegetable for 6 cups of soup.

Variations on the soup starter

   Before adding the vegetables, cook 2 slices of diced bacon in the butter.
   Add 1 tablespoon of paprika, chili powder, or curry powder to the vegetables as they cook, before adding liquid: 1 tablespoon of flour can be added at this time too, to give the starter a little body.
   Sherry, or dry red or white wine, about ⅓ cup, can be added before the other liquid and allowed to cook down to half. This gives a richness to the soup that will ensue.
   Add 2 tablespoons of finely chopped parsley to the vegetables.
   Add ⅓ cup finely chopped green pepper.

Once you have the starter, the rest of the liquid can be added. It can be more of the same, or perhaps milk. Heavy cream, yogurt, or sour cream are added at the end, to heat but not boil, to avoid curdling.
The solids you put in can be infinitely varied:

   Small pieces of stewing meat or soaked dried beans need about an hour to cook
   Fresh vegetables take from about 20 minutes for root vegetables to about 5 minutes for zucchini or tiny broccoli or cauliflower flowerets.
   Cooked vegetables should be put in just to warm, not to cook any further. If they are already overcooked, perhaps it would be better to add a little liquid and purée them.
   Soup can be thickened by puréing some or all of it, or for each cup of soup add 1 teaspoon of rice or 3 tablespoons of grated raw potato or 1 tablespoon of flour mixed with 2 tablespoons milk, water, or broth.
   Finely chopped cabbage can cook for hours in a soup, spinach goes in at the very end, for about a minute, remaining bright green.
   Cooked ham, in chunks or julienne, sliced frankfurters, and sliced garlic sausage have more flavor and give up some of their fat if they are lightly sautéed before being added to the soup.

Don't forget garlic, either mashed with salt or finely chopped.

Soups are, of course, more appetizing if they are presented attractively. A sprinkle of parsley, chives, or chopped scallions enhances any soup. Paprika improves the look of a creamy one. Chopped pimientos and chopped hard-boiled eggs add a bright note. A nice addition, which beautifies and also adds a delightful fresh taste, is a half-and-half mixture of chopped parsley and chopped scallions—a cupful of the mixture for 6 cups of soup, stirred in.

Seasoning

For seasoning ideas, you might consult the soup recipes and use the herbs and seasonings called for in soups that resemble your own. "Check seasoning" usually means adding salt and pepper. If there are hot seasonings like cayenne, crushed red pepper, or Tabasco, the phrase means adding as much more hotness as you can stand, or "to taste." Hotness fades somewhat after refrigeration or freezing and needs to be checked again.

When the soup or stew contains oregano or chili powder, or something like anise or fennel seeds, you might like more of that particular taste. Also, if herbs and spices are stale, the amount specified may be too little. When correcting seasoning, add small amounts at a time, stir, and cook a moment or two before tasting again. Repeat the process until the taste seems right to you.

If a soup or stew tastes too salty, possibly it has been cooked down too much. Try adding hot water in ½-cup amounts to bring the liquid back to its original level. If there is too much salt in the stew because of a mistake in measuring, add some potatoes, cut in large or small pieces, depending on the time they will have to cook. Take care when measuring the salt. The minimal amounts given in these recipes are usually enough, but individual preferences vary.

Use fresh herbs whenever possible. One tablespoon of fresh herbs equals 1 teaspoon of dried. Many herbs and spices keep their flavor better if they are kept in the refrigerator, particularly curry powder, fresh bulk Hungarian paprika, fresh chili powder, and cayenne pepper.

Herbs, spices and other flavoring or coloring items

Basic herbs: thyme, bay leaves, oregano, basil, marjoram
Curry powder
Chili powder
Paprika
Worcestershire sauce
Powdered stock, bouillon cubes: beef, chicken, vegetable
Hot pepper: cayenne, red pepper flakes, Tabasco
Dried leeks and chives: use fresh if possible, but these are not too bad
Turmeric—to add a little yellow color in a creamy soup that is a little gray
Brown coloring—for vaguely colored soups (page 51)
Freshly grated Parmesan cheese (can be frozen)
Vinegar—sometimes 1–2 teaspoons will be just the touch a soup needs
Pimientos, in can or jar: whole ones can be cut into whatever size you want—
strips, small or large pieces. Freeze leftovers in jar or twist of plastic or foil,
with remaining liquid.

Clarified Butter

Butter burns quickly, so if a lot of meat is to be browned, the butter is usually combined with olive oil or vegetable oil, either of which has a higher burning point.

Clarified butter, however, does not burn quickly and makes the addition of oil unnecessary. It is called *ghee* in India, and used in stews cooked in yogurt or buttermilk, it makes them less likely to curdle. Once clarified, the butter will keep indefinitely, so it is a good idea to make a fair amount at a time and store it in a jar or crock in the refrigerator.

To clarify 1 pound of butter, break it up in a saucepan and heat it very slowly so that it will melt but not brown. When it is all melted and foamy, remove it from the heat and place it in the refrigerator. When the butter has hardened, scrape off the foam, lift out the hardened block, and discard the milky sediment in the bottom of the pan. It is those milky solids which cause butter to burn quickly. Melt the block again and pour the now-clarified butter into a storage receptacle. The hardened foam can be used to butter vegetables.

To clarify a little butter when some is needed, melt slightly more butter than is called for. When it is foamy but not brown, skim off the foam and carefully pour off the butter, leaving the milky sediment in the bottom of the pan; discard. Clarified butter is great for sautéing croutons or large quantities of mushrooms and for anything that calls for cooking in butter alone. The flavor is properly buttery, and there is less danger of the off taste of burning.

Unless otherwise indicated, salted butter is used in this book.

About Wine

The wines suggested to have with the soups and stews are good ones to choose from for cooking. They are not the most expensive wines, but they are good to drink and are chosen to suit the dish. Not that the suggestions have to be followed to the letter; they are intended to give you clues to the type of wine the dish will taste best with and to the nature of the soup or stew if you have never had it before.

In case you wondered, the alcohol in the wine disappears in the first few minutes of cooking; only the flavor remains. Wine that has been open for a few days will have lost its freshness, but as long as it has no unpleasant characteristics of smell or taste will be fine for cooking. It is a good idea to put leftover wine into a smaller bottle, cork it well, and refrigerate it for use in cooking.

If you are interested in learning about wine, buy a mixed case, so you can try different wines and find the ones you like. You might make a list from the wines that go with these recipes, for a start.

TECHNIQUES

Storing and Reheating

Soups and stews can be refrigerated or frozen at the point marked by an ornament in the recipe. Reheat before continuing. The food must be at room temperature before being covered and refrigerated or frozen, or it may spoil. Bacteria thrive in the cozy warmth of a closed vessel in a cold place.

Cool with lid askew. With the lid off, the contents dry on the top. With the lid on, the soup or stew cooks a little more in its own heat. Also, steam accumulates and drips onto the food, not a disaster, but not desirable either. Once cool, cover well for refrigeration or freezing. If a stew has been transferred to a baking dish, cover the dish with foil—loosely to cool and tightly for storage.

A stew can be frozen in a foil baking dish and transferred to a hot serving dish when reheated.

If you have a favorite serving dish and do not want it immobilized in the freezer, refrigerate the food in the dish, and when it is cold and firm, wrap it in foil in the shape of the dish for freezing. It will then fit in the dish for reheating.

If you know ahead that you are going to freeze the dish, omit the finishing vegetables, which should not be overdone and are better added upon reheating. Egg and cream mixtures are added after thawing, too, and in the case of fish and seafood, it is best to freeze the sauce alone and to add the fish for its brief cooking after thawing. Heavy cream can be frozen in the dish, but sour cream and yogurt are apt to curdle, and should be added after thawing.

Most stews, unless otherwise stated, are improved by standing, and can be refrigerated for 2 or 3 days.

To reheat, I like to first bring the dish to room temperature, and then reheat in the oven at the original temperature or on top of the stove. As a general rule, reheat in the oven when the dish has a small amount of liquid, or bring to a simmer on top of the stove when there is plenty of liquid.

The dishes can be reheated before thawing, but they take at least twice as long and you have to control the desire to attack the frozen mass and mess it all up. There is also the danger of burning the outside before the inside is even thawed, much less heated.

Simmering

In soup and stew cookery, the liquid is usually brought to a boil and then turned down to a simmer. There is no trouble recognizing a boil, even a gentle boil. The simmer is below the gentle boil and above the point where nothing is happening at all. There should be movement, but no violent activity on the surface.

It is more difficult to maintain the simmer on top of the stove. Since slow, even cooking is what we want, using the oven is one way of coping.

You will have to test your oven a few times starting at 325° to find the temperature that will maintain the simmer. New stoves are probably better than the old ones I've used, and keeping a simmer may no longer be a problem. One gadget from a hardware store that helped me was a sort of upside-down covered pie-plate which raised the pot above the flame a bit for more successful top-of-the-stove simmering.

In general, I cook stews that have more liquid on top of the stove, and those with less in the oven.

Degreasing

This is a tiresome but necessary step for many soups and stews. The less expensive cuts of meat are apt to have more fat, and, although large outside pieces can be trimmed off, other fat is better left in to provide moistness and flavor. Fortunately, fat rises to the surface. The easiest way to remove it is to refrigerate the soup or stew, after cooling, until the fat hardens and can be lifted off.

To remove the fat before it hardens, tip the pot, to concentrate the fat, making it deeper and easier to skim. Use a large, shallow spoon and blot up the last bits with paper towel. Occasionally there will be enough fat to warrant the use of a bulb baster.

Timing

It is hard to give exact timing for the meat and the dried beans in soups and stews. The cut, the size of the pieces of meat, and the idiosyncrasies of stoves all make differences in cooking times. As for beans, I don't know why they take such widely differing amounts of time, unless it is simply age. Vigilance is required. Start checking at the shortest times given.

❋ This ornament throughout indicates the point to which a recipe can be prepared ahead. At this time the dish can be refrigerated or frozen for later serving. Be sure to read the instructions for storing and reheating on page 41.

I
MAIN-
COURSE SOUPS

2

Soups with Meat

CALDO VERDE

Travelers return from Portugal with a taste for Caldo Verde. The wonderful kale and potato soup they enjoyed there has found its way to this country, is recognized with joy by those familiar with it, and is a happy discovery for those to whom it is new.

As made in Portugal, Caldo Verde is a simple, delicate soup. The distinguishing flavor is the Portuguese olive oil, available in Spanish, Portuguese, or Mexican markets or specialty food shops here. To make the soup a little more substantial, and thus qualify as a main course, a few more sausages have been added in this version. Served with plenty of cornbread and preceded or followed by a hearty salad like the Salade Savoyarde (recipe follows), the soup makes a fine luncheon or supper.

Dessert should have Port in or on it. Baked Apples (page 277) could be basted with Port during their cooking, using 2–3 tablespoons per apple. Or serve slices of pound cake sprinkled with Port and topped with whipped cream; or the always delightful wedge of melon with Port poured into the hollow.

Serve the soup with a Portuguese white wine—Vinho Verde or Dão.

½ pound kale (about 4 cups shredded)	8 cups water
	¼ cup Portuguese olive oil
4 large potatoes, peeled and cut in ¼-inch rounds	¼ teaspoon freshly ground pepper
	6 ounces chorizo, or linguiça sausage
1 tablespoon salt	

Wash the kale thoroughly. Strip the leaves from the stems. Bunch the leaves together lengthwise and cut across into the finest possible shreds.

In a large kettle or saucepan, combine the potatoes, salt, and water. Bring to a boil, reduce heat and simmer, uncovered, until mashable, about 15 minutes. Transfer the potatoes to a bowl, using a slotted spoon. Reserve the cooking water. Mash potatoes coarsely with a potato masher or fork. Beat in the olive oil and pepper. Stir the mixture into the potato cooking water in the saucepan.

Prick the sausages in a few places. Put them in a small skillet with water to barely cover. Bring to a boil, reduce heat and simmer for 15 minutes. Drain and set aside on paper towel.

Bring the soup to a boil and add the kale. Boil, uncovered, for 3–4 minutes. Cut the sausages into thin slices, add to the soup, and simmer for 1–2 minutes.

6 servings

Variations (for non-purists): Use chicken broth instead of water, adjusting the salt accordingly; Use spinach, collard greens, or good dark green leaf lettuce instead of kale.

SALADE SAVOYARDE

This French salad, full of good solid ingredients to chew on, has curry in the dressing, giving it a delightful, hard-to-define, special flavor. Usually served as a first course, it is particularly pleasant before or after a soup with a rather thin base.

2 medium endives
1 medium apple
¼ pound Gruyère cheese

¼ cup chopped walnuts
8–10 pitted black olives

Trim endives, cut across in ½-inch rounds. Peel and core apple and cut into ½-inch cubes. Cut cheese into ½-inch cubes. Combine in a salad bowl with walnuts and black olives.

DRESSING

5 teaspoons vinegar
½ teaspoon Dijon mustard
5 tablespoons salad oil

1 teaspoon curry powder
Salt and pepper to taste

Beat dressing ingredients together and pour over salad. Toss gently.

4–6 servings

BEEF GOULASH SOUP

Those who know say that a true Hungarian goulash should never have: any flour, any wine, any spice but caraway. However, potatoes, green peppers, onions, garlic, and tomatoes are sanctioned. This recipe, adapted to make a substantial soup, has all the required ingredients and properly observes the taboos. Lard is the classic fat to use, but fortunately cooking oil is fine—who has lard around?

The soup is a main course in itself, needing only a salad and rye bread to accompany it. Any favorite salad would be fine. Radishes and Feta cheese or a firm goat cheese might precede the stew; dessert could be a fine selection of store-bought pastries.

We suggest a Beaujolais-Villages or a California Zinfandel to drink with the soup.

2 pounds boneless beef chuck, cut in ¾-inch pieces
2 tablespoons lard, or cooking oil
2 medium onions, chopped
3 garlic cloves, minced
2 teaspoons salt
⅛ teaspoon cayenne pepper
3 tablespoons medium Hungarian paprika
1 teaspoon caraway seeds

1 quart hot water
1 one-pound twelve-ounce can Italian tomatoes, undrained, crushed
4–6 medium potatoes, cut in ¾-inch cubes
2 medium green peppers, seeded and coarsely chopped
1 cup sour cream

Dry beef with paper towel. Heat the lard in a heavy saucepan or kettle and add the beef. Cook, stirring on moderately high heat until the pieces lose their color. Add the onions and garlic and continue cooking until onions have softened but not browned.

Stir in the salt, cayenne, paprika, and caraway seeds. Pour in the water and bring to a boil. Reduce heat and simmer, partially covered, for ½ hour. Add the tomatoes and continue to simmer, partially covered, for another ½ to ¾ hour, until meat is almost fork tender.

Add the potatoes and green peppers. Cover and simmer 20 to 30 minutes more, until potatoes are cooked and meat is tender.

Serve in large bowls; offer sour cream separately.   *6–8 servings*

PHILADELPHIA PEPPER POT

This famous all-American soup is said to have been invented by George Washington's cook at Valley Forge. Called upon to produce a hot and hearty meal for the troops when supplies were low after a hard winter, he did his best with what was on hand—tripe, bones, and peppercorns. Named after the cook's hometown, the soup is still dear to Philadelphians and has devotees everywhere.

The recipes vary, of course; some people put in celery, some add a few whole cloves or allspice, and some add dumplings. In this simple version, only lemon and parsley are my additions. It does need to be made a day ahead, though, for easy removal of fat—when cool, the soup will be firmly jellied from all the rich natural gelatin.

Hard-boiled eggs on Boston lettuce, with mayonnaise and a sprinkle of parsley or chives or capers, make a pleasant beginning for the meal. Serve some good crusty bread with the soup; a fine chunk of sharp Cheddar cheese with apples or pears will round out the feast.

Beer goes well with the soup, or a red wine—a Rioja or a Zinfandel.

1 calf's foot (about 2 pounds), cut up in 2-inch pieces	½ teaspoon thyme
2 pounds honeycomb tripe in 1-×-2-inch pieces	1 bay leaf
	2 teaspoons marjoram
7–8 cups water	3 medium onions, chopped
2 tablespoons salt	1 large garlic clove, chopped
Juice of 1 lemon	Freshly ground black pepper to taste
1 teaspoon peppercorns	2 medium potatoes
¼ teaspoon red pepper flakes	¼ cup flour
4 parsley sprigs	2–4 teaspoons meat coloring (recipe follows)
	½ cup finely chopped parsley

Wash the calf's foot and the tripe thoroughly. Put them in a large pot or kettle with the water to cover. Add the salt and lemon juice and simmer for 2 hours, partially covered.

Add the peppercorns, red pepper flakes, parsley sprigs, thyme, bay leaf, marjoram, onions, and garlic. Simmer, partially covered, for another 3 to 3½ hours, or until tripe is very tender. Add water to keep the solids barely submerged.

Drain, reserving liquid. Allow meat to cool until it can be handled.

Discard bay leaf and parsley. Remove and discard bones from the calf's foot and chop the meat, gelatinous part, and skin. Cut up the tripe if you prefer smaller pieces. Combine with the reserved liquid and when thoroughly cool, refrigerate, preferably overnight.

Remove hardened fat from the surface of the soup and discard. Bring soup to a simmer and add salt, pepper, hot pepper, and more marjoram to taste. Flavors are diminished by the long cooking.

Add the potatoes, peeled and cut into ½-inch dice, and cook for 20 minutes, or until tender. Add the flour mixed with a little cooled soup. Cook until soup thickens. Stir in the meat coloring until a satisfactory color is arrived at. If you do not mind the gray color, omit the coloring.

❀ The soup can be prepared ahead to this point and refrigerated for a few days, or frozen, after thorough cooling.

Garnish each serving with parsley.   *8–10 servings*

Note: Some people prefer the potatoes mashed into the soup, not left in cubes. Use an old-fashioned potato masher, or a fork. The soup is good this way too, but it has a different texture.

BROWN COLORING FOR SOUPS AND STEWS

Commercial coloring agents that are advertised as gravy makers are apt to have too much flavor and might affect the flavor of a delicate stew. Make your own brown coloring, which will not affect the taste of the stew:

½ cup sugar   **¼ cup boiling water**
¼ cup water

Cook sugar mixed with the ¼ cup of water, without stirring, until it turns a rich dark brown, about 5 minutes. Holding a pot lid as a shield to protect yourself from splatter, add boiling water. Remove from heat at once. If it is too gummy, add a little more boiling water. Stir, cool, and store in a covered jar—it keeps indefinitely, unrefrigerated.

LAMB AND SPLIT PEA SOUP

With ground lamb for texture and flavor and yellow split peas for body, this is a substantial soup. Seasoned with mint and dill and finished with yogurt, it has a distinctly Middle Eastern flavor. A garnish of chopped scallions and dill gives the soup a delightful freshness.

Small spinach and Feta cheese pastries would make a good first course, if you are able to find them or the phyllo pastry to make them (recipe follows). Hot pita bread goes well with the soup, and stewed dried fruit is a possibility for dessert.

Light wines like the clarets of Bordeaux suit this menu—regionals like St. Émilion or Graves. Similar, even drier wines are those of the Rioja and they are perhaps even better suited.

1 tablespoon cooking oil	¼ teaspoon white pepper
1 pound lean ground lamb	3 tablespoons chopped fresh dill
3 carrots, cut in ¼-inch dice	1 teaspoon crushed dried mint, or
2 celery stalks, finely chopped	1 tablespoon chopped fresh mint
1 medium onion, finely chopped	3 cups chicken broth
1 tablespoon salt	1 cup plain yogurt
4 cups water	6 scallions with crisp green tops,
1 cup yellow split peas	chopped

Heat the oil in a heavy, lidded saucepan or casserole, and crumble in the lamb. Cook, stirring and breaking up lumps, until lamb loses its color and begins to brown. Pour off fat.

Add carrots, celery, and onion, and continue stirring, until onions are transparent and a little soft. Add the salt and water and bring to a boil. Boil gently for about 5 minutes, skimming off foam as it forms.

Wash and pick over peas and add them to the pot. Add pepper, 1 tablespoon of the dill, the mint, and the chicken broth. Bring to a simmer, cover, and cook on low heat for 1 to 1½ hours, until split peas are very soft. Skim off fat. If possible, cool and refrigerate so fat will harden.

❊ Soup can be prepared ahead to this point.

To serve, bring the soup to a simmer. Put the yogurt into a small bowl and beat in a few tablespoons of the hot soup. Add to the soup and heat but do not boil or mixture will curdle. Sprinkle each serving with a mixture of the scallions and the remaining dill.

6–8 servings

SPINACH AND CHEESE PUFFS

I cannot claim that these phyllo pastry hors d'oeuvre are easy to make, but golden, flaky, and delicious they are—and worth the effort. They can be made ahead and frozen, before or after cooking, to be reheated as needed. Allow no more than 2 or 3 per person as a first course, so your guests will have room for the main course.

FILLING

8–10 ounces fresh spinach
8 thin scallions with crisp green tops, finely chopped
2 teaspoons butter
½ cup cottage cheese
¼ pound Feta cheese, patted dry with paper towel, crumbled

¼ teaspoon white pepper
1 tablespoon chopped fresh dill
1 tablespoon lemon juice
1 egg, beaten
Salt to taste

Wash spinach thoroughly and trim off thick stems. Chop finely and set aside.

Put scallions and butter in a large, heavy skillet or wide, shallow saucepan and cook on low heat, stirring, until scallions soften—a minute or two. Add the spinach, stir and cook until spinach wilts and dries. Allow to cool.

In a bowl, mix cottage cheese, Feta cheese, pepper, dill, lemon juice, egg, the cooled spinach, and salt to taste. Makes about 3 cups.

PASTRY AND ASSEMBLY

1 pound phyllo pastry (excess can be frozen)

¼ pound butter, melted
1 egg, well beaten

Melt the butter in a small saucepan and have a pastry brush ready.

Carefully open the package of phyllo pastry and unroll the pile of sheets. Working quickly, with scissors cut the sheets into quarters, cutting through the whole pile each time (strips should be about 4 × 12 inches). Cover at once with dampened kitchen towel.

Keeping the rest of the sheets covered, remove one and spread it out on wax paper, a short edge toward you. Brush with melted butter. Place a rounded teaspoon of the spinach-cheese mixture 1 inch from the bottom. Turn up the bottom over the mixture. Turn over the sides, the whole length of the sheet, and brush with melted butter. Roll loosely to the end, and butter the top. Place, seam side down, on an unbuttered cookie sheet.

Continue until the cookie sheet is filled without crowding. Brush each little roll with beaten egg and place in a preheated 400° oven for 12–15 minutes, or until golden, puffed, and crisp.

Repeat until all the mixture is used.

To freeze *after* baking: Cool thoroughly and freeze on a tray or cookie sheet, then pack rolls carefully in plastic bags or foil. To reheat: place in preheated 400° oven for 15–20 minutes, or until heated through—check by trying one.

To freeze *before* baking: Use same procedure as for freezing cooked rolls, but *do not* paint with egg. To reheat, paint with egg and place in 400° oven for 20–25 minutes, or until golden, puffed, and crisp.

makes about 50

CHICK PEA, CABBAGE, AND SAUSAGE SOUP

A hearty soup for a cold winter's day, this delectable concoction is easily and quickly made and can be expanded to serve any number. Chorizo or Polish sausages are suggested, either of which imbue the soup with good strong flavor. Serve with a big basket of assorted breads and a salad of greens, scallions, cucumbers, thinly sliced mushrooms, and some pitted black olives. Dessert could be something equally easy, and wonderful—ice cream with Cream Sherry and a sprinkle of toasted slivered almonds.

Drink a Rioja or an Italian jug wine with the soup, or beer.

¼ **pound chorizo or Polish sausage, cut in ¼-inch slices**
1 medium onion, finely chopped
¼ **pound of cabbage, finely shredded**
4 cups beef broth

1 one-pound can chick peas (garbanzos), undrained
Salt to taste
¼ **teaspoon freshly ground black pepper**
1 four-ounce jar chopped pimientos, with juice

Put the sausage into a wide, shallow flameproof casserole and cook over low heat to render some fat and brown slightly. Add the onion and cook, stirring, until the onion softens. Add the cabbage and ½ cup of the broth. Bring to a boil, reduce heat and simmer, covered, for 5 minutes. Add the rest of the broth and the chick peas with liquid. Cover and simmer for 15 minutes, or until cabbage is tender but still a bit firm.

Check seasoning and add salt to taste. Add pepper, stir in pimientos, and serve piping hot. *4 servings*

VEGETABLE SOUP WITH HAM

The addition of pasta makes this splendid soup substantial enough to serve as a main course for luncheon or supper. Thin spaghetti broken into small pieces will do, but some of the small pastas found in the markets are attractive and handy to have around for soup making, or to add to a stew. The tiny amount of ham called for gives the soup a satisfying tang. But packaged boiled ham, awash in its plastic container, will not add a thing. If good ham is not to be found, use Polish or some other garlic sausage.

Crusty bread and a leafy salad would go with the soup, but in the tomato season, just serve sliced tomatoes, with scallions and parsley, a dribble of olive oil, a squeeze of lemon, and salt and pepper. It is always a shame to miss a chance to enjoy the local tomatoes.

A cheese tray and fruit of the season would make an easy finish to the meal. You might like to try an assortment of Italian cheeses—3 would be enough: Taleggio, Asiago, Provolone, Fontina, Bel Paese, and a grating cheese too young to grate—Parmigiano or Pecorino Romano.

Serve with a light, young Italian wine, a Bardolino or Chianti.

⅓ cup uncooked small pasta, such as tubettini or small elbows
3 tablespoons olive oil
1 medium green pepper, cut in ¼-inch dice
1 small onion, finely chopped
2 garlic cloves, minced
Salt and pepper

1 large tomato, peeled, seeded, and cut in ¼-inch dice
4 cups beef broth
½ teaspoon oregano
⅛ teaspoon red pepper flakes
2 whole pimientos, chopped, with their juice
2 ounces baked ham, cut in fine julienne, 1-inch long

Cook the pasta according to package directions, but do not overcook. Drain and set aside.

Heat the oil in a large, heavy saucepan, or a flameproof casserole that can be brought to the table. Add the green pepper, onion, and garlic. Stir and cook over low heat for 4–5 minutes, or until onions are slightly transparent but not browned and peppers have softened. Sprinkle generously with salt and pepper. Add the tomatoes and cook for 1–2 minutes. Add the beef broth, oregano, and red pepper flakes. Bring to a boil, reduce heat, and simmer for 10 minutes.

Add the pimientos and their juice, the pasta, and the ham. Return to a boil and serve.

3–4 servings

SAUERKRAUT AND FRANKFURTER SOUP

This is something like Souse's soup, a popular Hungarian soup that is served as a late night supper, slightly sharp and reviving. As a main course for a regular meal, serve it with rye or pumpernickel bread, and surround it with compatible courses.

Hard-boiled eggs with mayonnaise make a good, simple first course before the piquant soup. Salad could be leafy greens, and dessert a soft cheese like a Brie, with ripe pears. Serve with beer.

2 slices bacon, diced	4 cups chicken broth (fat removed)
1 medium onion, finely chopped	2 cups water
1 pound sauerkraut, drained	4 frankfurters, cut in ¼-inch slices
½ cup dry white wine	4 cooked potatoes, peeled, cut in
½ teaspoon caraway seeds	½-inch dice
6 juniper berries	Salt to taste
6 whole black peppercorns	1 cup sour cream

Put the bacon in a heavy saucepan or kettle. Cook, stirring, over low heat until bacon is crisp and golden. Add the onion. Stir and cook until onion softens. Add the sauerkraut, wine, and caraway. Coarsely crack the juniper berries and peppercorns with a heavy knife or with a mortar and pestle. Add to the saucepan. Bring to a boil, reduce heat, cover and simmer for 30–40 minutes, until sauerkraut is tender. Add the broth and water and return to a simmer; add the frankfurters and simmer for 10 minutes.

❆ Soup can be prepared ahead to this point, and frozen after cooling.

Add the potatoes and simmer about 5 minutes, long enough to heat the potatoes through. Add salt to taste, and serve, piping hot, in warm bowls. Offer the sour cream separately. *4–5 servings*

Variation: When the onion has softened, stir in 1 tablespoon Hungarian paprika and 1 tablespoon flour, and proceed with the recipe as given.

Beef borscht is a glorious and traditional dish in both Russian and Jewish cuisines. This version has a versatility others do not have—it can be served in great soup bowls, with meat, potatoes, beets, and soup, all together in their beautiful redness, topped with snowy white sour cream; or the soup can be served as a course, with just sour cream, and the rest served as a stew, with horseradish, pickles, and rye bread.

Canned beets are quite acceptable to use here and make a splendid borscht. Beef broth is used to enrich the soup. The interesting balance of sweet and sour was worked out for me by Fannie Engel, author of the delightful *Jewish Festival Cookbook*.

To go with the soup-stew, broccoli or asparagus, when in season, would be good; otherwise, serve a green salad.

Strong tea in glasses, with lemon, is traditional, but beer or a red jug wine is good too. For dessert, serve a strudel or some other Viennese or Russian pastry.

2 pounds boneless shank or shin of beef, cut in 2-inch pieces
2 medium onions, quartered
3 cups beef broth
3 cups water
2 cups tomato juice
2 one-pound cans julienne beets
1 teaspoon salt
½ teaspoon pepper
Juice of 1 lemon
1 tablespoon cider vinegar
2 tablespoons brown sugar
6–8 potatoes, boiled, peeled, halved
1 cup sour cream
½ cup finely chopped parsley

Trim fat from the meat. Wash and drain the meat and bones; place in a 4-6-quart lidded flameproof casserole or kettle. Add the onions, broth, and water. Bring to a boil, reduce heat and simmer for 10–15 minutes, skimming off scum as it forms.

Add the tomato juice and juice from 1 can of beets. Purée the beets from this can and set aside.

Add the salt, pepper, lemon juice, vinegar, and sugar. Bring to a boil, reduce heat and simmer, covered, for 2 to 2½ hours, or until beef is tender.

To serve as two courses: Remove beef to an 8-X-10-inch baking dish. Discard bones (save the marrow to have on toast for a cook's treat). Skim off the fat from the liquid. Spoon out enough soup to barely cover the meat in the baking dish. Strain the other can of beets; reserve the liquid and strew the beets over the meat.

Place the potatoes on the meat, sprinkle with salt and pepper, and cover with foil. About 30 minutes before you need it, put the baking dish in a 325° oven.

Strain the soup and add the reserved puréed beets and the liquid from the second can. Bring to a boil and serve in soup bowls with a large dollop of sour cream and a sprinkle of parsley, or serve sour cream separately in a small bowl.

Then serve the meat and vegetables.

To serve as one course: When the meat is tender, skim off fat, add the reserved purée of beets, and the second can of beets, liquid and all. Add the potatoes, and cook just to heat through.

Serve in large soup plates or bowls with the sour cream and a sprinkle of parsley. Provide knives and forks as well as spoons.   *4–6 servings*

UKRAINIAN-STYLE BORSCHT

The innumerable versions of this wonderful soup-stew have only one thing in common—beets. Everything else is variable, and so is the spelling of its name. Is it borscht, borsch, borshch, bortsh, borsht? I have opted here for borscht, quite arbitrarily. In this version I have included cabbage and tomatoes, two of the controversial vegetables for use in borscht, because they are so good in the soup.

It all starts with some stewing beef, the vegetables added according to their particular cooking times. Beets are put in with some of their tops (to retain the color), and removed when cooked, to be peeled, and some puréed, some cut in julienne before being added to the soup.

The traditional sweet-sour balance comes from the lemon and sugar, and there are sour cream and fresh dill as a topping. Hot boiled potatoes, halved, could be offered to add to the soup if your party has been out in the snow for a long, cold afternoon.

Dark bread and beer or tea in a glass go with the soup. A first course could be fish roe on toast, with vodka; and dessert, a big fruit salad of apples, oranges, bananas, and any other fruits in the market at the time, with 2 to 4 tablespoons of an orange-flavored liqueur and some chopped walnuts added to the bowl—and perhaps thin slices of pound cake to go with it.

3 pounds stewing beef, cut in 1-inch pieces	1 small green cabbage (1 pound)
1 marrow bone	1 pound tomatoes, peeled, chopped, or 1 one-pound can tomatoes, undrained, chopped
3 quarts water	
5 teaspoons salt	
1 teaspoon pepper	4 carrots, cut in ½-inch slices
2 teaspoons sugar	4 white turnips, quartered
Bouquet garni (1 teaspoon thyme, 1 bay leaf, 3 parsley sprigs, tied in a cheesecloth bag)	¼ cup lemon juice
	Salt to taste
	2 tablespoons Dijon mustard
	Sour cream
3 medium onions, chopped	¾ cup chopped fresh dill
6–8 raw beets with tops	

Trim the fat from the beef and wash the bone. Put beef and bones in a large, lidded kettle with 3 quarts of water. Cook at a gentle boil for 30 minutes, skimming off scum as long as it appears.

Add the salt, pepper, sugar, bouquet garni, and onions. Wash the beets and cut off the leaf stems, leaving 2–3 inches on the vegetable (this prevents "bleeding"; tops will be trimmed off later). Add to kettle. Trim cabbage, quarter, and cut away the core. Coarsely chop and add to the kettle. Add tomatoes. Cover and simmer for about 40 minutes or until beets are tender. Remove beets and set aside.

Add carrots, turnips, and lemon juice. Cover and simmer for 20–30 minutes more, or until meat and vegetables are tender. Trim and peel beets, purée half and julienne the rest. Add to the soup. Stir in the mustard. Add salt if needed.

Serve hot, in large soup plates or bowls, with a large dollop of sour cream and a sprinkle of dill.   *8–10 servings*

SPLIT PEA SOUP

Pea soup is often a little too substantial to precede a hearty main course, but it can be a fine main course itself for luncheon or supper or a late night feast. This enjoyable version of the old classic is enriched with milk, fresh (or frozen) green peas and, for more body, frankfurters, sausage, or ham for something solid to chew on. Serve it with rye or pumpernickel bread, a salad, and cheese and fruit.

To be really classic, the soup should be made with a ham bone (recipe follows). A ham bone can be frozen until a convenient time for soup making.

4 slices bacon, diced	½ pound frankfurters or Polish
1 large onion, finely chopped	sausage, thinly sliced, or ham, in
3 cups beef broth	small chunks or julienne
4 cups water	2 cups fresh or 10-ounce package
1 teaspoon thyme	frozen green peas
1 bay leaf	Salt and pepper
2 cups split peas	1 cup sour cream (optional)
2 cups milk	

Cook the bacon in a large saucepan or kettle over low heat, stirring with a wooden spoon to separate the bits. When the bacon is golden brown, remove and discard all but 2 tablespoons of the bacon fat.

Add the onion to the bacon and cook over low heat until the onion is soft but not brown. Add the broth, water, thyme, and bay leaf. Wash and pick over the split peas and add them to the pot. Bring to a boil, stirring occasionally. Reduce heat and simmer, partially covered, for 1½ hours, or until peas are very soft. Stir from time to time during the cooking and add a little water if the soup becomes too thick, but remember milk is to be added.

Pick out the bay leaf and purée the soup in 2-cup batches. Return the soup to the kettle, add the milk, and bring to a simmer.

Cook the frankfurter or sausage slices briefly in a skillet to brown lightly and render some of their fat. Blot on paper towel to remove more. Sauté the ham in a little butter to intensify the flavor. Add the meat to the soup.

Add the peas, cover and cook for 5 minutes, or until peas are just tender. Fresh peas will take longer than frozen, unless you have just picked them, in which case they just need to warm up in the soup. Add salt and pepper to taste.

Serve very hot and offer a small bowl of sour cream for individual garnish. *6–8 servings*

SPLIT PEA SOUP WITH A HAM BONE

1 ham bone	1 teaspoon thyme
10 cups water	1 bay leaf
2 onions, chopped	2 cups split peas
2 celery stalks, chopped	Milk or cream
¼ cup chopped parsley	

Cut 1–2 cups of ham from the bone to add to the finished soup. Some ham should be left on the bone to add its flavor to the soup.

Put the bone into a large pot or kettle and add the water. Add onions, celery, parsley, thyme, bay leaf. Cover and simmer for 1 hour.

Wash and pick over the split peas and add them to the pot. Return to a simmer, cover and cook for 1½ to 2 hours, or until peas have almost puréed themselves. Add water during cooking if needed, and stir occasionally. Purée if you wish.

Remove the bay leaf and the bone. Any ham left on the bone will have given up all its goodies to the soup, but if it has any taste or texture left, use it. If there was not enough ham on the bone to provide the 1–2 cups to be added to the finished soup, use the meats suggested in the recipe above. Thin soup with milk or cream. *6–8 servings*

GARBURE-STYLE SOUP

A *garbure* is a wonderful, hearty main-course soup from southwestern France. I have called this version garbure-style because it is without the essential ingredient for a classic Béarnaise garbure—*confit d'oie* or *canard,* preserved goose or duck, not too easy to come by for most of us. It's such a splendid soup, even without the special quality imparted by the *confit,* it seemed a shame to leave it out.

Made mainly of beans, ham, and cabbage, the soup has other vegetables which can vary with the seasons. One essential item is a very large pot or kettle—of 6- or 8-quart capacity. The cabbage, although it cooks down, needs a lot of room at first.

Crusty white or brown bread, or rye, and a simple leafy salad go with the soup. A fruit dessert of thin, peeled rounds of oranges, sprinkled with Kirsch and sugar and chilled for an hour or two, is fine for any time of the year.

Serve a Bordeaux regional wine with the soup—a Graves or St. Émilion, for instance.

1 pound dried white beans, Great Northern or navy	¼ teaspoon freshly ground black pepper
¼ pound bacon, diced	¼ teaspoon red pepper flakes
2 pounds smoked pork butt	1 teaspoon marjoram
2 onions, chopped	1 teaspoon thyme
3 garlic cloves, finely chopped	1 bay leaf
1 leek	10 cups water
1 one-pound yellow turnip (rutabaga), peeled, cut in ½-inch cubes	1 green cabbage, about 2 pounds
2 carrots, cut in ¼-inch slices	2 medium potatoes, peeled, cut in ½-inch dice
1 tablespoon salt	½ cup finely chopped parsley

Wash and pick over the beans. Put them in a saucepan with water to cover, and bring to a boil. Remove from the heat and allow to stand for 1 hour. Drain and set aside.

The soup may now be started in the big kettle or pot in which it will cook, but it is easier to use a heavy skillet for the first steps.

Cook the bacon in a heavy skillet, stirring and separating the bits until they are golden. Remove the bacon with a slotted spoon to paper towel to drain. Set aside. Lightly brown the pork butt in the bacon fat and set it aside on paper towel to drain also.

Remove all but 2 tablespoons of fat from the skillet and cook the onions and garlic until onions are limp and transparent. Transfer them with a slotted spoon to the soup kettle. Add the bacon bits, the pork butt, and reserved beans.

Trim off the root end of the leek and remove all but the palest green. Split lengthwise, wash thoroughly between leaves, and cut in ½-inch slices. Add to the kettle. Add the turnip, carrots, salt, black pepper, red pepper, marjoram, thyme, bay leaf, and water. Bring to a boil.

Trim off the root end of the cabbage and discard any bad outside leaves. Cut in quarters and trim away the core. Cut across the leaves in ¼-inch slices. Add to the kettle. Cover and simmer for 1½ hours. Add the potatoes and continue cooking, covered, ½ hour longer, or until potatoes are done and the pork butt is tender.

Remove the pork butt and cut into ¾-inch cubes, trimming off excess fat.

Skim off fat from the surface, check seasoning, and add more salt and hot pepper if needed. Serve very hot in large soup plates and sprinkle with parsley. *8–10 servings*

VARIATION:
Some people like to purée 1–2 cups of the soup. Remove the meat from the portion to be puréed.

SHORT RIBS AND LENTIL SOUP

Short ribs and lentils, eminently compatible, produce a delectable, hearty soup-stew. It would be fine to take along in a big pot to a ski lodge, needing only warming up to provide a quick meal. A basket of assorted breads and a leafy salad go with the soup; dessert could be stewed fruit and ginger snaps, or store-bought pastry.

Equally good for chilly days at the shore or in the city, the soup might be preceded by a first course of shrimp or clams on the half shell for a sumptuous meal.

With the soup try mulled wine; red or white. Simmered, cut with water, sweetened with honey, and stirred with a cinnamon stick it is a comforting, but festive drink.

3 pounds meaty short ribs, cut in 2-inch pieces	1 bay leaf
3 slices bacon	1½ teaspoons savory
1 medium onion, chopped	¾ cup finely chopped parsley
2 garlic cloves, chopped	½ cup dry white wine
2½ teaspoons salt	2 cups beef broth
½ teaspoon freshly ground black pepper	Water to cover (3–4 cups)
	2 cups lentils

Wipe the meat and trim off large pieces of outside fat. Pat meat dry.

In large heavy skillet, cook the bacon until it is crisp. Set aside on paper towel to drain. Pour off all but a film of fat.

Brown ribs slowly in the same skillet, a few pieces at a time. When brown, blot them on paper towel and place in a heavy saucepan or kettle over low heat.

Stir in the onion, garlic, salt, pepper, bay leaf, savory, and ¼ cup of the parsley. Add the wine and cook for 5 minutes.

Pour in the beef broth, and add water to just cover. Bring to a boil, reduce heat, and simmer, covered, for 1¼ to 1½ hours, or until meat is tender but not falling off the bones. Skim off fat. Add lentils, cover and simmer another 30–45 minutes, or until beans are tender.

❄ For later serving, cool to room temperature and refrigerate or freeze.

Serve in large bowls, and sprinkle with the remaining parsley and crumbled bacon. Supply forks and knives as well as spoons.   *4–6 servings*

LENTIL AND SAUSAGE SOUP

Partial puréing makes this soup thick, rich, and satisfying, and a little cumin adds an interesting Middle Eastern flavor. It is served with the refreshing touch of a squeeze of lemon. The recipe is for quite a lot of soup, but, once made, it can be frozen in batches, for smaller gatherings.

Dark bread is practically a must with the soup, and crisp raw vegetables with a Savory Sour Cream Dip (see page 69) would be nice before it. To carry through with the Middle Eastern theme, the accompanying salad could have some crumbled Feta cheese in it, and dessert could be baklava.

Jug wines, red or white, go with this, as do cider, beer, and iced tea.

3 tablespoons butter
2 medium onions, finely chopped
4 garlic cloves, minced
1 eight-ounce can tomato sauce
1 cup dry red wine
2 cups lentils
6 cups water
4 cups chicken broth

2 teaspoons cumin
1 tablespoon salt
    Freshly ground black pepper
¼ pound Polish or other garlic
    sausage, cut in thin slices
2 hard-boiled eggs, chopped
2 lemons, each cut into 6 wedges

Heat 2 tablespoons of the butter in a heavy saucepan or kettle. Add the onions and garlic, and stir over low heat until the onions are soft and golden, but not brown. Stir in the tomato sauce. Add the wine and cook briskly for 3–4 minutes, to reduce it slightly.

Wash and carefully pick over the lentils, and add them, with the water, broth, cumin, salt, and several grindings of the pepper mill, to the kettle. Bring to a boil, reduce heat and simmer, partially covered, for 45 minutes, or until lentils are tender. Stir in the remaining tablespoon of butter.

Purée 2 cups of the soup in a blender or food processor (more, if you wish a smoother soup), and stir into the rest.

❋ At this point, the soup can be cooled and refrigerated or frozen for another time.

Reheat gently and check seasonings. Sauté sausage lightly in a dry skillet to render some fat. Blot on paper towel and add to the soup.

Serve in bowls and sprinkle with the chopped egg. Offer the lemon wedges in a small bowl. *8–10 servings*

ANGELICA'S BEEF AND BEAN SOUP

At Angelica's restaurant in New York's Greenwich Village, you might have a soup like this as a main course, with bread, wine, salad, and dessert, served with as much glamour as an eight-course dinner. Made at home, the soup can be the main attraction for a big party, or frozen in smaller quantities, for more intimate occasions during a long cold winter.

Soups like this, once peasant dishes, are now great treats. On a farm in the "old days," stock was no problem. There were always bones on hand and vegetables from the garden or the root cellar; the stock could simmer away for hours on the back of the wood stove. Beans and vegetables were then added to the strained stock at appropriate times for their cooking.

We can still do it all today, serving forth a wondrous bowl, and well worth the time and effort of making it. Make it on a weekend, when there are people around, not only to help but to be tantalized by the wonderful aroma of stock one day and be rewarded by the soup the next.

Dessert at Angelica's would be her genuine gelati or pastry, made right there. At home, we could serve Zabaglione (page 247) as a substitute for Angelica's marvels, or just have a fine cheese and fruit, Gorgonzola and apples, for instance.

The wine could be a Rioja or a good Chianti.

Note: To the beef stock recipe on page 32 add

1 pound marrow bones	1 tablespoon salt
1 quart water	1 bay leaf
2 medium parsnips	

Cook down to 3 quarts rather than 2 quarts. Rescue the marrow from the bones and add to the stock.

THE SOUP

½ cup each dried navy, pink, and red kidney beans	2 teaspoons salt
4 slices bacon	1 tablespoon oregano
3 medium onions, chopped	½ teaspoon ground coriander
3 garlic cloves, minced	½ cup each chopped carrots, chopped celery
1½ pounds boneless stewing beef, cut in ¾-inch pieces	2 leeks
2–4 tablespoons cooking oil	3 tablespoons chopped fresh dill
3 quarts beef stock (see Note)	2 cups fresh fava beans, or 1 ten-ounce package frozen baby lima beans
⅓ cup split peas, green or yellow	

Wash and pick over beans. Soak the beans overnight in water to cover. Drain and place in the pot or kettle in which you plan to make the soup. Or, prepare them the day the soup is being made: Put the beans in a saucepan with water to cover. Bring to a boil, remove from heat and allow to stand for 1 hour. Drain.

Cook the bacon until crisp in a large heavy skillet. Set aside on paper towel to drain. Cook the onions and garlic in the bacon fat until the onions are limp and transparent, but not brown. Transfer the onions and garlic with a slotted spoon to the pot containing the soaked beans.

Pat the beef dry with paper towel; it does not brown well if it is wet. Add 2 tablespoons of the oil to the bacon fat in the skillet and brown the beef, a few pieces at a time. Add them to the soup pot as they are browned. Use more oil if needed.

Add the stock, bring to a boil, reduce heat and simmer for ½ hour. Add split peas, salt, oregano, and coriander. Simmer, partially covered, for ½ hour, stirring occasionally.

Add carrots and celery. Cut off dark green tops of leeks and trim root ends. Split lengthwise and wash well between leaves. Chop across in ½-inch pieces. Add to the soup with 2 tablespoons of the dill. Cook, partially covered, for ½ to ¾ hour more, or until beef and beans are tender. Add salt if needed.

To finish, bring soup to a boil, add fava beans, cover and cook another 5 minutes, or until favas are tender but not too soft. Sprinkle with remaining dill and serve.

10–12 servings

SAVORY SOUR CREAM DIP

1 egg	4 teaspoons lemon juice
1 teaspoon salt	1 teaspoon grated onion
⅛ teaspoon white pepper	2 tablespoons chopped fresh dill
Pinch of sugar	1½ cups sour cream

Beat the egg until it is fluffy and lemon colored. Add everything else, stirring to mix well. Chill for at least 1 hour before serving.

COUSCOUS

This famous North African specialty so popular in France is about to become the rage in New York. Couscous is the name of this dish as well as the grain, usually semolina, around which all the luscious ingredients are heaped.

Don't be discouraged by the length of the recipe—there are a lot of vegetables.

In this recipe, quick-cooking couscous grain is used, taking less time and fuss than regular and eliminating the need for special equipment. In Morocco, where it is the national dish, couscous is cooked traditionally in a *couscousière*. This two-part vessel resembles a large double boiler. The lower part is for the stew; the upper part, with a perforated bottom, holds the grain. The grain steams slowly over the stew and requires special handling to prevent it from becoming lumpy or soggy.

Couscous is served with a little very hot sauce called harissa. It can be found in small cans in specialty food shops, or you can make it from Pierre Franey's recipe given here.

Pita bread, buttered in the pockets, quartered and heated, is a good accompaniment. Cucumbers, scallions, and parsley in a lemon and oil dressing would make a cool, pleasant first or salad course.

Dessert could be baklava from a Greek bakery, or nuts, dates, and figs with Tawny Port.

Serve the couscous with a Rioja, or a not-too-sweet rosé.

2 tablespoons olive oil
2½ pounds meaty lamb neck, with bones, cut in 2-inch pieces
4 medium onions, coarsely chopped
2 garlic cloves, minced
4 cups chicken broth
6 cups water
1¾ teaspoons salt
½ teaspoon freshly ground black pepper
1½ teaspoons cumin
½ teaspoon turmeric
½ teaspoon crumbled saffron
½ teaspoon ground cinnamon

2 cups yellow turnip, cut in ¾-inch cubes
3 medium carrots, cut in 2-inch pieces (split thick ends)
3 small zucchini, cut in ¾-inch slices
1 red or green pepper, seeded, cut in 1-inch pieces
1 cup canned chick peas, drained
½ cup raisins
1 four-ounce jar pimientos, coarsely chopped
1½ cups couscous grain
2 tablespoons butter
Harissa sauce

Heat the oil in a large, heavy pot that has a lid. Put in the lamb pieces and stir over moderately high heat until the meat loses its color. Add the onions and garlic and continue cooking and stirring until onions are transparent and softened.

Add the chicken broth, 3 cups of the water and 1 teaspoon of the salt. Cook at a gentle boil for 20 minutes, skimming off foam as it forms.

Add the pepper, cumin, turmeric, saffron, and cinnamon. Reduce heat and simmer, covered, for 30 minutes.

Add the turnip and carrots. Return to simmer, cover and cook for 10 minutes.

Add the zucchini, red pepper, chick peas, raisins, and pimientos. Return to a simmer, cover and cook for 10 minutes, or until lamb and vegetables are tender.

When the stew is almost ready, bring the remaining 3 cups of water to a boil in a saucepan with the 2 tablespoons of butter and the remaining ¾ teaspoon of salt. Add the couscous gradually, stirring constantly. Cook and stir for about 2 minutes, being careful as it is thickening and plopping. When the water is almost all absorbed, cover and allow to stand, off heat, for 15 minutes, or until all the water is absorbed. Fluff with a fork.

Check the stew for salt and add more if needed. Stir in less than 1 teaspoon of the harissa (hot sauce) and serve the rest in a small bowl. Place a mound of couscous in each heated bowl and ladle stew meat and vegetables onto and around the grain. Moisten with stew liquid and serve at once.

4—6 servings

PIERRE FRANEY'S HARISSA

12 long hot fresh green or red
  peppers
3 large cloves of garlic
¼ cup olive oil

⅛ teaspoon ground cumin
Tabasco or Louisiana hot sauce
  to taste, optional

Cut off stems of peppers. Split peppers and trim away veins and discard seeds. Chop peppers. There should be ½ cup.

Place peppers, garlic, oil, and cumin into the container of a blender. Blend at high speed to fine liquid. Add Tabasco or Louisiana hot sauce to taste.

about ½ cup

3

Soups with Chicken

MULLIGATAWNY

This chicken soup-stew probably got into the Western cuisine from India via England in the days of the Empire. The name means "pepper water," and pleasantly spicy, mildly curried it is, toned down at the end with rice.

Hot pita bread, chutney, and a cool Cucumber and Yogurt Salad (recipe follows) would go well with the Mulligatawny. Dessert could be fresh fruit in season.

Beer is good with this—or Pimm's Cup.

1 tablespoon butter
2 pounds chicken drumsticks
   and/or thighs
1 medium onion, finely chopped
1 medium green pepper, chopped
2 celery stalks, chopped
1 medium green apple, finely
   chopped
1½ teaspoons salt

⅛ teaspoon each ground cloves and
   cayenne
2 tablespoons flour
1 tablespoon curry powder
6 cups chicken broth
   Juice of 1 lemon
   Hot boiled rice
¼ cup chopped parsley

Heat the butter in a heavy casserole or saucepan and brown the chicken pieces lightly. Add the onion, green pepper, celery, and apple. Stir in salt, cloves, and cayenne. Stir and cook until onions are slightly soft. Sprinkle flour and curry over all and mix well. Pour chicken broth in gradually, stirring to clear the bottom of the pan. Bring to a boil, reduce heat and simmer covered for 45–60 minutes, until chicken is very tender.

Tip casserole and skim off fat, or cool and refrigerate and remove fat when it has hardened.

❁ At this point it can be frozen.

When soup is hot and ready to serve, stir in lemon juice. Serve the soup in large bowls or soup plates with a mound of hot rice in the middle, and sprinkle parsley over all. Serve with knives and forks as well as soup spoons.

6 servings

CUCUMBER AND YOGURT SALAD

2 medium cucumbers, thinly sliced
¼ teaspoon salt, or to taste
⅛ teaspoon freshly ground black pepper
2 tablespoons finely chopped fresh dill
½ to 1 cup plain yogurt
2 tablespoons finely chopped parsley

Put the cucumbers into a small serving dish. Sprinkle with salt, pepper, and dill. Stir in the yogurt for desired consistency, and sprinkle with parsley.

6 servings

MIDDLE EASTERN CHICKEN SOUP

Mint and yogurt give this rather sturdy rice and chicken soup a lovely lightness. Suitable for luncheon or supper, any time of the year, it is a useful item for your repertoire.

Served with pastry cheese straws or Popovers (recipe follows), the soup has a kind of elegance; with French or hot pita bread it is a little more homey. The salad could have some Feta cheese in it, as well as lemon and a pinch of oregano, to carry through the Middle Eastern theme.

Since the soup is not a bit heavy, dessert can be wickedly rich—assorted pastries, for instance.

Serve with a light white wine—a Muscadet or an Alsatian Sylvaner.

1 tablespoon butter	¼ teaspoon white pepper
10 scallions with crisp green tops, chopped	6 cups chicken broth
½ teaspoon thyme	¼ cup rice
2 teaspoons crumbled dried mint, or 2 tablespoons fresh mint, finely chopped	2½ to 3 cups cooked chicken, cut in bite-size pieces
1¼ teaspoons salt	1 cup yogurt
	¼ cup finely chopped fresh dill, or parsley

Heat the butter in a saucepan or kettle and add the scallions. Cook on low heat until the scallions are wilted but not brown. Stir in the thyme, mint, salt, pepper, and broth. Bring to a boil, stir in the rice, cover, reduce heat and simmer for 15–20 minutes, or until rice is tender.

Add the chicken and cook for 2–3 minutes to heat the chicken through. Put the yogurt in a small bowl and carefully stir in a few tablespoons of the hot soup to make a smooth mixture. Add the mixture to the soup, taste and add salt if needed. Heat gently, but do not let it boil. Serve sprinkled with dill or parsley.

6 servings

POPOVERS

1¼ cups milk at room temperature
Butter for pans
2 eggs at room temperature

½ teaspoon salt
1 cup flour

In a 4-cup measuring cup beat the milk, eggs, salt, and flour until smooth.

Generously butter the cups of the popover pan and heat in 450° oven. When pan is hot, remove from oven and fill each cup ⅔ full.

Bake 10 minutes at 450°, then lower heat to 350° for another 20–25 minutes until popovers are puffed and golden. *Do not* open oven until 30 minutes baking time has elapsed.   *for 11-cup iron popover pan*

WATERZOOIE

Waterzooie is a Belgian soup-stew, sometimes made with fish. This version is adapted to our little frying chickens rather than the customary, but hard-to-find, stewing hen. The recipe looks long, but the dish is simply chicken, stewed in a well-seasoned broth, made rich and elegant with eggs and cream at the end. To our taste the cloves are enough spice, but add a pinch of nutmeg if you like.

It is a meal in itself with just dark bread and a salad, perhaps of endive and beets in oil and vinegar. Dessert could be Gingerbread (page 173) with applesauce and sour cream.

Beer is probably the best drink with this, or red or white wine.

2 tablespoons butter	6 cups chicken broth (fat removed)
1 three-pound chicken, cut up	½ teaspoon salt
½ cup dry white wine	Freshly ground black pepper
2 leeks	1 onion stuck with 2 cloves
2 stalks celery, coarsely chopped	4 egg yolks
½ cup finely chopped parsley	¼ cup heavy cream
1 teaspoon thyme	1 lemon, cut in thin slices
1 bay leaf	

Heat the butter in a heavy saucepan or kettle and lightly brown the chicken pieces. Add the wine and stir up the bits in the bottom of the pan.

Trim the leeks down to the palest green. Split them lengthwise, wash thoroughly, and cut across in ½-inch pieces. Add to the chicken, along with the celery, 2 tablespoons of the parsley, thyme, and bay leaf. Pour in the broth. Add salt, a few grindings of the peppermill, and the onion with its cloves.

Bring to a simmer, cover and cook for 30–45 minutes, or until chicken is tender. Skim off fat (or remove fat after it has been hardened by refrigeration). Take out and discard bay leaf and onion.

❊ For later serving, cool to room temperature and refrigerate or freeze, covered.

At serving time, return soup to a simmer. Lightly beat together the egg yolks and cream in a small bowl. Add a little hot broth to the eggs and cream and stir the mixture into the soup. Heat carefully without boiling.

Serve in large bowls and garnish with lemon slices and the remaining parsley. Provide forks and knives as well as spoons. *6 servings*

4

Vegetable Soups

GARBANZO AND PASTA SOUP

The Italians have a gift for combining beans, pasta, and sometimes rice with vegetables, to produce delicious, satisfying main-course soups. This one is mainly flavored with rosemary, and it has the unusual addition of anchovies, which give a special taste, hard to identify—even by anchovy-haters.

A salad of interesting greens, including some arugula with its good strong taste, and plenty of Italian bread would go well with the soup. When pears are to be found, and real Gorgonzola, the combination makes a splendid dessert.

Serve a red jug wine from Italy.

1 cup small pasta
2 tablespoons olive oil
1 large onion, finely chopped
2 garlic cloves, minced
⅓ cup finely chopped parsley
1 small (1¾-ounce) can flat
   anchovies
1 eight-ounce can tomato sauce
1 one-pound can tomatoes,
   chopped, or 2 cups fresh
   tomatoes, peeled, chopped

5 cups water
2 teaspoons rosemary, crumbled
1 teaspoon oregano
¼ teaspoon freshly ground black
   pepper
2 teaspoons salt
2 one-pound cans garbanzo beans
   Freshly grated Parmesan cheese

Cook pasta according to package directions. Drain and set aside.

Continued

In a large, heavy, lidded saucepan or casserole, heat the oil, add the onion and garlic, and cook over low heat until the onion is transparent. Stir in ¼ cup of the parsley.

Drain, cut up and mash the anchovies, and add them with the tomato sauce and tomatoes. Cook for 1–2 minutes.

Add the water, rosemary, oregano, pepper, and salt. Bring to a simmer, cover and cook for 20–30 minutes, stirring occasionally. Stir in beans and their liquid. Heat, uncovered, for about 5 minutes. Add cooked pasta and cook another 5 minutes, or until soup is piping hot. Check seasoning and add salt and pepper if needed.

❋ The soup can, at this point, be cooled and refrigerated or frozen for later use. At serving time, bring soup to a boil, sprinkle with parsley and offer Parmesan cheese to be added to each serving.   *6–8 servings*

SUCCOTASH CHOWDER

A fine way to use up cooked corn, after a feast of it on the cob, is to make a chowder. Corn time is also tomato time, and a big platter of luscious sliced tomatoes, seasoned with nothing but a squeeze of lemon, salt and pepper, and fresh basil leaves, makes a good accompaniment.

At other times of the year, frozen or canned corn can be used. Corn is one of the few vegetables that freeze and can well. Frozen lima beans are a fine substitute when the fresh ones are not available.

A summer mélange of berries, slices of different kinds of melons, or any fruit in season would be a refreshing finish to the meal. On a cold winter's day Baked Apples (page 277) would be nice and homey.

Chilled Spanish Sherry—a Fino or Amontillado—goes well with the chowder.

3 slices bacon, diced	3 cups cooked corn scraped from
1 medium onion, finely chopped	the cob, or 1 one-pound can
3 potatoes, peeled, cut in ½-inch	creamed corn and 1 eight-
dice	ounce can Niblets
2 cups water	3–4 cups milk
½ teaspoon thyme	2 cups cooked baby lima beans
½ teaspoon salt	1 tablespoon butter
⅛ teaspoon white pepper	¼ cup finely chopped parsley

In a heavy saucepan or casserole, cook bacon until it is golden and crisp. Remove the bits with a slotted spoon to paper towel to drain. Set aside. Pour off all but 1 tablespoon of fat and add the onions. Cook, stirring, until onions are soft, but not brown.

Add the potatoes, water, thyme, salt, and pepper. Cover and cook for 15 minutes, or until potatoes are just tender.

Add the corn and milk; cook, uncovered, for 10 minutes. Add the lima beans and cook to heat them through.

Stir in butter and serve sprinkled with parsley and bacon bits.

6 servings

SOUPE AU PISTOU

Pistou is the French Riviera's version of Italy's minestrone, full of vegetables and beans and a little pasta. Unlike minestrone, though, this soup has a sauce that goes with it and gives the soup its name. Pistou, the sauce of garlic, basil, oil, and cheese, gives this vegetable soup plenty of taste.

In France the soup is a salute to the beginning of summer, with fresh basil and local vegetables from the markets or your garden. Other times of the year vegetables of the season go into the soup to cook as long or as little as required, and dried basil instead of fresh is used in the Pistou.

Here is a basic version; other vegetables may be substituted or added, according to availability: white or yellow turnips, parsnips, squash, broccoli or cauliflower, fresh white beans, zucchini, and green peppers. Root vegetables take longer to cook; zucchini and peppers take a very short time. Potatoes should be new or regular, not baking.

Plenty of crusty bread, a big salad, and a cheese tray make a meal of this soup. Dessert, after such a wholesome dish, could be fabulous and fattening.

Any simple table wine is good with the Pistou; so is beer.

2 cups carrots, cut in ½-inch dice	Salt and pepper
2 cups potatoes, cut in ¾-inch dice, or little new potatoes in skins, halved or quartered	2 cups fresh green beans, cut in 1-inch pieces
2 cups chopped onion	½ cup vermicelli broken into 2-inch pieces
1 leek	2 cups fresh peas, or 1 ten-ounce package frozen peas
2 cups tomatoes, peeled and chopped, or 1 one-pound can tomatoes, undrained, chopped	1 one-pound can kidney beans, drained
1 quart chicken broth	½ teaspoon crumbled saffron threads (optional)
2 quarts water	

Put the carrots, potatoes, and onions into a large kettle. Cut off the green part of the leek, down to the palest green. Split lengthwise, clean thoroughly, and chop across in ½-inch pieces. Add the leek, tomatoes, the broth and the water to the kettle. The liquid can also be all water, but add 1 tablespoon salt.

Add salt and pepper to taste. More may be needed later. Bring to a simmer and cook, uncovered, for 10–15 minutes, until vegetables are almost tender.

Add the green beans and vermicelli. Continue to simmer, uncovered, for 10–15 minutes, or until beans and pasta are cooked. Add peas, kidney beans, and saffron and cook just until soup is hot.

PISTOU SAUCE

    4 garlic cloves, chopped
    ¼ cup chopped fresh basil, or 1
       tablespoon dried

    ¼ to ½ cup olive oil
    6 tablespoons freshly grated
       Parmesan cheese

Put all the ingredients for the Pistou Sauce into the blender. Blend to the consistency of mayonnaise, using more oil if necessary.

Put the sauce in the bottom of a soup tureen. Stir or beat 1 cup of soup into the sauce and add the rest gradually.

Pistou sauce may also be passed separately for diners to help themselves.   *6–8 servings*

WHITE AND GREEN BEAN SOUP

Rosemary and garlic give this hearty and handsome main-course soup a pleasantly strong taste; lemon and crisp green beans add a freshness. Like all soups with cooked dried beans in them, puréing 1–2 cups of the finished soup gives it a thickness some people like. Otherwise, the beans, white and green, are intact in a beautiful, almost clear broth.

Serve a big basket of assorted breads because white, brown, or dark bread goes equally well with the soup. Crisp romaine could be the main ingredient in a salad with cucumbers, radishes, celery, tomatoes, if they are in season, and an oil and vinegar dressing with a generous amount of Dijon mustard in it.

Fruit is always a good dessert after a fine soup, but sometimes a light, Lemon-Walnut Cake might be the proper ending (recipe follows).

With the soup drink a light, thirst-quenching dry white wine—a Soave or French jug wine.

1½ cups dried white beans, Great
   Northern, navy, or baby lima
6 cups water
3 garlic cloves, chopped
2 teaspoons salt
4 cups beef broth
¼ teaspoon freshly ground black
   pepper

1 teaspoon rosemary, crumbled
2 cups fresh green beans (about ¾
   pound), cut on the diagonal in 1-
   inch pieces
1 tablespoon butter
Juice of ½ lemon

Wash and pick over the dried beans. Put them into a large saucepan or kettle with the water and bring to a boil. Remove from the heat, cover, and allow to stand for 1 hour.

Return to the heat and bring to a boil again. Reduce heat and simmer, partially covered, for ½ hour. Using a heavy fork, mash the garlic with the salt until no large chunks remain. Add to the saucepan with the beans. Add the broth, pepper, and rosemary.

Simmer, partially covered, until beans are tender. This can take 15 minutes or as long as 1 hour; timing for beans is hard to predict—keep checking.

❀ Soup can be made ahead to this point, and refrigerated or frozen after thorough cooling.

Cook the green beans uncovered in 2 quarts of boiling salted water until they are tender-crisp and bright green. Drain and add to the soup when the white beans are tender but not mushy. If green beans are not to be added right away, rinse in cold water to retain color. Stir in the butter and lemon. Serve at once, while green beans are still bright.

Note: If you want some of the soup puréed, do it before adding the green beans—the color will be better. *6–8 servings*

LEMON-WALNUT CAKE

Light, white, tart with lemon and full of nuts, this is a fine dessert by itself; but do try it with fresh or stewed fruit.

½ cup butter	1 teaspoon baking powder
1 cup plus 1 tablespoon sugar	½ cup milk
2 eggs	2 lemons
1½ cups flour	½ cup walnuts, coarsely chopped

In a large mixing bowl, cream together the butter and 1 cup of the sugar. Add the eggs, 1 at a time, beating well. Sift together the flour and baking powder. Add to the mixing bowl, in 3 batches alternating with the milk. Stir in the grated rind of 1 of the lemons and the walnuts. Turn into a greased 9-inch square pan. Bake in preheated 375° oven for 30–40 minutes, or until a skewer comes out clean after being plunged into the center of the cake.

Mix together the grated rind of the other lemon, the juice of both lemons, and the remaining tablespoon of sugar. Dribble evenly over the cake while it is still hot. Cut into squares in the pan, and remove to serving platter with a spatula. *for 9-inch square pan*

PASTA, BEANS, AND SPINACH SOUP

In this delectable, robust soup the clear liquid is a delightful foil for the pasta and beans. And the addition of spinach and lemon at the last minute gives it a marvelous freshness.

A tray of assorted cheeses would be a good first course; salad could be crisp raw vegetables in a vinaigrette—zucchini, mushrooms, scallions, and cucumbers, for instance—all with crusty French or Italian bread.

Try Lemon Mousse for dessert—a cool, cloud-light concoction made with egg whites (recipe follows). It's just right after the soup.

White wine's best here—a lemony Sicilian white, or a sprightly Pinot Grigio.

1 cup dried red kidney beans	¼ teaspoon white pepper
6 cups cold water	1 tablespoon olive oil
½ cup small pasta	10–12 ounces fresh spinach,
3 garlic cloves, chopped	chopped
2 teaspoons salt	Juice of 1 lemon
4 cups beef broth	
1 teaspoon rosemary, crumbled	

Wash and pick over beans. Place in a large saucepan or kettle with the cold water and bring to a boil. Turn off the heat, cover and allow to stand for 1 hour.

Cook the pasta in boiling water according to package directions. Drain and set aside.

Bring the beans back to a boil. Reduce heat and simmer, partially covered, for ½ hour. Using a heavy fork, mash the garlic with the salt until it is a paste and no large chunks remain. Add to the saucepan with the beef broth, rosemary, and pepper. Simmer, partially covered, until beans are tender. This can take 15 minutes or as long as 1 hour; it is hard to predict cooking time for beans—keep checking. Stir in the olive oil and the cooked pasta.

❀ The soup can at this point be cooled and refrigerated or frozen for later use.

At serving time, bring soup to a boil, put in the spinach and cover for about 1 minute.

Sprinkle the lemon juice over the top and serve at once in warm bowls.

6 servings

LEMON MOUSSE

1 cup whipping cream	2 tablespoons grated lemon rind
3 eggs	2 teaspoons plain gelatin
Salt	Lemon zest for garnish
¾ cup sugar	
½ cup lemon juice	

Whip the cream until stiff and refrigerate. Separate the eggs, putting the yolks into the top of a double boiler. Beat the whites until they are stiff. Add a pinch of salt and ¼ cup of the sugar. Keep beating until whites are satiny. Refrigerate.

Add ½ cup of sugar, the lemon juice, lemon rind and gelatin to the egg yolks. With water boiling in the bottom of the double boiler, but not touching the upper pan, beat the mixture until it thickens enough to coat a spoon and gelatin is thoroughly dissolved. Remove from heat and beat until it is just warm, not hot.

Fold the beaten egg whites into the yolk mixture, and then fold in the whipped cream. Turn into a serving dish or individual parfait glasses. Garnish with slivered zest of lemon, and chill for 2 hours.   *6 servings*

MINESTRONE

This wonderful rich soup, replete with vegetables, cooked dried beans, and pasta, and topped with Parmesan cheese, lends itself to almost infinite variations. Not being Italian—and having only been there once—I am no authority, but it seemed, from my research, that I could feel free to make the soup to my liking. This is the result.

I chose red kidney beans, although navy or pea beans can be used, because of their color and flavor. I've used beef broth and a whole can of tomato paste (none left over to wonder what to do with) instead of whole tomatoes because I thought a smooth base was needed for all those vegetables. The list is long, but it is the very abundance that makes the soup so good.

Any time of the year is minestrone time. The vegetables will change, but the basics are the same. This recipe is a summer one, but it could be for any season.

The leafiest of salads is called for following the soup, and a tray of Italian cheeses—Bel Paese, Taleggio, for example—and beautiful fresh fruit of the season.

An Italian red jug wine would be good to drink with the soup and the cheese.

¾ cup dried red kidney beans	½ teaspoon black pepper
½ cup small pasta	2 carrots, cut in ¼-inch dice
1 medium onion, finely chopped	2 cups finely shredded cabbage
⅓ cup salt pork, cut in ¼-inch dice	2 small potatoes, peeled, cut in ½-inch dice
1 tablespoon olive oil	1 cup green beans, cut in 1-inch pieces
1 six-ounce can tomato paste	
4 cups beef broth	1 small zucchini, cut in ¾-inch pieces
4 cups water	
1 large garlic clove, chopped	1 small green pepper, cut in ¾-inch pieces
2 teaspoons salt	
½ teaspoon oregano	½ cup finely chopped parsley
1 teaspoon dried basil, or 1 tablespoon chopped fresh	Parmesan cheese, freshly grated

In order to have the beans and pasta at just the proper point of firmness, I am suggesting that they be cooked separately and added to the soup to heat through at the end.

Wash and pick over the beans. Put them in a saucepan with 2 cups of water. Bring to a boil, remove from the heat, cover and allow to stand for 1 hour. Bring to a boil, reduce heat and simmer, partially covered, until beans are tender but not too soft. Timing for beans is infuriatingly hard to predict: They can take 15 minutes or 1½ hours—keep checking until they are the way you want them. Drain and set aside, reserving the liquid.

Cook pasta according to package directions. Drain, discard liquid, and set aside.

In a large, heavy kettle or casserole that has a lid, cook the onion, salt pork, and oil together until the onions are golden and softened. Stir in the tomato paste, broth, and remaining 2 cups of water. Mash the garlic with the salt until no large pieces remain and add to the casserole. Bring to a simmer, cover and cook for 1 hour. To keep the soup at the merest simmer it may be necessary to uncover partially.

Add the oregano, basil, pepper, carrots, cabbage and potatoes. Simmer, partially covered, for ½ hour.

Add the green beans and continue cooking, partially covered, at the merest simmer for ½ hour. Add the zucchini and green pepper and simmer another 15 minutes, or until zucchini and pepper are cooked but not too soft.

Carefully stir in the beans, the reserved cooking liquid from the beans, and the pasta. Simmer for about 5 minutes, or until beans and pasta are heated through. The soup should be thick, but if you prefer it thinner, add a small amount of hot water. Check seasoning and add salt and pepper if needed.

❀ The soup keeps in the refrigerator for about a week, after cooling, and even improves. It might need a little water on reheating, and an adjustment of seasonings. The soup can also be frozen, after cooling.

Serve sprinkled with parsley, and offer a bowl of Parmesan for individual serving.

6–8 servings

COLD DILLED YOGURT SOUP

Half-and-half smooths this lovely soup; raisins provide subtle sweetness and a bit of chewiness. In addition, there are cucumbers, scallions, and fresh dill. Served icy cold the soup can be the star of a happy deck, patio, or terrace summer luncheon or supper. Scandinavian dark bread goes with the soup, as well as with a leafy salad and a soft cheese like Brie. If it is corn and tomato time, the soup could follow a feast of fresh corn on the cob and be followed by sliced tomatoes with fresh basil. Apple pie could be the dessert.

When the soup is served in a cooler season, the first course could be the cheese, and the apple pie could be hot.

This might be the time to serve a rosé wine from Provence or the Loire.

¾ cup raisins	8 ice cubes
4 cups plain yogurt	1 tablespoon salt
1½ cups half-and-half	¾ teaspoon white pepper
2 medium cucumbers	¼ cup finely chopped parsley
½ cup finely chopped scallions, including green	2 coarsely chopped hard-boiled eggs
¼ cup finely chopped fresh dill	

Soak the raisins in hot water. Set aside.

In a tureen or serving bowl, mix the yogurt and half-and-half. Peel, halve lengthwise, and scoop out the seeds of the cucumbers. Chop them into ¼-inch cubes and stir into the soup. Add scallions, dill, ice cubes, salt, pepper, and the drained raisins.

Refrigerate for 2 or 3 hours. Serve garnished with the parsley and eggs. If soup has thickened too much, add ice water a little at a time—but not more than 1 cup—until it is correct consistency. *6–8 servings*

SUGGESTIONS FOR SALADS WITH FRUIT

An oil and vinegar dressing tastes surprisingly good with fruit, particularly citrus fruit.

BASIC OIL AND VINEGAR DRESSING
This dressing is easily adapted to taste with more salt, pepper, or mustard.

⅛ teaspoon salt	2 tablespoons wine or cider vinegar
¼ teaspoon dry mustard	6 tablespoons olive oil or salad oil,
⅛ teaspoon freshly ground black pepper	or a combination

Mix the seasonings with the vinegar and beat in the oil.   *½ cup dressing*

These salads give you a chance to try some of the fruit vinegars, such as raspberry and blueberry, and different oils—walnut, for instance.

Proportions are variable but here are some ideas for combinations.

Grapefruit sections, endive and watercress: Peel grapefruit, remove fruit from membranes; cut endive across, or into slivers, or just separate the leaves. Trim stems from watercress, break up but do not chop.

Sliced oranges, cucumbers, scallions, lettuce: Peel, seed, and slice the oranges in thin rounds. Score the cucumbers with a fork and cut in thin rounds. Chop scallions including crisp green tops. Place on a bed of Boston lettuce.

Grated carrots, raisins, apples, grated onion, parsley: Grate, shred, or finely julienne the carrots. Soak raisins in boiling water to cover for 10 minutes before adding. Peel and core apples, cut in ½-inch dice. Add 1 teaspoon grated onion to the dressing. Finely chop the parsley.

Kiwi fruit, grapefruit sections, scallions, Boston lettuce: Peel and slice kiwis, peel grapefruit and remove pulp from membranes, chop scallions, wash and dry lettuce.

Endive, radishes, watercress, orange sections, chopped walnuts: Cut endive across in rounds, slice radishes. Trim stems from watercress, break up but do not chop. Peel oranges, cut pulp from membranes. Chop walnuts into ½-inch pieces.

Apples, endive, cooked beets, blueberries, walnuts: Peel, core and dice apples (tart if possible), cut endive across in rings, dice beets, toss in blueberries and nuts.

COLD MINTED CUCUMBER SOUP

Cold soups are not only good served around an umbrella-shaded table on a patio or deck; they make marvelous luncheon or supper dishes indoors. This one is handsomely white, accented with the purple of "red" onion, gold of raisins, bright yellow of hard-boiled egg yolks, and green of parsley. There is no cooking involved, and little work. But the soup needs to be made ahead to thoroughly cool and blend the flavors.

Dark bread is good with this—firm Scandinavian rye or pumpernickel. If you think the soup is more Eastern, serve pita bread, buttered in the pocket, quartered and heated in the oven. For a taste of Provence serve plain or toasted French bread. In the summer, fresh fruit and a soft cheese, like a Brie or Explorateur, would be a fine dessert; in the winter, a Chocolate Almond Mousse (recipe follows).

A white wine like Pinot Grigio or Chenin Blanc would complement the soup.

⅓ cup yellow raisins	1 tablespoon crumbled dried mint
2 medium cucumbers	1 teaspoon salt
2 cups plain yogurt	White pepper to taste
2 cups milk	4 hard-boiled eggs, coarsely
⅓ cup minced red onion	chopped
¼ cup coarsely chopped walnuts	½ cup finely chopped parsley

Pour boiling water over raisins and set aside.

Peel cucumbers, cut in half lengthwise, and remove seeds with a spoon. Grate the cucumbers into a large bowl. Add yogurt, milk, onion, walnuts, mint, salt and pepper to taste. Drain raisins and stir them in. Refrigerate for 1–2 hours.

Serve from a beautiful large bowl or tureen or in individual bowls with the chopped eggs and parsley added at that time.   *4–5 servings*

CHOCOLATE ALMOND MOUSSE

8 ounces white chocolate   **2 teaspoons almond extract**
4 tablespoons water   **6 eggs, separated**
2 tablespoons ground almonds   **1 cup whipping cream**

Melt the chocolate with the water over low heat. Off heat, add the almonds and extract and beat in the egg yolks, 1 at a time. Beat the egg whites until stiff but not dry. Fold into the yolk mixture. Whip the cream until it forms soft peaks, and fold in. Place in a large serving bowl or in individual parfait glasses. Refrigerate for several hours or overnight.   *6–8 servings*

Note: For a glamorous touch, top with candied violets.

GAZPACHO

Fresh and cold, light but satisfying, this justly famous Andalusian soup is perfect on a hot summer's day. It has to be summer for the tomatoes to be at their best and for the delicious coolness of the soup to be properly anticipated and appreciated.

Like a meal with a curried dish, this soup has the fun of a variety of garnishes in little bowls to accompany it. Some of the garnishes are a diced version of vegetables puréed in the soup—a nice contrast in textures.

Whenever I have gazpacho, it takes me back to a lovely summer day in Seville, when the soup was served in precious china, on a snowy table-cloth, bathed in the special light that comes through those yellow and white striped canvas canopies. I can't remember what the occasion was, but I remember the beauty of the soup and its garnishes, the sandwiches made of a strong ham with a bland cheese like a Muenster on small hard rolls and the dessert Caramel Custard (page 279). The whole marvelous feast can be reproduced for serving on deck or patio table or a checked tablecloth at a beach or country picnic—and the gazpacho tastes just as wonderful.

Serve the driest of Sherries, Manzanilla, or a less dry Fino or a medium Amontillado. Serve a sweet one, Oloroso or Cream, with the custard.

2 medium green peppers, ribs and seeds removed
1 large Spanish onion, peeled
4 medium-size ripe tomatoes, peeled
1 medium cucumber, peeled and seeded
4 garlic cloves, peeled, chopped
½ cup crumbled stale French or Italian bread, crustless
3 cups water
6 tablespoons olive oil
3 tablespoons red wine vinegar
4 teaspoons salt
Tabasco sauce
Freshly ground black pepper

Cut the peppers, onion, tomatoes, and cucumber into chunks and place in a large mixing bowl. Mix in the garlic and bread. Purée in batches of about 2 cups each, using a food processor with the metal blade, or a blender. Gradually add some of the water, oil, and vinegar to each batch. Do not over-purée—leave a little texture.

As each batch is done, pour the purée into a tureen or handsome bowl that can go to the table. Stir in the salt, a few drops of Tabasco, and pepper to taste. Cover and refrigerate for a few hours or overnight.

Add some ice cubes just before serving, and check the seasoning; chilling masks some flavor. Offer garnishes in small bowls (list follows).

6 servings

GARNISHES FOR GAZPACHO

Except for the croutons, which can be as large as ¼ inch, everything should be very finely chopped to have the right taste and texture.

> Tomato: peeled, seeded, chopped in ⅛-inch dice
> Green pepper: deribbed, seeded, chopped in ⅛-inch dice
> Red onions: peeled, chopped in ⅛-inch dice
> Cucumber: peeled, seeded, chopped in ⅛-inch dice
> Hard-boiled egg: finely chopped
> Croutons: ¼-inch cubes

CROUTONS

> **¼ cup olive oil**
> **1 cup crustless French or Italian**
> **bread, cut in ¼-inch cubes**

Heat olive oil in a heavy skillet until a light haze forms. Put in bread and stir and turn in oil until croutons are golden on all sides and crisp. Drain on paper towels.

1 cup

SUMMER VEGETABLE SOUP

This soup was made one summer day at a small cottage by a lake, to serve two hungry people, with a little left over to test when it was cold. It's good either hot or cold. I have set it down as I made it that day even though this is not the usual family amount. The recipe is easy to double to make 4 large or 6 adequate servings.

No French or Italian bread was to be found in the area, but we were able to get unsliced homestyle bread from a local bakery. Brought to freshly baked warmth and crustiness in the oven, it was perfect with the soup.

Dessert was a bowl of assorted plums—red, yellow, and purple—and the crisp sugar cookies that are a staple in small family bakeries all over Canada.

1 tablespoon butter	4 small potatoes, cut in
1 small onion, finely chopped	½-inch dice
4 small carrots, cut in ¼-inch dice	1 cup milk
1 stalk celery, finely chopped	1 tablespoon flour
2 cups beef or vegetable broth	1 cup very small cauliflower
Salt and pepper	flowerets
¼ teaspoon crumbled rosemary	¼ cup finely chopped parsley
1 cup fresh green beans, cut in	Sour cream
½-inch dice	

Heat the butter in a lidded saucepan and add the onion, carrots, and celery. Cook, stirring, on low heat until onions soften, about 5 minutes. Add broth, salt and pepper to taste, and rosemary. Bring to a simmer, cover, and cook for 10 minutes. Add beans and potatoes, unpeeled if they are new. Cover and simmer for 10–12 minutes, or until beans and potatoes are just tender.

Add the milk gradually to the flour to make a smooth mixture and stir into the soup. Add the cauliflower, cover and simmer 5 minutes, or until cauliflower is barely tender. Serve sprinkled with parsley, and offer sour cream in a small bowl. *2–3 servings*

COLD DILLED SOUP WITH ZUCCHINI

The fresh dill permeating this creamy soup imparts a distinguishing freshness. Because it is not heavy in taste or texture, the soup might not seem substantial enough for a main course, but the hidden enrichment—mashed hard-boiled eggs—makes it very satisfying.

The soup requires no cooking at all and practically no time at all to prepare—it is easily done in the food processor. Many breads go with the soup: crusty rye, pumpernickel or pita—serve several different kinds. Pita bread, its pocket buttered, can be cut in quarters and heated.

Instead of a salad and dessert, the two could be combined in a salad with fruit. Some suggestions follow the recipe.

Beer would be a suitable drink with the soup, or a dry white jug wine.

4 hard-boiled eggs	2 cups plain yogurt
6 sprigs parsley, without stems	2 cups milk
6 scallions with crisp tops, cut in 2-inch pieces	2 teaspoons salt
1 tablespoon Dijon mustard	¼ teaspoon white pepper
½ cup sour cream	1 small zucchini, cut in ¼-inch dice
2 medium cucumbers, peeled, seeded, cut in 2-inch pieces	¼ cup chopped fresh dill

Peel the eggs, cut them in two and place in a food processor equipped with the metal blade. Add the parsley, scallions, mustard, and sour cream. Process briefly. Stop when parsley and scallions are still in about 1-inch pieces. Add the cucumbers and stop when cucumbers are not quite liquefied. Add the yogurt and process to combine everything, but stop while there is still texture in the soup.

Remove from the processor and stir in the milk, salt, pepper, zucchini, and dill. Add more salt and pepper if needed.

Chill for an hour, or serve at once with ice cubes in it—2 per bowl.

6 servings

PASTA AND KIDNEY BEAN SOUP

Oregano and a sprinkle of Parmesan at the end give this soup an Italian accent. It is a substantial soup but not heavy. A first course of hard-boiled eggs with anchovies would not be too much, and the accompanying salad could have plenty of crisp raw vegetables in it. Crusty Italian bread is called for, and dessert could be Pears in Madeira (recipe follows).

A light wine suits this soup—Bardolino, Valpolicella, or Chianti for red, Soave or Pinot Grigio for white.

¾ cup small pasta
2 tablespoons butter
2 onions, finely chopped
2 garlic cloves, chopped
1½ teaspoons salt
   Freshly ground black pepper
½ teaspoon thyme
¾ teaspoon oregano

½ cup dry red wine
1 one-pound can Italian tomatoes, crushed
4 cups beef broth
2 one-pound cans kidney beans, undrained
¼ to ½ cup freshly grated Parmesan cheese

Cook the pasta in the water according to package directions. Drain and set aside.

Melt the butter in a heavy saucepan or kettle and put in the onions. Stir and cook on low heat until onions are soft but not brown. Mash the garlic with the salt to make a paste. Stir into onions with a few grindings of the peppermill, the thyme, and oregano. Add the wine and cook down to half. Add the tomatoes and cook 5 minutes. Add the broth and simmer, partially covered, for another 15 minutes.

Add the undrained beans, cover and cook 5 minutes to heat the beans. Add the pasta and cook, uncovered, until the soup comes to a simmer and pasta is heated.

Serve in large bowls with Parmesan cheese on the side, to be sprinkled on each serving.

4–6 servings

PEARS IN MADEIRA

8 unblemished, not-too-ripe pears	**1 cup Madeira**
1 tablespoon lemon juice	**4 cups water**
Slivered zest of 1 orange	**1 cup sugar**

Peel the pears, cut in half, and scoop out the cores carefully. Put halves instantly into a bowl of water with the lemon juice or they will darken.

Put the orange zest, Madeira, water, and sugar into a wide, enamelware or stainless steel saucepan. Bring to a simmer and cook for 5 minutes.

Drain the pears and add to the syrup. Cover and cook until the pears are tender but not too soft, about 10 minutes. Serve chilled or at room temperature.

4–6 servings

VEGETABLE SOUP WITH CUCUMBERS

A clear soup, jam-packed with vegetables, this should satisfy the most ardent vegetable-lover. Like all vegetable soups, timing is paramount. The soup only cooks about ½ hour altogether, but you almost have to stand over it to add the ingredients, which cook at different rates, and to wait for the soup to return to a boil or a simmer each time. A nice addition at the end is a fine dice of cucumbers, for texture and a fresh taste. Another is pimientos for a bright color accent.

A salad seems hardly necessary with all those vegetables in the soup, but a platter of deviled eggs (page 297) on a bed of watercress would be enticing before, with, or after the soup. Serve a basket of dark bread for the soup and thin Scandinavian crisp bread with some soft cheese like Pont l'Evêque, Pyramide, or Bucheron.

The vegetables for this soup are in the market or your garden in early fall, when there are wonderful fruits. A platter of seedless grapes, green, red and purple; assorted plums; different melons, in slices or large cubes; or a large bowl of one fruit—apples or pears or nectarines—would be beautiful not only for their color but also for the lavishness of the number presented.

Drink a white wine—a Chenin Blanc, or Sauvignon Blanc—or a rosé with the soup and the cheese.

1 leek	1 medium parsnip, cut in ⅓-inch dice
2 tablespoons cooking oil	1 medium carrot, cut in ⅓-inch dice
1 medium onion, finely chopped	1 cup small broccoli flowerets
1 cup finely shredded cabbage	1 cup small cauliflower flowerets
2 cups water	2 whole pimientos, chopped, with their juice
1 teaspoon salt	½ cup peeled, seeded cucumbers, cut in ¼-inch dice
¼ teaspoon white pepper	
½ teaspoon savory	
4 cups chicken broth	

Trim the root end of the leek, cut off the dark green, tough tops and split lengthwise. Open up and clean thoroughly between the leaves and cut across in ½-inch pieces.

Heat the oil in a heavy saucepan or flameproof casserole and put in the onion and the leek. Stir over low heat for 4–5 minutes, until onion is soft.

Add the cabbage, water, salt, pepper, and savory. Bring to a boil, reduce heat, and simmer for 10 minutes. Add the chicken broth, parsnip, and carrot. Bring to a boil, reduce heat and simmer for 10 minutes, or until parsnip and carrot are almost tender enough.

Add the broccoli and cauliflower and cook about 5 minutes, until the flowerets are tender but still slightly crisp. Add the pimientos and cucumbers and cook just to heat through.   *4–6 servings*

VEGETABLE SOUP WITH WATERCRESS

Potatoes and squash contribute heartiness to this flavorful mélange of vegetables. Onions, green beans, carrots, and a julienne of zucchini cook in a mixture of water and chicken broth. Cooking time is only about ½ hour, but you have to stand guard so the vegetables will not overcook. Preparing the vegetables takes a bit of time, but the resulting rather elegant luncheon or supper main-course soup makes the effort worthwhile.

French or Italian bread, particularly whole wheat Italian, goes well with the soup. A regular salad seems redundant; serve instead a big fruit salad after the soup: pineapple, strawberries, blueberries, and bananas; oranges, pears, bananas, and kiwi fruit; or plums, apples, peaches, and seedless grapes. A few tablespoons of liqueur—Kirsch, Cream Sherry, or an orange liqueur like Grand Marnier—will add a luscious flavor.

Serve a white wine, Chenin Blanc or Sauvignon Blanc, or a rosé.

2 tablespoons butter
1 small onion, finely chopped
1 cup green beans, cut on the diagonal in 1-inch pieces
2 cups water
2 teaspoons salt
¼ teaspoon white pepper
½ teaspoon thyme
4 cups chicken broth
1 cup Hubbard squash, cut in ⅓-inch dice

2 medium potatoes, cut in ½-inch dice
1 medium carrot, cut in ¼-inch dice
½ cup zucchini, cut in fine julienne
½ cup coarsely chopped watercress leaves, or ¼ cup finely chopped parsley

Melt the butter in a large heavy saucepan or flameproof casserole that can serve as a tureen. Add the onion and cook 1–2 minutes, until onion softens.

Add the green beans and stir to coat with butter. Add the water and 1 teaspoon of the salt, pepper, and thyme. Bring to a simmer and cook 5 minutes.

Add the chicken broth, squash, potatoes, carrot, and the remaining 1 teaspoon salt. Return to a simmer and cook for 10–15 minutes, or until vegetables are tender. Add the zucchini and cook for another 1–2 minutes. Sprinkle with watercress and serve at once.   *4–6 servings*

Note: The soup is cooked uncovered for the most part. It is covered after adding fresh ingredients to hasten return to simmer and then uncovered to continue cooking.

II
FISH AND SEAFOOD SOUPS AND STEWS

5

Chowders and Gumbos

NEW ENGLAND CLAM CHOWDER

New England Clam Chowder is one of America's greatest dishes—even when canned clams have to be used (see note following recipe).

For those who live in the country near the sea, clam chowder is a natural combination with a great feast of fresh corn. Salad and a selection of cheeses and, of course, good French or Italian bread go with the chowder. Apple pie with Calvados and coffee make a fine finish.

Any white wine suits the chowder as long as it is dry—a Muscadet or Chardonnay. A light Pilsener beer is also good.

2 dozen medium-size chowder
    clams
    Dry white wine, or water
¼ pound salt pork, cut in ¼-inch
    dice, or ¼ pound thick bacon,
    cut in ¼-inch dice
1 medium onion, finely chopped
4 medium potatoes, cut in ½-inch
    dice

¼ teaspoon white pepper
    Pinch of thyme
    Dash of Tabasco (optional)
4 cups liquid from the clams
2 cups heavy cream, half-and-
    half, or milk, heated
1–2 tablespoons Cognac (optional
    but good)
    Paprika

Make sure all clams are tightly shut when you buy them. Scrub them thoroughly and place them in a heavy 4-quart, lidded flameproof casserole. Pour in the wine to a depth of ½ inch. Cover and cook on medium heat, shaking the pot occasionally, for 10–15 minutes, or until clams open; discard those that have not opened. Strain through sieve lined with dampened kitchen towel, and reserve liquid. If it is less than 4 cups, add water to make 4 cups. Remove clams from shells. Mince the hard parts, which will be obvious to the touch. Leave the rest whole.

Wash the pot to eliminate any sand. Put in the salt pork and cook slowly until fat is rendered and pork or bacon is crisp. With a slotted spoon, remove it to a paper towel for draining. Pour off all but 2 table-spoons of the fat.

Slowly cook the onion in the pork fat until limp but not brown. Stir in the potatoes, pepper, thyme, and Tabasco. Add the clam liquid. Cook gent-ly until potatoes are tender, 10–15 minutes.

Add the hot cream; add the pork, and the clams, minced and not minced. Stir in the Cognac.

Serve sprinkled with paprika. *4–6 servings*

Note: For 4 to 6 servings, and 2 dozen clams, you need about 6 cups of soup. When the clams are steamed with wine or water, they produce about 4 cups of liquid. Cream is added to make up the 6 cups. If canned clams have to be used, buy 2 eight-ounce cans, drain and measure their liquid. Add enough water or wine to make 2 cups, add 1 cup of bottled clam juice and 1 cup of water. Follow the recipe then, as given.

MANHATTAN CLAM CHOWDER

Manhattan puts tomatoes in clam chowder and leaves out the cream, although it is considered a crime east of the Connecticut River. The dish came originally from the Atlantic coast of France, where a *chaudière* was the large pot in which the fisherman dropped his share of the day's catch, to be turned into a seaside stew for the enjoyment of the whole community. With its arrival in New England, via Canada, *chaudière* became chowder. When the dish came south to New Amsterdam, the tomatoes crept in.

After a feast of corn on the cob, the chowder needs only lots of French or Italian bread, a salad, some good cheese and an excessive amount of the fruit of the moment, like a huge bowl of cherries, or half a watermelon full of fruit salad—truly a salute to summer.

Beer is almost traditional with the chowder, but a white wine is good too—a Muscadet or Chardonnay.

2 dozen medium-size chowder clams
Dry white wine, or dry Vermouth, or water
¼ pound salt pork, or thickly sliced bacon, diced in ¼-inch pieces
2 medium onions, chopped
1 medium green pepper, chopped
2 leeks, white part only, chopped (optional)
2 stalks celery, chopped

2 medium carrots, cut in ¼-inch dice
3 medium potatoes, cut in ¾-inch dice
3 cups tomatoes, peeled, chopped, or 3 cups canned tomatoes, undrained, chopped
½ teaspoon freshly ground black pepper
½ teaspoon thyme
1 bay leaf
⅓ cup finely chopped parsley

Make sure all the clams are tightly shut when you buy them. Scrub them well and place in a wide 4- to 4½-quart pot or kettle, preferably enameled ironware with a well-fitting lid. Pour ½ inch of wine, Vermouth or water in the bottom of the kettle. Bring to a boil and put in the clams. Cover and cook on medium heat about 10 minutes, or until all clams are open (discard those which have not opened).

Strain through sieve lined with dampened kitchen towel, and reserve the liquid. Remove the clams from the shells. Mince the hard parts; they will be obvious to the touch. Leave the rest whole. Set aside.

Continued

Rinse the pot and slowly cook the salt pork or bacon until it renders its fat and is golden brown. Pour off all but 2 tablespoons of the fat.

Put in the onions, green pepper, leeks, if used (clean well between the leaves), celery, carrots, and potatoes. Stir and cook gently together for 5 minutes.

Add the tomatoes, pepper, thyme, bay leaf, and 2 tablespoons of the parsley. Bring to a simmer, cover and cook for 15–20 minutes, or until vegetables are almost tender.

Measure liquid from clams. If it is less than 4 cups, add water to bring it to 4 cups. Add to the pot. Return to a simmer, cover and cook for another 5 minutes, until vegetables are tender and flavors have melded.

❁ The chowder can be prepared ahead up to the addition of the clams. Add the clams and cook 1–2 minutes, just to heat the clams. Check for salt and pepper.

Serve sprinkled with the rest of the parsley.   *4–6 servings*

FISH CHOWDER WITH DILL

This light and pleasant soup, good any time of the year, has potatoes for body, milk for enrichment, and plenty of fresh dill for flavor. The fish should be one of the less expensive ones, which hold up better in soups and stews than delicate ones like sole. A few choices are given in the recipe, but ask the fish merchant.

A dark Scandinavian bread goes with the soup, perhaps with some Edam cheese as a first course. Salad could be sliced beets and red onions in a vinaigrette, with a pinch of cloves.

The soup is not too heavy so it could be followed by pastry or cake, but fruit of the season is always good.

Serve Italian white jug wine or beer.

2 slices bacon, diced
1 tablespoon butter
8 scallions with crisp green tops, chopped
½ cup chopped fresh dill
¼ cup chopped fresh parsley
1 teaspoon ground cardamom
2 cups clam juice
1 cup water

6–8 small new potatoes, or 3–4 regular potatoes (not baking potatoes)
2 cups milk
2 tablespoons flour
1 teaspoon salt
Freshly ground black pepper
1½ pounds fish fillets, weakfish, tile, blackfish, cod, monk fish

Put the bacon and butter into a large, wide saucepan or flameproof casserole with a lid. Cook on low heat, stirring, until bacon is golden. Add the scallions; cook for 1–2 minutes until they soften. Stir in half the dill, half the parsley, and the cardamom.

Pour in the clam juice and water. Peel and cut the potatoes, either kind, into roughly ¾-inch dice (although little new potatoes do not even have to be peeled). Cover and cook on low heat for 15–20 minutes, until potatoes are almost tender.

Mix ¼ cup of the milk with the flour. Stir into the pot. Add the rest of the milk, the salt and pepper to taste, and bring to a simmer.

Cut the fish fillets across at 2-inch intervals and put them into the pot. Cover and cook on low heat for 5–8 minutes, until fish is cooked (it will be very tender and flake easily).

Serve sprinkled with the remaining dill and parsley.

6 servings

FISH CHOWDER

Fish merchants can be a big help when you are choosing fish for a soup or stew: The fish which hold up best are often the least expensive.

A tray of assorted cheeses with crusty French or Italian bread before the soup and a salad full of good things—mushrooms, radishes, sprouts, hard-boiled eggs, et cetera, with or after, makes an interesting meal. Orange Cake (recipe follows) is a not-too-sweet dessert.

Beer is good with this or a white jug wine, preferably one of those from France, which are generally the driest of the lot.

1½ to 2 pounds white fish fillets: tile, monk, cod
2 slices thick bacon, diced
2 onions, finely chopped
1 medium green pepper, finely chopped
2 garlic cloves, minced
½ teaspoon fennel seeds
1 bay leaf
4 medium potatoes, peeled and cubed
3 cups water
2 cups clam juice
Salt and pepper
Pinch of red pepper flakes
½ cup finely chopped parsley

Cut fish fillets across at 2-inch intervals.

In a heavy saucepan or casserole, cook the bacon pieces until they are golden and crisp. Remove them with a slotted spoon to paper towel and set aside.

Put the onions, green pepper, and garlic into the pan and stir over low heat until onion softens slightly, but does not brown.

Add the fennel, bay leaf, potatoes, water, clam juice, salt and pepper to taste, and red pepper flakes. Bring to a boil, reduce heat and cook, partially covered, for 15–20 minutes, or until potatoes are barely tender.

Add the fish and bring to the merest simmer. Cover and cook 6–8 minutes, or until fish is white and opaque throughout.

Serve in large soup bowls and garnish with parsley and bacon bits.

4–6 servings

ORANGE CAKE

½ cup butter
1 cup white sugar
1 egg
1 teaspoon baking powder
1 teaspoon baking soda

1 cup sour milk (see note)
Rind of 1 orange, grated
1¾ cups all-purpose flour
Juice of 1 orange
1 orange for garnish

Cream butter and sugar. Beat in egg. Add baking powder. Add soda to sour milk and add to mixture. Stir in orange rind. Stir in flour.

Butter and flour 9-inch square cake pan. Pour in batter and bake 40 minutes at 350°, or until golden brown, and a small knife comes out clean after being plunged in the center.

When cake comes from the oven and while it is still hot, sprinkle evenly with the orange juice. Cut into squares in the pan and remove to serving plate.

Serve with a thin slice of orange on each portion.

9-inch square pan

Note: To sour milk, put 1 tablespoon vinegar in a cup and add milk to make 1 cup.

PERUVIAN FISH CHOWDER

Chowder is not peculiar to New England. Peruvians probably had it long before there was a New England. Like ours, the Peruvian chowder has cubed potatoes and milk in it, plus corn and hotness. An unusual ingredient is a small amount of cream cheese, mixed with the milk in the soup, to give a subtle richness. It sounds crazy, but it isn't. Try it.

This is a substantial soup, a fine main course for luncheon or supper, year-round. In corn season, corn on the cob could be a first course—it's too good to miss—as well as provide Niblets for the soup. In autumn, pumpkin pie would be an appropriate dessert, squash being an important item in most South American cuisines.

A big round loaf of Italian brown bread would be a good bread to have with the soup, and salad could be shredded spinach with an oil and vinegar dressing with lots of Dijon mustard in it.

The meal might start with Margaritas and continue with a pitcher of Sangría (recipe follows).

2 tablespoons cooking oil	2 cups potatoes, peeled, cut in ½-inch dice
2 garlic cloves, minced	1¼ cups milk
1 medium onion, finely chopped	2 ounces cream cheese, at room temperature
1 pound tomatoes, peeled, chopped, or 1 one-pound can tomatoes, undrained, chopped	1 cup cooked corn Niblets
2 teaspoons chili powder, or to taste	1½ pounds fish fillets: flounder or cod
1 tablespoon salt	Fresh mint sprigs, or Italian parsley sprigs
¼ teaspoon red pepper flakes	
3 cups water	

In a heavy, lidded saucepan or flameproof casserole, heat the oil and add the garlic and onion. Cook on low heat until onion is golden and limp, but not brown.

Add the tomatoes, chili powder, salt (it sounds like too much but isn't), and red pepper flakes. Simmer for 10 minutes. Add the water, potatoes, and 1 cup of the milk. Bring to a boil, stirring occasionally, reduce heat and simmer, covered, for 15 minutes, or until potatoes are almost tender.

Make a smooth mixture of the remaining ¼ cup of milk and the cream cheese, beating them with a fork or whisk. Stir the mixture into the soup with the corn. Bring to a simmer. Add more salt, chili powder, or hot pepper, if desired.

Cut the fish across into 6 pieces. Place in the soup, cover and cook for 5–6 minutes, or until fish flakes and is opaque inside. Serve with mint or parsley sprigs.   *4–6 servings*

SANGRÍA

1 orange
1 lime, or lemon
1 bottle Spanish red wine

1 ounce brandy
Sugar or honey to taste
Club soda (optional)

Remove the peel from the orange and lime with a carrot peeler, and put in a pitcher, together with their juice. Add wine, brandy, and sugar to taste. Chill and serve over ice. Club soda can be added or not, depending on how strong a taste is desired.

If mussels with—or in—potato salad are so good, why not put some potatoes in with the mussels? This recipe proves that it works very well. Not only does it make a few mussels go a long way, but it results in a fine, flavorful main course that is extremely edible hot or cold.

Mussels have more protein than steak and no fat at all, reason enough to use them, but people often worry about sand being in their mussels. Mussels from rocky tidewaters are usually free of sand; the ones from sandy beaches and mudflats are likely to have it. Careful scrubbing and rinsing should solve the problem and straining the broth should eliminate whatever little sand remains.

A salad with lettuce, tomatoes, red onion rings, and a little yogurt in the dressing would be a good companion for the mussels. Crusty bread is necessary for mopping up the sauce and for the cheese course that could follow the salad. A first course could be *oeufs durs mayonnaise,* hard-boiled eggs on lettuce, with mayonnaise and a grating of pepper on top, an old-fashioned but satisfactory first course if the main course is not too heavy. Fresh fruit is the best dessert.

For wine—serve a Muscadet or an estate-bottled Chablis from France, or a Chenin Blanc from California.

4 dozen mussels	3–4 medium-size regular
1 clove garlic, mashed	potatoes (not baking potatoes)
1 cup dry white wine	½ teaspoon salt
1 sprig fresh dill	Freshly ground black pepper
1 bay leaf	1 teaspoon mustard
1 tablespoon butter	1 cup yogurt
¼ cup shallots, minced	¼ cup chopped chives or parsley
6–8 small new potatoes, or	

Scrub the mussels thoroughly, remove the beards, and rinse in several waters. In a pot with a tight-fitting lid, and large enough to hold the mussels, put the garlic and wine. Bring to a boil, put in the dill, bay leaf, and mussels. Cover and cook on high heat 3–5 minutes, shaking the pot occasionally, until mussels have opened. Remove mussels with a slotted spoon to a platter. When the mussels are cool enough to handle, remove the top shells, discarding any mussels that have not opened or look funny. Set the good ones aside.

Pour off mussel broth, straining through a dampened clean kitchen towel to catch any remaining sand. Add water if needed to bring broth up to 2 cups.

Rinse pot to eliminate any sand. Melt the butter, add the shallots and cook until they are transparent. Pour in the mussel broth. If the potatoes are new, scrub, and cut into ¼-inch slices, without peeling. If regular potatoes are used, peel, cut in half and then in ¼-inch slices. Put the potatoes into the broth, add salt and a few grindings of the pepper mill. Bring to a simmer, cover and cook 20–30 minutes, or until potatoes are done.

Return mussels to the pot, stir in the mustard and yogurt mixed together, heat but do not boil and serve at once, sprinkling with chives or parsley.   *4 servings*

Variation: To serve cold, omit the addition of yogurt, mustard and garnish until serving time.

GUMBO WITH OKRA

Okra-haters should reserve judgment until they have tasted this gumbo, but the okra must be fresh, not canned or frozen. This gumbo contains sausage, chicken, and oysters—a magic Creole combination—and okra to add its special quality.

Folks in New Orleans like to serve potato salad with their gumbo—which is very good—but since rice is served with the soup, some people might prefer a green salad. French or Italian crusty bread is essential, and a nice cool sherbet or Lime Snow (recipe follows), could round out the meal.

Jug wines, red or white, go with gumbo, and so does beer.

½ pound Polish or other garlic sausage, cut in ½-inch slices, quartered
¾ to 1 pound fresh okra, cut in ½-inch slices
3 tablespoons cooking oil
2 medium green peppers, chopped
1 large onion, chopped
2 cloves garlic, minced
2 cups tomatoes (or 1 one-pound can), chopped, undrained

1 teaspoon thyme
2 bay leaves
½ to 1 teaspoon cayenne
2 cups chicken broth
3 cups water
1 tablespoon salt
2½ to 3 cups cooked chicken or turkey, cut in small pieces
1 pint shucked oysters with liquid
1 cup hot rice per serving

In a large, heavy saucepan or kettle, cook the sausage on low heat until it renders its fat and is lightly brown in places. Set aside on paper towel to drain.

Stir okra into the sausage fat and cook, stirring, until okra dries out and browns in spots. Add the oil, and stir in the peppers, onions, and garlic. Stir, scraping the brown bits from the bottom of the pot, and cook until peppers and onions have softened slightly.

Add tomatoes, thyme, bay leaves, and cayenne (I find the whole teaspoon not too much) and simmer, partially covered, for 15 minutes.

Add chicken broth, water, and salt. Simmer, partially covered, for 1 hour.

Stir in sausage and chicken and bring to a simmer again. Stir in oysters and their liquid, cover and cook 5–8 minutes longer, until oysters puff up and edges curl.

Serve around mounds of hot rice in large soup bowls.   *6–8 servings*

LIME SNOW

This snowy white dessert with its raspberry sauce makes a lovely finish to a meal. It will keep for a day or two because gelatin keeps the mixture from collapsing.

2 envelopes plain gelatin	⅔ cup lime juice (4 or 5 limes)
3 cups water	4 egg whites
⅔ cup sugar	1 ten-ounce package frozen
Grated rind of 2 lemons	raspberries

Soften gelatin in ½ cup of the water for 2–5 minutes.

Bring remaining 2½ cups of water to a boil in a saucepan, and stir in the sugar and lemon rind. Boil gently for 5 minutes. Add the gelatin, and stir until dissolved.

Add the lime juice and pour into a bowl. Chill until the mixture has the consistency of unbeaten egg whites. Stir occasionally, and when it has cooled enough, beat until foamy.

Beat 4 egg whites until stiff peaks form; combine with gelatin and beat until mixture begins to set. Setting the bowl in a pan of ice while beating will hasten this process. Pour into a serving bowl or individual parfait glasses and chill for 1–2 hours.

To make the sauce, partially thaw the raspberries and purée in a blender or food processor. Strain and serve over Lime Snow.

8 or more servings

CREOLE JAMBALAYA

Jambalaya is one of the great dishes of Creole cooking, combining meat, seafood, and rice. It has the famous brown roux, that strange mixture of oil and flour, cooked to a nutty brown, and the inevitable fillip of cayenne among its seasonings.

Although the word comes from *jambon,* French for ham, other meats are used, too, notably a New Orleans sausage called *andouille,* hard to find elsewhere. In this recipe we have substituted hot Italian sausage, because of its good strong taste.

Oysters on the half shell would be a fabulous first course, and a salad with avocados and lime juice in the dressing would be quite splendid.

Dessert could be a Chocolate Almond Mousse (page 91) followed by Café Royale—black coffee is set aflame by putting a sugar cube in a spoonful of Cognac, lighting it and sliding it onto the surface of the coffee.

The wine should be plentiful and thirst quenching, a jug wine, white, red, or a dry rosé, if you can find one. Beer is also good.

1 pound Italian hot sausage
2 tablespoons cooking oil
2 tablespoons flour
2 medium onions, chopped
3 garlic cloves, minced
2 medium green peppers, chopped
2 celery stalks, chopped
1 bay leaf
1½ teaspoons thyme
¼ teaspoon cayenne

1 tablespoon salt
2 cups (1 one-pound can) Italian
   tomatoes, undrained, crushed
3 cups water
2 cups uncooked rice
1 to 1½ pounds fresh shrimp,
   shelled and deveined
½ cup each chopped parsley,
   chopped scallions

Heat ½ inch of water in a large skillet. Prick the sausages and cook in it until water evaporates, then cook until sausages are browned. Set aside on paper towel to drain.

In a heavy saucepan or casserole, make a smooth mixture of the oil and flour. Stir over moderate heat until mixture is a rich, nutty or butterscotch brown and creamy in texture. This takes about 10 minutes or more of careful attention.

Add the onions, garlic, peppers, and celery. Stir and cook until onions are slightly soft but not brown.

Add bay leaf, thyme, cayenne, salt, tomatoes, and water. Bring to a boil and add the sausages, cut into bite-size pieces. Cover and simmer for 15 minutes.

Add rice, bring to a boil again, stir once and cover. Reduce heat and simmer for 30–35 minutes, or until rice is cooked. The dish should be moist but not watery. If more liquid is needed, add a little hot water. If there is too much, cook briefly uncovered.

Carefully stir in shrimp, cover and cook 6–8 minutes, or until shrimp are pink and opaque.

Stir the mixture of parsley and scallions into the top 2 inches of the jambalaya.   *8 servings*

LOUISIANA FISH SOUP-STEW

This was to have been an all-shrimp soup-stew with 2 pounds of shrimp and potatoes instead of rice to give it substance. However, on the day of the testing, the price of shrimp hit a new high, and it seemed unduly extravagant to use all shrimp. So we bought only ½ pound of the shrimp and 1 pound of the least expensive fish on the market, which happened to be monk fish. Monk, tile, and blackfish are usually relatively inexpensive and are actually better in soups and stews (less apt to fall apart) than the more delicate and costlier fish, such as sole or flounder.

The soup is started with the classic brown roux—oil and flour cooked together to a smooth nutty brown, giving the dish that special New Orleans flavor.

Crisp slivers of celery with some sharp Greek olives and a small dish of toasted nuts could start the meal, a mixed green salad could follow the soup, and fruit of the season end the meal. On testing day for the soup, the high price of shrimp was offset by the arrival of cherries on the market, and we had a feast of them.

Serve with a thirst-quenching French jug wine—white and dry.

5 tablespoons cooking oil	2 cups fresh tomatoes, peeled, coarsely chopped, or 1 one-pound can tomatoes, undrained, coarsely chopped
5 tablespoons flour	
½ cup finely chopped shallots, or white part of scallions	
1 large onion, chopped	3 cups water
2 stalks celery, finely chopped	6–8 medium potatoes, peeled, cut in 1-inch cubes
4 garlic cloves, minced	
1 teaspoon black pepper	1 pound monk fish, tile, or blackfish fillets
⅛ teaspoon cayenne	
1 large bay leaf	½ pound medium-size fresh shrimp, peeled, deveined
1 teaspoon thyme	
1 tablespoon salt	2 teaspoons lemon juice
	½ cup finely chopped parsley

Mix the oil and flour together in a large heavy saucepan or casserole, with a lid. Cook over low heat, stirring all the time (it must not stick or burn), until the mixture is smooth, creamy and a rich nutty, butterscotch brown. This can take up to 15–20 minutes.

When the roux is nut brown, stir in the shallots, onion, celery, and garlic. Stir and cook for 10 minutes. Add the pepper, cayenne, bay leaf, thyme, and salt, and mix well. Add the tomatoes and water. Simmer, partially covered, for 1 hour, stirring occasionally.

Add the potatoes, cover and simmer for 10 minutes on low heat. Put in the fish, cut into pieces about 2 inches square and 1 inch thick. Cover and simmer another 10 minutes. Add the shrimp, cover and simmer about 2 minutes more. Stir in lemon juice.

Serve in large soup plates or bowls and sprinkle with parsley. Serve with forks as well as spoons. *6 servings*

GUMBO FILÉ

The feature of New Orleans cooking which gives some of their dishes a special texture and taste is the brown roux. The usual French roux is a simple mixture of flour and butter, cooked together briefly before acting as a thickener. Brown roux is a mixture of flour and oil, cooked slowly, for a long time, until it is a rich nutty or butterscotch brown color. Filé powder also supplies a slight thickening and completes the unique Creole taste. Filé powder can be found in spice or specialty food shops.

Served around a mound of hot rice, this is a substantial concoction and needs only good bread, salad, and fruit to complete the meal.

Red or white jug wines go well with gumbos. They should be dry and thirst quenching. Beer is also good.

1 pound Polish or other garlic sausage, cut in ¼-inch slices and halved	2 quarts water
	¼ cup chopped parsley
	1 pint oysters and their liquid
8 chicken thighs	1 tablespoon salt
½ cup cooking oil	¼ teaspoon cayenne
½ cup flour	1½ teaspoons thyme
2 medium onions, chopped	2 bay leaves
2 medium green peppers, chopped	¼ teaspoon mace
2 stalks celery, chopped	1 tablespoon filé powder
2 garlic cloves, minced	Hot rice, 1 cup per serving

Cook sausage in a dry skillet to render its fat and to brown lightly. Set sausage aside on paper towel to drain. Brown chicken pieces lightly in sausage fat and set aside.

Mix the oil and flour together in a large pot or kettle. Cook on moderate heat, stirring constantly, until the mixture is smooth, creamy, and a rich nutty or butterscotch brown color, 10 minutes or longer.

Stir in onions, peppers, celery, and garlic, and cook until vegetables soften slightly.

Add ½ cup of the water and the parsley. Cook and stir for 5 minutes. Add the oyster *liquid* and the salt, cayenne, thyme, bay leaves, and mace.

Gradually add the rest of the water, the sausages, and the chicken. Bring to a boil, reduce heat and simmer, partially covered, for 1 hour, or until chicken is done. Add oysters, cover and cook 5–8 minutes until oysters puff up and edges curl. Remove from the heat and stir in filé powder.

Serve around mounds of hot rice in large bowls. Provide knives and forks as well as spoons.   *8–10 servings*

6

Soup-Stews

ZUPPA DI PESCE

A fresh Italian fish stew, light enough to be preceded by a small course of pasta with a simple sauce of oil, garlic, and chopped parsley. Good crusty bread and a salad go with the stew. Dessert could be Gorgonzola with pears or apples.

Italian wines, particularly those from Sicily, suit this soup.

¼ cup olive oil
1 large onion, finely chopped
1 bay leaf
1 teaspoon oregano
¼ teaspoon fennel seeds
½ cup finely chopped parsley
1 cup dry white wine
2 pounds scrod, cut across in
  2-inch pieces

2 quarts boiling water
1 tablespoon salt
¼ teaspoon freshly ground black
  pepper
1 dozen small clams
2 garlic cloves, minced
  Minced zest of 1 lemon

Heat the oil in a heavy saucepan and add the onion. Cook, stirring, over low heat until onion is soft but not brown. Add bay leaf, oregano, fennel, and 2 tablespoons of the parsley. Add the wine and cook down to half.

Put in the fish and stir carefully. Add the boiling water, salt, and pepper. Bring to a simmer and put in the clams. Cover and cook for 8–10 minutes, or until clams open and fish is opaque and flakes easily.

Mix remaining parsley with the garlic and lemon zest and sprinkle over the soup. Serve immediately. *6–8 servings*

SEAFARE SOUP-STEW

Stew or soup? This can be called either one, but it is a main course, whatever it is called. If the fish cooks for such a short time, the sauce it cooks in has to be marvelously flavorful, which this one is. Redolent of the Mediterranean, with tomatoes, garlic, wine and saffron, it is further enhanced by the subtle taste of Pernod or similar liqueur that goes in. Crusty bread, plain or with garlic, goes with the dish.

Crisp raw vegetables with a Sour Cream and Dill Dip (recipe follows) could either precede the dish or replace a salad. Salty cheeses like Feta or a selection of goat cheeses could follow with fresh fruit for dessert.

A white wine from Italy suits the Mediterranean character of the dish—Soave or Orvieto.

FISH STOCK

Fish stock is easy to make, and made with scraps the fish merchant usually throws away, it costs nothing. Some merchants make their own stock, in which case, of course, it is no longer free.

1–2 pounds fish heads and scraps   **2 quarts unsalted water**

Wash the fish heads and scraps thoroughly. Place in a saucepan with water and simmer gently for 40–60 minutes, or until liquid has reduced to half. Strain stock, discard solids. If there is less than 1 quart liquid, add water to make 4 cups, and reserve.

2 tablespoons olive oil
¼ cup chopped shallots
1 green pepper, cut in strips
2 garlic cloves, minced
2 cups tomato purée
1 cup dry white wine
4 cups fish stock
½ cup finely chopped parsley
⅛ teaspoon crushed red pepper, or to taste
1 teaspoon saffron threads, crushed
½ teaspoon dried basil, or 1 tablespoon chopped fresh basil
2 teaspoons salt
½ teaspoon freshly ground black pepper
12 small clams
1 pound fillet of haddock, cut in 2-inch squares
½ pound raw shrimp, shelled, deveined
½ pound fresh bay scallops, or quartered sea scallops
2 tablespoons Pernod, Ricard, or Pec
1 four-ounce can or jar pimientos, drained and chopped

In a wide, lidded flamproof casserole, heat the oil and lightly cook the shallots and green pepper until they are tender but not brown. Stir in the garlic.

Add the tomato purée, wine and fish stock. Add ¼ cup of the parsley, red pepper, saffron, basil, salt, and pepper. Bring to a simmer, partially cover and cook 15 minutes. Check seasoning; add up to 1 teaspoon more salt to taste. For more hotness, add more red pepper flakes or a pinch of cayenne or a dash of Tabasco.

❀ The soup can be made ahead up to this point.

With the liquid at a simmer, put in the clams. Cover and cook 5 minutes. Put in the haddock, cover, and cook 4 minutes. Put in the shrimp and scallops and cook another 2 minutes. Clams should be open; discard those that have not opened.

Stir in the Pernod, Ricard, or Pec. Sprinkle in the pimientos and remaining parsley.

4 servings

SOUR CREAM AND DILL DIP

1 cup sour cream	¼ teaspoon salt
3 teaspoons chopped fresh dill, or 1 teaspoon dried	¼ teaspoon white pepper
	1 teaspoon lemon juice

Mix all ingredients together.

makes 1 cup

SPANISH FISH SOUP-STEW

A tomato-based sauce, with cumin, saffron, and paprika for the Spanish flavor, envelops fish, shrimp, and clams or mussels in this rich stew.

Instead of serving a salad, offer a sort of Spanish antipasto before the stew. Called tapas in Spain, these appetizers are enormously varied and can be complicated. But the stew is the star of this show so a list of some easy ones follow.

A wonderful dessert would be *flan*, a Caramel Custard. (page 279)

Spanish white wine from the Rioja or Penedés district would complement this stew nicely. Beer is also good, as is Manzanilla, the driest of Sherries.

½ pound small raw shrimp
1 pound firm white fish fillets
1 dozen small clams or mussels, or
  6 of each
3 tablespoons olive oil
2 medium onions
1 medium green pepper
2 garlic cloves, minced
1 teaspoon cumin
½ teaspoon saffron threads,
  crushed

1 tablespoon paprika
1 cup dry white wine
2 one-pound cans tomatoes,
  undrained, crushed
2 teaspoons salt
¼ teaspoon freshly ground black
  pepper
Pinch of red pepper flakes
8–10 pitted black olives

Remove shells from shrimp, leaving tails on. Cut fish fillets across in 2-inch pieces. Scrub clams or mussels well.

Heat the oil in a heavy saucepan or casserole. Add onions, green pepper, and garlic. Stir and cook over low heat until onions are soft but not brown.

Stir in cumin, saffron, and paprika. Pour in wine and cook for 5 minutes on medium heat. Add tomatoes, salt, pepper, and red pepper. Bring to a boil, reduce heat and simmer, covered, for 30 minutes. Uncover and cook 10 minutes.

Add clams to simmering sauce, cover and cook 5 minutes. Add fish, shrimp, and olives. Cook 4 minutes, or until clams open (discard any unopened clams). Serve in large soup plates or bowls. *4 servings*

TAPAS

In Spain tapas are wonderfully varied, hot and cold and often complicated. It is possible to make a meal of just tapas. These are served in small bowls, and 3 or 4 will do, but the more the merrier is the idea. The ones listed are simple, easy to assemble, pleasantly light with drinks.

Kidney beans in vinaigrette, with minced parsley, pimiento, and onion and red pepper flakes

Whole pimientos with minced garlic

Bread cubes fried in olive oil and garlic

Black olives with lemon and oregano

Pickled beets

Sliced boiled potatoes with mayonnaise and garlic

Fried green and red pepper strips

Sardines

Raw mushrooms with lemon, chopped parsley and minced garlic

CREAM OF FLOUNDER SOUP

This is a subtly rich soup. The main liquid is not heavy cream but milk which is given a little body with flour and extra flavor with clam juice. This soup is a handsome sight—with the bright green parsley and scallions afloat in its almost pure whiteness. It would look marvelous on a summer table next to a mound of corn on the cob and a platter of ripe tomatoes. It is enough to send you out to buy a tureen.

Good as it is for a main course, this soup makes a fine first course, serving twice as many people.

Different breads go with the soup—crusty white or brown, dark breads, or Melba toast—a basket of them would be nice.

A Soave or a dry white jug wine goes well with the soup.

3 tablespoons butter
2 tablespoons chopped shallots
3 tablespoons flour
½ teaspoon fennel seeds, crushed
1 quart milk
1 cup clam juice
1 teaspoon salt

¼ teaspoon white pepper
1 pound flounder fillets, or other white-fleshed fillets
½ cup finely chopped parsley
½ cup scallions with crisp green tops, chopped

Melt the butter in a heavy saucepan or casserole, preferably wide and shallow, rather than deep. Add the shallots and stir them over low heat until they soften. Off the heat, mix the flour with the butter and shallots. Stir in the fennel and add the milk gradually, stirring to keep the mixture smooth.

Back on the heat, return mixture to a simmer, stirring constantly. Add the clam juice, salt and pepper, and return to a simmer. Almost constant stirring is required or it will stick on the bottom.

Lay in the fish, cut up if it is too long for the pan. By the time the soup comes back to a simmer the fish is done if the fillets are thin. Cook another few seconds, breaking the fish into small pieces. As soon as the fish flakes and breaks up it is done.

Stir in the parsley and scallions—and top with a few grindings of pepper from the mill, if you like—and serve at once.   *4–5 servings*

SHRIMP AND JAPANESE NOODLE SOUP

Noodles and broth—a combination dear to both East and West—is more noodles than broth in the East. Japanese noodles are no longer hard to find; the noodles used for this soup are the straight ones, about 8 inches long, looking very much like fine but shorter spaghetti.

The shop that sells the noodles will have a wonderful variety of crisp crackers, just the right accompaniment for the soup. The sweet crackers might be good with a jar of preserved kumquats for dessert. A large platter of sliced pineapple, when pineapples are at their best, with other colorful fruit is another possibility.

Beer or the customary tea are most suitable for the accompanying beverage.

1 tablespoon sesame oil	½ pound fine Japanese noodles,
1 teaspoon minced fresh ginger	cooked, drained
2 garlic cloves, minced	½ pound cooked shrimp
1 green pepper, cut in thin strips	2 scallions with crisp green tops,
1 tablespoon soy sauce	chopped
4 cups chicken broth	

Heat the oil in a heavy saucepan or casserole. Add the ginger and garlic. Stir briefly, not long enough to brown. Add the green pepper strips. Stir and cook for 30 seconds. Add the soy sauce and broth. Stir and bring to a boil.

Add the noodles, cooked according to package directions. When the noodles are hot, add the shrimp, just to warm. Serve sprinkled with chopped scallions.

4 servings

COACH HOUSE STRIPED BASS

This main-course soup has always been a favorite at Leon Lianides' famous Coach House restaurant in New York's Greenwich Village. The soup must be made with the freshest vegetables and impeccably fresh fish, to taste the way it does at the Coach House.

A French pâté of chicken livers, made with a touch of Cognac and Madeira (page 137), would make a fine first course, along with some good French bread.

At the Coach House, a salad which could go with or after the soup probably would have a little crumbled Feta cheese in it, Bibb or Boston lettuce, and certainly the best possible olive oil and wine vinegar. French pastry purchased from your favorite bakery would be a splendid finish; or Caramel Custard (page 279) would also be just right.

The most elegant of white wines suits this soup—a Meursault or Corton from Burgundy, one of the white Graves, or a Sauvignon Blanc from California.

1 whole fresh striped bass, about 3 pounds	1 cup dry white wine
4 cups fish stock	1 cup tomatoes, peeled, seeded, and chopped
1 tablespoon olive oil	⅛ teaspoon thyme
1 tablespoon butter	1 ounce Pernod
1 cup each carrots, celery, onions, leeks (white parts only), all julienne	Freshly ground pepper, salt
8 fresh clams, scrubbed and cleaned, or 1 cup clam broth	2 tablespoons finely chopped parsley

Have the bass filleted and skinned at the fish market. Ask for all the trimmings, except the gills.

Wash the fish trimmings and place them in a saucepan with 4 cups of water. Bring to a boil, reduce heat, and simmer for 15 minutes. Strain and reserve broth; discard residue.

Cut the fillets in half.

Heat the oil and butter in a wide, shallow saucepan which will hold the 4 portions without overlapping. Put in the carrots and celery. Cook on low heat for 2 minutes. Add the onions and leeks and cook until they soften, about 3 minutes. Add the clams and wine and cook another 3 minutes.

Stir in the tomatoes, thyme, Pernod, and pepper and salt to taste. Cover and simmer 5 minutes longer.

Remove the clams and shells (discard unopened ones). Stir in the reserved fish broth and simmer for 8 minutes.

Carefully place the fish in the soup. Cover and cook at the merest simmer for 6–8 minutes, until fish is opaque and flakes easily.

Gently lift the fish to soup plates and ladle the soup over the fish. Sprinkle with parsley.   *4 servings*

CURRIED FISH SOUP-STEW

Like any curry dish, fish takes on a new dimension in the succulent sauce from the cuisines of the East. Curry is a mixture of spices; Indian women grind and mix fresh spices every day to suit the dish they are to make. In this recipe, a prepared curry is used, but the sauce as it cooked seemed to need more cumin, which I added—feeling rather Indian.

Elsewhere in this book there is a Lamb Curry recipe (page 252) that uses no prepared curry powder but gives all the spices—one of an infinite number of combinations.

The fish used here was blackfish, recommended by the fish merchant, and the best bargain that day. The other fish listed as alternatives are all suitable for fish soups and stews, holding up better than the more delicate flounder and sole.

Plenty of crusty bread, a leafy salad, a tray of interesting cheeses, and fruit make a meal around the stew.

Beer, tea, or thirst-quenching spritzers are good to drink with the meal. Spritzers are ½ white wine and ½ club soda, with plenty of ice, and a slice of lemon.

3 tablespoons butter	3 cups water
1 small onion, finely chopped	2 cups clam broth
2 garlic cloves, minced	1 teaspoon salt
1 tart apple, peeled, cored, finely chopped	¼ cup rice
2 tablespoons curry powder	1 pound fish fillets, such as blackfish, tile, monk fish, cod
1 teaspoon cumin	½ pound sea scallops, cut in half
2 tablespoons flour	½ cup heavy cream (optional)
1 cup dry white wine	½ cup finely chopped parsley

In a heavy, wide saucepan or casserole that has a lid, melt the butter. Add the onion, garlic, and apple and cook on low heat until onions soften.

Stir in the curry powder, cumin, and flour, and add the wine, stirring with a whisk. Bring to a simmer. Add the water, clam broth, and salt and return to a simmer. Cook on very low heat, partially covered, for 45 minutes, stirring occasionally. If some liquid cooks away, replace it with water.

Turn up the heat and stir in the rice. Cover tightly and cook on low heat again for 15–20 minutes, or until rice is cooked.

Cut fish fillets across at 2-inch intervals. Add them to the pot. Cover and cook for about 4 minutes, or until fish is white and opaque and flakes easily. Put in the scallops, cover and cook for 1–2 minutes. Scallops are so tender they are cooked as soon as they are warm; further cooking only toughens them.

Stir in cream if used. Cream adds extra richness and makes the soup go further.

Serve the soup in large hot bowls or soup plates and sprinkled with parsley. *4 servings*

CIOPPINO

California's great fish stew must have been invented by a homesick Mediterranean who found himself with the bounty from another sea at hand. The secret, as with many great fish stews, is to use a variety of fish and seafood and to cook it briefly in a well-seasoned, previously prepared sauce. Traditionally crab is included because the dish originated on the California coast where Dungeness crabs are found.

Bruschetta, Italian garlic toast (recipe follows), is almost an essential companion, as is a leafy salad with a slightly piquant dressing. The first course could be asparagus or artichokes vinaigrette, and dessert fresh fruit or a fruit sherbet.

A California white wine like Grey Riesling or Mountain White goes well with the Cioppino.

1 pound firm white fish: cod, sea bass, et cetera	1½ teaspoons oregano
2 large crab legs, fresh or frozen	1 bay leaf, crumbled
¼ to ½ pound medium shrimp	½ teaspoon sage
8 sea scallops	1 cup dry red wine
1 dozen small clams or mussels	4 tablespoons tomato paste
2 tablespoons olive oil	1 one-pound can tomatoes, undrained, crushed
1 large onion, chopped	2 teaspoons salt
1 large green pepper, coarsely chopped	Red pepper flakes
2 garlic cloves, minced	¼ cup each chopped parsley and scallions

Cut fish across into 2-inch pieces. Cut crab legs into 3-inch lengths, and split shell on one side. Shell shrimp, leaving tails on, and scrub clams or mussels.

In a heavy saucepan or casserole, heat the olive oil. Put in the onion, green pepper, and garlic, and cook on low heat until the onions are soft, but not brown. Add the oregano, bay leaf, and sage. Add the wine and cook briskly for 5 minutes. Stir in tomato paste and tomatoes. Cover and simmer for 1 hour, stirring occasionally. Add salt and pepper flakes to taste.

❀ The sauce can now be cooled to room temperature, and refrigerated or frozen.

At serving time, bring the sauce to a boil and put in the clams and crab. Reduce heat. Cover and cook 3–4 minutes. Add fish, shrimp, and scallops, and cook covered about 6 minutes, or until clams open (discard unopened ones). Sprinkle with the parsley and scallions and serve in hot bowls.

Leftovers can be refrigerated for 1 or 2 days, or frozen, after cooling. It is better to refrigerate or freeze the sauce alone, adding perfectly fresh fish and seafood upon reheating.   *4 servings*

BRUSCHETTA

Slice Italian or French bread in ¾-inch slices. Place on cookie sheet in a preheated 350° oven for about 10 minutes, until slices are lightly brown. Remove and rub each slice with a garlic clove. Brush the top with olive oil and return to the oven for 5 minutes.

LA MOUCLADE

It may seem to be stretching the term to call this bowl of beautiful mussels, in their creamy, rich sauce, a soup—and a main-course one. Whatever you call it, it certainly can be the star of a luncheon or supper, with plenty of crusty bread. The bread is essential to sop up the last vestiges of the sauce and to have with a tray of French cheeses. The accompanying salad could be a variety of greens, and dessert, fruit tarts or Orange Soup (recipe follows).

White wine is called for here, and the suggestions are a Meursault or a California Chardonnay.

4 pounds mussels	¼ teaspoon thyme
1 garlic clove, mashed	1 tablespoon flour
1 bay leaf	½ to 1 cup heavy cream
1 cup dry white wine	1 egg yolk
1 tablespoon butter	¼ cup finely chopped parsley
¼ cup finely chopped shallots	Freshly ground black pepper
2 celery stalks, chopped	1 lemon, cut in 6 wedges

Scrub the mussels well and rinse them in several waters, debearding them in the process.

Put the garlic, bay leaf, and wine in a heavy pot that is large enough to hold the mussels and has a tight-fitting lid. Bring to a boil and put in the mussels. Cook over high heat, shaking the pot occasionally, for 3–6 minutes, or until the mussels open.

Remove the mussels with a slotted spoon to a platter. When they are cool enough to handle, snap off and discard the top shells. Discard any that have not opened or that look peculiar. Set the good ones aside.

Pour off the broth, straining through a dampened clean kitchen towel, to catch any sand or mud. Rinse out and wipe the pot and return to the stove, over medium heat. Add the butter, shallots, celery, and thyme. Stir and cook until shallots have softened. Sprinkle flour in and add broth, a little at a time, stirring to make a smooth mixture. Simmer for 5 minutes, add cream and stir. Turn off the heat and stir in the beaten egg yolk with a whisk.

Put the mussels into warm soup bowls or plates, pour the sauce over them, sprinkle with parsley and pepper, and pass a small bowl of lemon wedges.

4–6 servings

ORANGE SOUP

This refreshing concoction was found in Biras Creek, in the British Virgin Islands, where it was served as a first course. It makes a fresh cool dessert. Although it has gelatin in it, it is more soupy than jellied.

2 cups orange segments
3 cups orange juice
½ cup grapefruit juice

½ cup lemon juice
2 tablespoons plain gelatin

Break up the orange segments in a serving bowl and add the orange juice. Mix the other juices with the gelatin in a small saucepan and stir over low heat until the gelatin is dissolved. Stir into the bowl. Chill for at least 2 hours.

6 servings

MOULES MARINIÈRE

Devotees of bistros and checked tablecloths consider a mounded, steaming bowl of mussels as a first course. But double the amounts and you have one of the finest meals from seashore cuisine. The sailor's way with mussels is to steam them as quickly as possible in a closed pan so that they produce their own juice; Italians add red pepper flakes and tomatoes to the pot, along with basil or oregano; others call for bacon fat and onions; and the French want shallots, thyme, and bay. Everybody uses wine and garlic. None of these are absolutely necessary, of course, for mussels taste wonderful by themselves. Oh, maybe a grating or two of pepper, a sprinkle of chives or parsley.... And have you ever tried thickening the broth with a little cream?

Affectionate familiarity makes mussels one of the most versatile of seafoods. Perhaps the most delightful characteristic is that mussels can be served hot or cold, before lunch or dinner or, with a few more per serving, as the meal itself, along with salad and cheese and dessert. Dessert could be a cool lime sherbet and cookies.

Any white wine will do, but best may be a Muscadet from the Loire, or even an estate-bottled Chablis from Burgundy. Portuguese Vinho Verde or a Sicilian white would also serve.

4 pounds mussels	1 bay leaf
1 tablespoon butter	¼ teaspoon thyme
3 tablespoons shallots, minced	1 cup dry white wine
1 garlic clove, mashed	Freshly ground black pepper

Scrub the mussels thoroughly, remove the beards, and rinse in several waters. In a pot large enough to accommodate the mussels, with a tight-fitting lid, melt the butter. Add the shallots, garlic, bay leaf, and thyme. Stir and cook over low heat until shallots are soft, 1–2 minutes. Turn heat to high, pour in mussels and wine. Cover tightly and cook 3–5 minutes, shaking the pot occasionally, until mussels have opened.

Remove mussels with a slotted spoon to a platter. When they are cool enough to handle, remove the top shells, discarding any mussels that have not opened or look funny. Set aside. Strain the broth through a dampened, clean kitchen towel Clean the cooking pot if there is any sign of sand. Return the broth and the mussels to the pot. Reheat and as soon as the mussels are hot pour into 4 large bowls or soup plates and serve sprinkled with pepper.

4 servings

PÂTÉ DE FOIE DE VOLAILLE

Easy to make in the blender, this delightful pâté can be made the day it is to be served as long as it has time to chill for at least 2 hours.

½ pound chicken livers
5–6 tablespoons butter
⅛ teaspoon salt
⅛ teaspoon freshly ground black pepper
2 tablespoons Cognac
½ clove garlic (the size of a pea)

1 tablespoon heavy cream (more if needed)
Pinch each of thyme, basil, and allspice
1 teaspoon lemon juice
¼ teaspoon Madeira

Pat the livers dry and trim off any yellow fat or membrane that clings to them; also any black or greenish spots. Cut them into uniformly sized pieces, about 1 inch square.

Heat 2 tablespoons of the butter in a small skillet, and when the foam has almost subsided, put in the livers. Cook for 3 or 4 minutes, or until the livers have turned light brown but are still pink inside. Sprinkle with salt and pepper, and remove livers from the pan to a plate or small bowl. Turn off heat. Pour the Cognac into the pan and stir to mix with the pan juices and to incorporate bits on the bottom. Pour this liquid into the blender.

Add 2 more tablespoons of butter, softened, to the blender, and the garlic, heavy cream, pinches of thyme, basil, and allspice, lemon juice, and Madeira. Cover and start blender, then add the livers through the hole in the top, a few at a time. Add any juice in the bowl from the cooked livers.

Blend until just smooth, stopping to scrape down occasionally. Add a little more cream if mixture gets too dry. It should be a soft pudding texture; it firms up when cold. Taste and add salt and pepper if needed.

Pour into a 1-cup jar or pot, smooth the surface, and cover with a layer of remaining butter, melted. Refrigerate for at least 2 hours. Serve from the pot.

makes 1 cup

SOLIANKA

In this remarkable Russian soup-stew, salmon is cooked in a simple home-made fish stock with onions and tomatoes, and the added fillip of dill pickles, olives, and capers. The taste is unexpectedly subtle and indefinable. The soup looks beautiful—pink salmon in a broth colored faintly by the tomatoes, garnished with green and black olives and lemon slices.

Dark bread goes with the stew. A possible first course is pickled herring and drafts of icy vodka. Salad of cucumbers and dill would be a nice accompaniment. Dessert could be brandied peaches on ice cream, with a sprinkle of walnuts.

Drink beer, tea in a glass, hot or iced, or more vodka—to continue the Russian theme.

FISH STOCK

2 pounds fish trimmings (preferably donated by fish dealer)
2 quarts water

1 teaspoon salt
¼ teaspoon white pepper

Wash trimmings and put in a saucepan with remaining ingredients. Bring to a boil, reduce heat and simmer for 30 minutes. Strain through cheese-cloth-lined strainer and reserve the stock.

2 tablespoons olive oil
3 large tomatoes, peeled, seeded, chopped, or 2 one-pound cans tomatoes, well drained, juice reserved for another use
2 medium onions, finely chopped
4 small or 2 large dill pickles, finely chopped
6 pitted green olives
6 pitted black olives

1 teaspoon drained capers
2 quarts fish stock
1 bay leaf
2 sprigs parsley
Salt and pepper
1 pound salmon, cut in 2-inch strips
2 tablespoons butter (optional)
Lemon slices

Put the oil in a 3-quart, wide, shallow flameproof casserole. Add the tomatoes and cook slowly, stirring until a paste is formed. Add the onions and pickles. Chop 2 green olives and 2 black olives and add them with the capers. Stir to mix well.

Pour in the stock gradually, stirring. Add the bay leaf, parsley, and salt and pepper to taste. Bring to a simmer and cook on low heat for 10 minutes.

❀ The sauce can be made ahead.

Return sauce to a simmer, put in the salmon and cook for 3–5 minutes, or until salmon is just done. Timing will depend on thickness of salmon. It is done when flesh is pink and flakes easily.

Stir in the butter. This is for enrichment and can be omitted.

Pick out and discard the bay leaf and parsley. Slice the remaining olives and strew over the soup and serve with lemon slices on top.

4 servings

BOUILLABAISSE

Rascasse and other fish essential to bouillabaisse in Marseilles are not to be found here, but this is a splendid version of the justly famous dish. Like the original, it has a variety of fish and seafood, cooked together but added according to their slightly different cooking times. This may be one of the reasons it is so good. And it has saffron. Saffron is so expensive I rarely use it, but this is one case where I splurge. Leeks are optional, but not the saffron.

Along the Mediterranean the dish varies endlessly with the day's catch, but it is pretty well agreed that there must be eel, the fish should be a mixture of firm- and soft-fleshed fish, and there should be some shellfish. This recipe has clams and shrimp, but no crab or lobster, but by all means use them if you wish. Buy them live if you can, split them, and add them with the firm-fleshed fish.

Plenty of good French bread, a leafy salad and fruit in season complete the meal. Beforehand you might serve pastis, which is Pec, Pernod, or Ricard, with ice and water, and antipasto for the starving.

Any dry white wine, young and fresh, is fine with this glamorous dish.

3–4 pounds fish fillets, ½ firm-fleshed (eel, cod, haddock, halibut, sea bass), ½ soft-fleshed (sole, red snapper, flounder, sea perch, hake, mullet, whiting)
3 dozen small clams
½ pound small shrimp
⅓ cup olive oil
2 large onions, chopped
3 garlic cloves, finely chopped
3 leeks, white part only, about ¾ inch in diameter (optional)
3 large, ripe tomatoes, peeled, seeded, and chopped
½ teaspoon thyme
1 bay leaf
⅓ cup finely chopped parsley
¼ teaspoon crumbled rosemary
¼ teaspoon crushed fennel seeds, or 2 tablespoons of a licorice-flavored liqueur (Pec, Pernod, or Ricard)
1 teaspoon grated orange rind
Fish stock, or 1 quart water and 1 quart clam juice
1 teaspoon crumbled saffron threads
¼ teaspoon freshly ground black pepper
¼ teaspoon cayenne pepper

At the fish store, select fish from the two categories, preferably 6 different kinds. Ask the fish dealer to prepare the fish in uniform, bite-size pieces and to peel the eel (keep the firm fish separate from the soft fish). Also ask for the trimmings.

THE STOCK

Fish trimmings　　　　　　　　　　**2 teaspoons salt**
2 quarts water

Wash the trimmings and place in pot with water and salt. Boil gently for 30 minutes; strain, pressing out juices.

Wash and scrub clams well until washing water is clean and clear. Shell and devein shrimp. Set aside.

Heat the olive oil in a high, narrow, lidded kettle or deep, lidded flameproof casserole. Use a stove-to-table vessel if possible. Add the onions, garlic, and leeks (if used) and cook until they are tender but not brown. Add tomatoes and simmer for 5 minutes.

Stir in thyme, bay leaf, 2 tablespoons of the parsley, rosemary, fennel, and orange rind (if liqueur is being used, add it after the saffron).

Add the fish stock. Bring to a boil, uncovered. Reduce heat and simmer for 20 minutes. Add the saffron, rubbing the threads between the fingers; add the black pepper and the cayenne. The saffron and peppers are added later than the other seasonings so the flavor won't fade. Taste for salt.

❋ The soup can be prepared ahead to this point. Refrigerate the fish in 3 separate containers: firm, soft, and shellfish. Return broth to simmer before proceeding.

Put in the firm-fleshed fish and simmer for 5 minutes. Add the soft-fleshed fish and simmer for 5 minutes.

Add the clams, cover and cook for 5 minutes. Add the shrimp, cover and cook another 5 minutes, or until clams open and all the fish is tender but not overdone.

Serve in large soup plates or bowls and sprinkle with the rest of the parsley. Provide forks as well as soup spoons.　　　　*6–8 servings*

FISH AND ONION SOUP WITH ROUILLE

This Basque soup seems to break all the rules for cooking fish. Instead of the usual 2 or 3 minutes cooking time, this soup cooks for 1 *hour*. Unbelievable as it may seem, this long slow cooking on very low heat is not too much.

With water as the liquid, not wine or stock or tomatoes, the taste of the soup is very mild, so it seemed a good one with which to serve the strong hot garlicky *rouille sauce,* made of garlic, hot pepper, and bread crumbs with olive oil beaten in as for mayonnaise. A small amount is spread on the toast which lies on the bottom of the soup plate under the fish. The rest is served in a small bowl, to be used judiciously by diners, to their own taste—and at their own risk.

Good black olives, some red and green pepper strips, and round slices of orange, cut in half, make an attractive hors d'oeuvre platter. A simple lettuce salad is best, and dessert could be blue cheese (strong enough to be noticed after the *rouille*) and apples.

Since the sauce gives the soup the flavor of Provence, a wine from there would be appropriate—red, white, or rosé.

4 medium onions, sliced	½ teaspoon oregano
¼ cup olive oil	1 tablespoon salt
2 quarts water	6 thick pieces (about 1½ pounds)
½ teaspoon thyme	hake, cod, haddock, weakfish,
1 bay leaf	boned
⅓ cup finely chopped parsley	6 slices toasted French bread

Choose a wide, heavy pot with a lid. Sauté the onions in the oil until they are golden but not brown.

Add the water, thyme, bay leaf, 2 tablespoons of the parsley, oregano, and salt. Bring to a simmer, cover and cook for 15 minutes. Add the fish, cover and cook on very low heat for 1 hour.

ROUILLE SAUCE

2 garlic cloves	¼ cup fine bread crumbs
2 hot red peppers, or 1 teaspoon	3 tablespoons olive oil
red pepper flakes	½ to 1 cup broth from the soup

Pound the garlic and red peppers or flakes in a mortar. Mix in the bread crumbs to make a smooth paste. Add the olive oil, beating it in, drop by drop. Add the broth gradually until sauce is thick and creamy.

Spread a thin layer of sauce on each piece of toast, place the toast in hot bowls or soup plates. With a slotted spoon or egg turner, carefully take the fish from the pot and place a piece in each bowl, on top of the toast.

Serve, sprinkled with the remaining parsley, and offer the extra sauce in a small bowl.   *6 servings*

GRAND CENTRAL OYSTER STEW

Recipes for this great New York City landmark stew abound—all slightly different, all perfectly good. For the genuine one, I went to the source—the people at the Oyster Bar Restaurant in Grand Central Station. They sent it to me promptly, and it is given here exactly as it came—a recipe for 1 serving. I have supplied instructions to expand the recipe for more servings.

I first encountered this superb soup-stew as a late night supper, served with hot, crisp French bread and Champagne—still my favorite combination. For luncheon or dinner a salad and dessert seem to be called for, to complete the meal. Salad should be delicate—endive and watercress, for instance, with a light oil and lemon dressing. Dessert should be some fabulous pastry, from the best bakery in town—your own?

Champagne is splendid, of course, but a less expensive sparkling wine, from California or Spain, would be very festive too.

8 freshly opened oysters	1 teaspoon Worcestershire sauce
2 tablespoons butter	1 ounce of clam juice
¼ cup oyster liquor	½ teaspoon paprika
Dash of celery salt	1 cup half-and-half

Place all ingredients except half-and-half and 1 tablespoon of the butter in the top part of a double boiler over boiling water. Don't let the top pan touch the water.

Whisk or stir briskly and constantly for about 1 minute, until oysters are just beginning to curl.

Add half-and-half and continue stirring briskly, just to a boil. *Do not boil.*

Pour stew into a soup plate.

Serve piping hot topped with the remaining 1 tablespoon butter and sprinkled with paprika.

1 serving

Note: To make more servings do 2 at a time. Have bowls hot, and heat half-and-half before adding.

III
STEWS

7

Beef Stews

BASIC BEEF AND VEGETABLE STEW

For a snowy winter's day there is nothing like a comforting, well-seasoned basic beef stew made with broth and red wine to which the vegetables are added toward the end of the cooking so they do not overcook and lose their own texture and taste. Green vegetables are best cooked separately and added upon serving the stew, thereby doing double duty as a handsome bright green garnish. You could substitute a side dish of noodles, rice, kasha, or dumplings for the potatoes. The dumplings should be the kind that can be made apart from the stew, so they will not interfere with the cooking of the stew vegetables.

A salad of different greens served after the stew in the French way, followed by soft Brie or Fontina with the last of the wine, along with good French or Italian bread, and a bowl of brightly colored apples—Cortlands, Golden Delicious, Granny Smiths—for dessert could complete the meal.

Wine suggestions are a Côtes du Rhône, one of the less expensive ones; a Chianti Riserva, a wine of some age and elegance (worth the higher price); a Rioja from Spain, one of the driest of red wines.

Continued

2 pounds boneless beef shoulder or chuck fillet, cut in 1½-inch cubes
1 tablespoon butter
1 tablespoon cooking oil, more if needed
2 tablespoons flour
2 cloves garlic, chopped
1½ teaspoons salt
½ teaspoon thyme
1 bay leaf
2 tablespoons finely chopped parsley
5–6 grindings of the pepper mill
1 cup dry red wine
½ to 1 cup beef broth
4 medium carrots, cut in ½-inch diagonal slices
2 medium onions, cut in 8 wedges
4–6 medium potatoes, halved
1 ten-ounce package frozen peas, cooked

Turn on oven to 325°.

Dry meat on paper towels; it won't brown if it is wet. In a heavy skillet, heat the butter and oil and carefully brown the beef pieces, a few at a time. Do not crowd the pan or the meat will not sear. Transfer to a heavy, lidded flameproof casserole, with a very low flame under it.

Sprinkle flour on the meat in the casserole and stir, with a wooden spoon until the flour is absorbed.

Mash the garlic with 1 teaspoon of the salt until no large pieces remain and a sort of paste is formed. Add to the casserole with the thyme, bay leaf, parsley and pepper.

Add the wine, allow stew to simmer for 5 minutes, add the beef broth to barely cover the meat. Stir to clear bottom of pan. Return to a simmer, cover and place in the oven. Reduce heat to 300° or whatever temperature will just maintain the simmer.

Cook 1 to 1½ hours, or until beef is barely fork tender. Check the stew occasionally to be sure broth has not evaporated. Add a little hot water if needed.

Add the carrots, onions, and potatoes, sprinkle with the remaining salt and a few grindings of the pepper mill. Cover and return to the oven for ½ to ¾ hour, or until meat is tender and vegetables are cooked but still a bit crisp. Tip pot, skim off fat (or remove hardened fat after refrigeration).

❈ At this point stew can be refrigerated after cooling.

Check seasoning and add salt if needed. Scatter the peas on top.

4–5 servings

DUMPLINGS

1½ cups all-purpose flour	1 tablespoon butter
3 teaspoons baking powder	¼–½ cup milk
½ teaspoon salt	1 egg, well beaten

Sift together flour, baking powder and salt into a bowl. Cut in the butter with knives or pastry blender, then stir in enough milk to make a soft dough. Add the egg.

Bring 3–4 quarts of water to a simmer with 1 teaspoon of salt per quart, preferably in a wide pot, but one with a good lid. Wet the hands with cold water and form the dough into large walnut-sized balls. Place them carefully, in batches if necessary, into the simmering water. Cook for 8 minutes uncovered and 10 minutes covered. Place on the stew.

STIFADO

A delectable whiff of clove, cinnamon, and allspice fills the kitchen as this Greek stew cooks. Strangely, the spices do not end up tasting of themselves, but give the stew a unique and indescribable flavor. Like many European stews, it is made with equal weight of meat and onions. The resulting sauce is rich indeed.

Plain rice and a salad of cucumbers with a touch of dill go with the stew. The lemony taste of the Greek soup Avgolemono (recipe follows) would make a good first course, and fresh fruit with Feta cheese a fine dessert.

A full wine is needed for this stew, a California Zinfandel or an Hermitage from France's Rhône Valley, 5 or 6 years old.

2 pounds boneless shoulder or top round of beef, cut in 2-inch cubes	**¼ teaspoon each cinnamon, allspice**
3 tablespoons olive oil, more if needed	**1 bay leaf**
⅔ cup dry red wine	**⅛ teaspoon freshly ground black pepper**
2 cups Italian-style canned tomatoes, drained, chopped, juice reserved	**⅓ cup parsley**
	2 tablespoons tomato paste
2 garlic cloves	**2 pounds tiny white onions, or coarsely chopped regular onions**
1 teaspoon salt	**2 tablespoons butter**
2 whole cloves, broken	**10–12 Greek olives**

Turn oven on to 325°.

Dry meat on paper towels; it won't brown if it is wet. Heat the oil in a heavy skillet and brown the beef pieces well on all sides, a few pieces at a time. As they are browned, transfer the pieces to a lidded flameproof casserole, with a very low flame under it. Rinse the skillet with the wine and pour the wine into the casserole. Cover and cook for 10 minutes. Stir in the tomatoes.

Using a heavy fork, mash together the garlic and salt, and stir into the stew with the cloves, cinnamon, allspice, bay leaf, pepper, 2 tablespoons of the parsley, and the tomato paste.

Drop onions into boiling water for about 5 seconds, drain and run under cold water. Trim the ends and slip off the skins. Make a shallow cross cut at root ends. Heat the butter in the skillet and cook the onions slowly, stirring to coat them with butter and to brown here and there, in spots. Do them in batches and add to the casserole as they are browned.

Cover casserole and place in the oven. Reduce heat as low as possible to just maintain the simmer. Check in 10 minutes and adjust oven temperature if necessary. Cook for 2 to 2½ hours, or until meat is fork tender. Add juice from tomatoes or hot water if stew gets too dry during cooking. Tip the pot and skim off fat. Check and add salt if needed.

❀ At this point stew can be refrigerated or frozen; after cooling transfer to a clean casserole or baking dish if the cooking vessel looks messy. Serve sprinkled with the remaining parsley and olives.

6 servings

AVGOLEMONO SOUP

6 cups chicken broth	**¼ cup lemon juice (about 2 small**
¼ cup rice	**lemons)**
3 eggs	**Salt and freshly ground black**
	pepper

Bring broth to a boil and add rice. Cover and cook on low heat for 15 minutes, or until rice is tender. Remove from the heat.

Beat the eggs until frothy, adding the lemon juice gradually. Beating constantly, add a cup of the broth, a tablespoon at a time. Beat this egg, lemon, and broth mixture into the soup gradually. Stir over very low heat for a minute or two.

❀ Soup can be made ahead up to the point of adding egg and lemon.

6 servings

STEWED SHIN BEEF, PEKING STYLE

This lovely, very different stew has been adapted from *Jim Lee's Chinese Cookbook*. It calls for the subtle flavor of star anise, once found only in Chinese stores and now appearing in supermarkets. Star anise is a beautiful brown star, about an inch in diameter, with eight points, each holding a seed.

Serve with plain rice and a green vegetable—snow peas or the new sugar peas, spinach, or Jim Lee's Chinese Green Beans (recipe follows).

Dessert could be a bowl of fresh fruit or a rich and crumbly tart or pastry served with glasses of chilled Poire from Switzerland and small cups of black coffee.

Beer or tea goes with the stew; for wine, try a rosé from Anjou or Tavel.

2½ pounds shin beef, boned, cut in 1½- to 2-inch pieces	2 tablespoons brown sugar
2 tablespoons cooking oil	½ teaspoon sesame oil (optional)
¼ teaspoon salt	2 tablespoons vinegar
2 cloves garlic, peeled, crushed	¼ cup soy sauce
3 slices peeled fresh ginger	¼ cup Amontillado Sherry
1 medium onion, chopped	6 scallions
½ teaspoon cracked black pepper	2 tablespoons cornstarch mixed with ¼ cup water
2 star anise seeds	

Wipe the meat and dry it for browning. Trim off fat.

Heat a heavy skillet, add the oil, then the salt. Reduce heat to medium, add garlic, ginger, and onions. Stir-fry until just golden. Remove the garlic, ginger, and onion. Reserve for later use.

Brown the pieces of beef, a few at a time, in the skillet. As they are browned, transfer them to a heavy, lidded, flameproof casserole or Dutch oven. Add the pepper, star anise, sugar, sesame oil, vinegar, soy sauce, and Sherry. Cover and simmer 2–3 minutes. Put in the reserved garlic, ginger and onions. Add 3 of the scallions (sauce will be strained later).

Add water to barely cover the meat. Bring to a boil, reduce heat, cover and simmer for 2 to 2½ hours, or until meat is tender.

❋ Stew can be prepared ahead to this point, and refrigerated or frozen.

To serve: Remove fat. Reheat and remove the meat to a clean casserole. Strain the sauce, discard solids. Stir the cornstarch mixture into the sauce and cook gently 1–2 minutes to thicken. Pour the sauce over the meat in the clean casserole. Bring to a simmer.

Serve sprinkled with the remaining 3 scallions chopped across in ¼-inch slices to make little circles.

4 servings

CHINESE GREEN BEANS

Bright green and still crisp, these beans are just right with a Chinese stew.

1½ pounds green beans, cut in 1-inch pieces	⅓ cup cooking oil
	⅛ teaspoon salt
1 teaspoon sugar	2 slices fresh ginger, finely chopped
1 tablespoon cornstarch	
2 tablespoons soy sauce	1 clove garlic, minced
½ cup water or chicken broth	2 tablespoons Amontillado Sherry

Dry the beans after washing and cutting into 1-inch pieces. If they are wet, they will sputter in the oil.

In a bowl, mix together the sugar, cornstarch, soy sauce, and water. Set aside.

Heat a large, heavy, lidded skillet and put in the oil and salt. Reduce heat to medium and add the ginger and garlic. Stir-fry until they are golden.

Add the beans; stir-fry until beans change to a deeper green color. Add the Sherry, cover, and cook on low heat for 2 minutes.

Remove the cover and add cornstarch mixture. Stir-fry until sauce has thickened.

6–8 servings

BEEF AND KIDNEY STEW

By not making a pie of this, or topping it with pastry, calorie-worried folks like me can enjoy the mashed potatoes that go so well with it. Green peas suit the stew, but any green vegetable would be good and look pretty with the brown of the stew and the white of mashed potatoes. A salad of grated carrots, chopped scallions, and finely chopped green pepper makes another attractive color note. Add about 1 teaspoon of grated onion and ½ teaspoon of Dijon mustard to an oil and vinegar dressing for the salad, if you like a little extra piquancy.

Beef kidneys are used here because, compared to lamb or veal kidneys, they take the longest to cook. This allows the beef and kidney to cook together the entire time, thus blending their flavors. Mushrooms are lightly sautéed and added at the end of the cooking time.

An English approach to dessert could be Stilton cheese and crackers, walnuts, fresh fruit, and a glass of Port.

Red wine goes with the stew—a Côtes du Rhône or a Zinfandel, for instance.

1½ pounds stewing beef, cut in 1-inch pieces	⅛ teaspoon cayenne
1- to 1½-pound beef kidney (whole)	1 teaspoon thyme
4 tablespoons cooking oil, more if needed	1 bay leaf
2 medium onions, coarsely chopped	1 teaspoon Worcestershire sauce
2 garlic cloves, minced	2 cups beef broth
2½ teaspoons salt	3 tablespoons flour
¼ teaspoon freshly ground black pepper	2 tablespoons Amontillado Sherry
	½ pound mushrooms, coarsely chopped, sautéed in 1 tablespoon butter and salted and peppered
	¼ cup finely chopped parsley

Pat the beef pieces dry with paper towel; they will not brown if they are wet. Cut the beef kidney down the middle, lengthwise, and remove the fat. Cut into pieces more or less the same size as the beef pieces. Cut away any little bits of fat or gristle. Pat the kidney pieces dry with paper towel.

Heat 2 tablespoons of the oil in a heavy skillet. When a slight haze appears, put in the beef, a few pieces at a time, and brown on all sides. As they are browned, transfer them to a heavy saucepan or flameproof casserole equipped with a lid. Turn heat on low under the vessel.

When all the beef is browned, heat the rest of the oil in the skillet and brown the kidney pieces, also a few at a time. Add them to the beef pieces. Add the onions and garlic to the beef and kidney in the casserole, and cook over moderate heat, stirring, until onions have softened. Add the salt, pepper, cayenne, thyme, bay leaf, and Worcestershire sauce.

Pour in the beef broth, stirring to blend everything and to clear the bottom of the pot. Bring to a boil, reduce heat, cover, and simmer for 1 to 1¼ hours, or until beef and kidneys are tender. Tip the pot and skim off fat. Taste and add salt and pepper if needed.

Remove ½ cup of liquid from the stew, let it cool, and mix with the flour until smooth. With the stew at a simmer, stir in the flour mixture and cook for 1–2 minutes, until sauce thickens. Stir in the Sherry and mushrooms.

❀ At this point the stew can be cooled and refrigerated or frozen for later.

Serve sprinkled with parsley. *6 servings*

CHILI CON CARNE

Everybody loves their own chili, and claims only theirs is authentic. I know better than to claim authenticity for mine, but I do love it. It is made with small chunks of beef rather than ground beef, giving it more texture. The recipe is given with canned beans, but if possible, start with dried beans.

Serve with rice and tortillas or crusty bread. A bowl of grated sharp Cheddar cheese and a bowl of sour cream can be offered, to be added to individual servings. The salad could be big and green, with avocado slices, red onion, and green pepper rings.

Margaritas and corn chips with a dip (page 273) would make a fine beginning for the meal, and a Lemon Granita (page 201), or lemon sherbet would make a cool ending.

Serve beer as the beverage, Mexican if possible, or a red jug wine.

2 pounds beef, top or bottom round or chuck fillet, cut in ½- to ¾-inch cubes
2 tablespoons cooking oil
1 medium onion, chopped
1 medium green pepper, chopped
2 tablespoons flour
2 cloves garlic, chopped
1 tablespoon salt
½ teaspoon cayenne
1 teaspoon oregano
½ teaspoon cumin
2 tablespoons or more chili powder

1 tablespoon paprika
Juice from 3 one-pound cans pinto or kidney beans, beans reserved
1¼ cups (10½-ounce can) tomato purée
Hot water as needed
1 small can (3½ ounces) chopped green chilies (see note)
2 tablespoons chopped pimientos

Turn on oven to 325°.

Pat beef pieces dry with paper towel; they won't brown if they are wet.

In a large, heavy skillet, heat the oil and brown the meat, a few pieces at a time, removing them as they are done to a lidded, flameproof casserole.

Cook onion and green pepper in the skillet, adding more oil if needed. Cook until onion is golden and wilted. Add to the casserole. Turn heat on low under the casserole. Sprinkle in flour and stir until it is absorbed and no white shows.

Mash the garlic and salt together and add to the casserole with the cayenne, oregano, cumin, chili powder, and paprika. Stir to mix well.

Add the bean liquid and the tomato purée. Add a little hot water if liquid is too thick (or if you are using cooked dried beans). Liquid should almost cover the casserole contents.

Bring to a simmer, cover, and place in the oven; reduce heat to 300° so simmer is just maintained. Check after 10 minutes and adjust temperature if necessary. Cook for 1½ to 2 hours, or until beef is tender. Stir occasionally and add hot water in small quantities if liquid gets too thick. Check seasoning and add more chili powder if desired.

Add the beans, stirring in carefully. Add the chilies. Bring to a simmer on top of the stove, cover, and return to the oven. Cook another 15–20 minutes or until beans are well heated. Check seasoning again after adding beans.

Sprinkle pimientos over the stew.   *6–8 servings*

TO COOK DRIED BEANS

    2 cups (1 pound) pinto or red   **6 cups water**
       kidney beans   **2 teaspoons salt**

Wash and pick over beans. Place them in a saucepan with water and bring to a boil. Remove from the heat and allow to stand for 1 hour, covered. Bring to a simmer, cover and cook for ½ hour. Add salt, cover and simmer for another 15–30 minutes, or until beans are tender but not too soft. Timing is hard to predict; keep checking. Drain and add to the stew as directed.

Note: Jalapeños are hot chilies. If you do not want that much hotness, use the kind not labeled "jalapeños."

DAUBE DE BOEUF À LA PROVENÇALE

Like so many French dishes, this beef stew is named after the vessel it is cooked in. It is called a *daube*, after the *daubière* it used to be cooked in, an oval pot with a flat, tight-fitting lid on which coals were heaped, rather in the manner of a chuckwagon bean pot. White wine is usually used in a *daube* in Provence, but in one region nearer the Rhône they use red wine, which we prefer. The other Provençale touches are black olives, anchovies and pimientos. A good big pot is needed for this, with a well-fitting lid.

This is a hearty dish. The beef and vegetables are marinated in a tasty concoction, then layered with bacon and cooked in the marinade.

Rice is good with this stew, but the essential crusty bread might be enough. The first course might be an antipasto, the salad a simple green one, the cheese a salty Chèvre or Feta. Ice cream with fresh fruit would make a nice dessert, with chilled Kirsch and black coffee.

Wine could be red, from the Côtes de Provence or from California—Mountain Red or Zinfandel.

BEEF AND MARINADE

3 pounds boneless shoulder or chuck fillet of beef, cut in 2-×-2-×-1-inch pieces
1½ cups dry red wine
¼ cup Cognac
2 tablespoons olive oil
2 teaspoons salt
½ teaspoon freshly ground black pepper
1 teaspoon thyme
1 large bay leaf, broken up
2 tablespoons finely chopped parsley
2 garlic cloves, minced

Trim off outside fat and wipe the beef pieces with damp paper towels. Place the meat in a large non-metallic bowl. Stir in the marinade ingredients and allow to stand for 1 hour.

2 medium onions, cut in ¼-inch slices
2 stalks celery, coarsely chopped
6 medium carrots, cut in ½-inch slices
8 slices lean bacon
Sifted flour on a plate, about ½ cup
Salt and pepper
¾ pound mushrooms, coarsely chopped
2 one-pound cans Italian tomatoes, drained, chopped
20–24 pitted black olives
Beef broth to barely cover (if needed)
1 small can of flat anchovy fillets, chopped
4 pimientos, cut in ½-inch squares
⅓ cup finely chopped parsley

Add the onions, celery, and carrots to the beef and marinade and allow to stand another 2 hours, stirring occasionally.

If the bacon is very strong (which it rarely is these days), blanch it by simmering in water for 5 minutes, then drain and dry. Blanched or not, cut the strips in half, crosswise

Line the bottom of a large heavy, flameproof casserole with half the bacon. The pot should have a lid that fits well.

Turn on oven to 325°.

Drain the beef and vegetables, reserving the liquid. Pick out the pieces of beef and roll them in flour, shaking off excess as you go. Arrange pieces close together in a layer over the bacon. (You should have enough for at least one more layer, depending on the diameter of the pot.) Sprinkle with salt and pepper.

Mix the mushrooms, tomatoes (save the juice from the tomatoes for another use), and olives with the marinated vegetables. Strew some of them over the meat. Make as many layers of beef, vegetables and bacon as possible, but it may be only two of each. After that first layer of bacon on the bottom, just a few strips per layer are enough. Sprinkle the meat layers with a little salt and pepper as you go.

Pour in the marinade liquid and enough beef broth to barely cover. Bring to a boil on top of the stove. Reduce heat to a simmer, cover and place in the oven. Check the stew after 10 minutes, and adjust temperature, if necessary, to just maintain a simmer. Cook 2 to 2½ hours, or until meat is fork tender. Take the pot out of the oven, tip it up and skim off fat.

❈ Stew can be prepared ahead to this point, and refrigerated or frozen after cooling.

Serve with anchovies, pimientos, and the ⅓ cup of parsley sprinkled on top.   *8 servings*

SHORT RIB STEW WITH MUSHROOMS

The preparation of this succulent stew is designed for ribs with a lot of fat, which is the way they come sometimes. Thorough browning renders some of the fat, and a little more cooking without liquid eliminates more. The ribs are then simmered in stock with onions, red wine vinegar, lemon rind, caraway, and herbs. Mushrooms are added at the end. Noodles with poppy seeds are a good accompaniment.

Rye bread goes with the stew; black bean soup would make a fine first course. Salad could be lettuce with green pepper rings and black olives. Fresh fruit, cut up and steeped in Kirsch or Cointreau, is a refreshing dessert.

A California Zinfandel or Mountain Red would be a good wine choice for the ribs.

4 pounds short ribs of beef, cut in 2-inch pieces	3 cups beef broth
1 tablespoon cooking oil	¼ cup red wine vinegar
2 medium onions, chopped	3 tablespoons flour, mixed with ¼ cup cold water
2 teaspoons salt	½ pound mushrooms, coarsely chopped
1 teaspoon pepper	1 tablespoon butter
½ teaspoon marjoram	2 whole pimientos, coarsely chopped
1 teaspoon caraway seeds	
1 bay leaf	
Grated rind of 1 lemon	

Turn on oven to 475–500°F.

Wipe the ribs with paper towels to remove any splinters and to dry; they won't brown if they are wet.

Oil a shallow roasting pan and place in the hot oven for 5 minutes. Put the pieces of beef in the pan, leaving them far enough apart so the meat will brown rather than steam. Cook 10–15 minutes, turning once or twice to brown on all sides. Reduce oven temperature to 325°.

Transfer beef from roasting pan to a 4-quart Dutch oven. Cover and place in the oven for 20 minutes.

Pour off fat, add the onions. On top of the stove stir and cook until onions are limp.

Add salt, pepper, marjoram, caraway, bay leaf, and lemon rind. Add broth and vinegar, stirring to blend seasonings and clear the bottom of the pot.

Cover and return to the oven. Cook 1–2 hours or until beef is fork tender. Cooking time depends on the quality of the meat and how much it cooked during the browning.

Remove the ribs to a baking dish and keep warm. Skim any fat off the liquid in the pot. Make a smooth mixture of the flour and water and stir into the liquid. Cook on top of the stove 2–3 minutes until it thickens. Pour over beef in baking dish.

❋ For later serving, cool, cover baking dish well and refrigerate or freeze.

At serving time, lightly sauté the mushrooms in the butter and sprinkle with salt and pepper. Spread over the stew. Scatter the pimientos over all.
6 servings

Variation: Instead of pimientos, use 10–12 cherry tomatoes, peeled or unpeeled. To peel, spear them 1 at a time on a long-tined fork and dip in boiling water for a moment or two. Skins will peel off quickly and easily.

SPICY SHORT RIBS

The bony cuts of meat have gained prestige as meat prices have climbed so unmercifully. The price is no longer quite so beautifully low, but the meat is still full of flavor. Beef short ribs are usually rather fat, even the leanest ones, but there are various ways of getting rid of it. In this recipe the ribs are cooked for 1 hour with no liquid just to render their fat. They are then cooked in a spicy barbecue sauce, to make a splendid stew.

Boiled potatoes go with the ribs, and when it is the season, corn on the cob. Other times of the year, green beans are good, or Ginger Corn (recipe follows), and any time of the year a fine big salad with a variety of crisp vegetables as well as lettuce and perhaps lemon in the dressing is appreciated. Fresh fruit of the season is what you will want for dessert: fresh pineapple slices with strawberries; blueberries and bananas; oranges and kiwi fruit; slices of different kinds of melons.

Beer is good with this meal. If you prefer wine, make it a sturdy red that will stand up to the spiciness of the stew—a Premiat from Rumania, or a Zinfandel from California.

2 tablespoons cooking oil	3 tablespoons vinegar
4 pounds short ribs	2 tablespoons Worcestershire
2 tablespoons flour	sauce
1½ teaspoons salt	2 teaspoons paprika
Freshly ground black pepper	2 teaspoons chili powder
1 small onion, finely chopped	¼ teaspoon cinnamon
1 cup tomato juice	⅛ teaspoon ground cloves
1 cup beef broth	¼ cup finely chopped parsley

Heat the oil in a heavy, lidded flameproof casserole, preferably enameled ironware. Brown the ribs on all sides in the oil, a few at a time. Shove them to one side of the pan as they are done. When they are all browned, spread them out, cover and cook on very low heat for 1 hour. Pour off the fat. Sprinkle the flour over the meat and stir to spread it throughout. Sprinkle in 1 teaspoon of the salt and several grindings of the peppermill.

While the ribs cook to render their fat, combine the remaining ½ teaspoon of salt with the rest of the ingredients, except the parsley, in a saucepan. Simmer this mixture for 10 minutes.

When the ribs have been defatted and floured, the salt and pepper added, pour the sauce over the meat. Stir to clear the bottom of the casserole and bring to a simmer.

Cover and simmer on very low heat for 1 to 1½ hours, or until ribs are tender. Stir occasionally to prevent their sticking.

Check seasoning and serve sprinkled with parsley.

❋ Stew can be frozen after cooling.   *6–8 servings*

GINGER CORN

This is a way to make a good vegetable out of corn on the cob that isn't absolutely right out of the garden. The ginger and butter seem to bring it back to life.

6 cobs fresh corn, uncooked   **1 tablespoon grated fresh ginger**
2 tablespoons butter   **Salt and pepper**

Shuck the corn and scrape the kernels from the cobs with a sharp knife. Melt the butter in a skillet and add the corn and ginger. Stir and cook until heated through, sprinkling with salt and pepper. Serve in a warmed bowl.

ARMENIAN BEEF AND CABBAGE

An unusual and flavorful stew, this beef and cabbage combination cooks in a tomato sauce, seasoned with paprika, cayenne, and the surprise of dill. Dill is usually associated with lamb, but it works well with beef.

Brown rice or bulgur and a green vegetable go with the stew. Artichokes would be a possibility, either hot, with butter and lemon, or cold, in a vinaigrette. The cold version could take the place of salad. Hot pita bread or dark breads suit the stew.

A glamorous but simple first course you might be glad to have in your repertoire is suggested here—Seviche, a fresh and lively scallop dish. To finish this splendid repast, dessert could be as simple as Feta cheese and fresh fruit or as rich as a Greek pastry.

Serve a dry white wine, like a Muscadet with the Seviche, and a light red with the stew, such as a Côtes du Rhône or a Valpolicella. Beer would also go with the stew.

1½ pounds boneless stewing beef, cut in 1-inch pieces	1½ teaspoons salt
4 tablespoons butter	⅛ teaspoon cayenne
2 medium onions, finely chopped	1–2 cups hot water
4 tablespoons tomato paste	1 small (2 pounds) cabbage, coarsely shredded
1 tablespoon paprika	½ cup chopped fresh dill

Turn on oven to 325°.

Pat meat dry with paper towels or it will not brown. Melt the butter in a heavy, lidded saucepan or casserole, large enough to accommodate the cabbage before it cooks down. Cook and stir meat over moderately high heat until its red color disappears. Add onions and cook, stirring, until they soften. Stir in tomato paste to coat meat and onions. Stir in paprika, salt, and cayenne. Add hot water, enough to barely cover meat.

Bring to a simmer on top of the stove. Cover and place in the preheated oven. Reduce temperature to 300°, or whatever temperature will just maintain the simmer. Check occasionally. Cook for 30 minutes.

Stir in cabbage and ⅓ of the dill. Cover and return to the oven for 30–60 minutes, or until meat is tender. Taste and add salt if needed.

❋ Stew can be prepared in advance and refrigerated or frozen after cooling.

Serve sprinkled with remaining dill.

4–6 servings

SEVICHE

A refreshing start for a meal, these scallops are "cooked" by standing in citrus juices for a few hours. The scallops must be very fresh, with absolutely no fishy odor.

1 pound fresh bay scallops, or quartered sea scallops
1 small red onion, finely chopped
1 small garlic clove, minced
1 teaspoon salt
⅛ teaspoon freshly ground black pepper
½ cup fresh lime juice (3 or 4 limes) or ⅔ cup fresh lemon juice (about 3 medium lemons) or a combination
2 tablespoons olive oil
½ teaspoon thyme
2–3 dashes Tabasco
1 whole pimiento, chopped
1 avocado

Combine everything but the avocado in a glass or porcelain bowl. Allow to stand for 4 hours in the refrigerator, stirring gently occasionally.

At serving time, peel, seed, and slice the avocado and sprinkle with a little of the lime or lemon juice to prevent discoloration. Stir gently into the scallops.

6 servings

ÖKÖRFAROK RAGÚ

In the cuisine of almost every country there seems to be a rich oxtail stew. This Hungarian version, with the strange name, has an extra savor from the paprika, and is most attractive with the novel arrangement of its vegetables. The stew's being Hungarian is an excuse to have sour cream with it, if sour cream needs any excuse.

The first course to precede the stew might be a pâté or terrine, because there isn't a great deal of meat on the oxtails. After the stew try a salty cheese, like Feta, or a couple of goat cheeses, like Valençay and Sainte Maure. With or after the cheese, fresh fruit of the season would be good, as well as beautiful. A big bowl of one kind of fruit has an especially bountiful look: pears, cherries, peaches, nectarines, purple plums with a few white flowers tucked in among them, grapes. Have plenty, even if you have to eat the rest all week.

A hearty red wine like a fruity young Beaujolais or a fuller, older Rhône is a good companion for this, and very cold plum brandy, Slivovitz, could come with coffee.

2 oxtails, disjointed, or 4 pounds packaged oxtails (3–4 sections per person)
4 tablespoons cooking oil, more if needed
2 tablespoons flour
2 cloves garlic, chopped
2 teaspoons salt
2 tablespoons Hungarian paprika
½ teaspoon freshly ground black pepper
1 medium onion, chopped
2 cups ripe tomatoes, peeled and chopped, or 1 one-pound can tomatoes, undrained, chopped
1 cup beef broth
½ cup dry red wine
16 scallions with green tops, coarsely chopped
¾ pound large mushrooms, sliced
6 medium carrots, cut in ½-inch dice
2 cups potatoes, cut in 1-inch cubes
2 whole pimientos, chopped
1 cup sour cream

Dry oxtails for browning and to remove any splinters of bone.

In a large skillet, heat the oil and brown the pieces of oxtail, a few at a time, removing them as they are done to a lidded flameproof casserole. Turn the heat on very low under the casserole. Sprinkle flour on the meat and stir until it is absorbed.

Using a heavy fork mash the garlic and salt together until no large pieces remain. Stir into the meat with the paprika, pepper, and onion. Cook and stir until onion softens slightly, 3–4 minutes.

Turn on oven to 325°.

Add the tomatoes, broth and wine and carefully stir up the bits from the bottom of the casserole. Bring to a simmer, cover and place in the oven. Check after 10–15 minutes and adjust temperature to maintain simmer. Cook 2 to 2½ hours or until meat is almost coming off the bones. (The stew may be cooked on top of the stove if you wish; the timing is the same. Simmer on low heat, covered.) Check for dryness during cooking. The stew should be rather thick, but not dry or in danger of sticking.

Tip the pot and skim off fat; check seasoning and add salt and pepper if needed.

❋ Stew can be prepared ahead to this point and refrigerated or frozen after cooling.

If the casserole is not large enough to accommodate the vegetables to be added, transfer the stew to a larger one, also equipped with a lid.

With the stew at a simmer, add the vegetables, keeping each kind in its own section. Sprinkle lightly with salt and pepper. Cover and simmer 30–45 minutes, or until meat and vegetables are tender.

Serve sprinkled with pimientos, and offer sour cream in a small bowl.

6 servings

OXTAIL RAGOUT

This savory boiled stew of oxtails with vegetables has come out of Central Europe, by way of Canada. The liquid is water and tomato purée, and the simple seasonings bring out the special flavor of the oxtails. A splendid first course would be smoked salmon with cucumbers in a sour cream (or yogurt) and dill sauce (page 73). With all those vegetables in the stew, salad is hardly needed, but Boston lettuce and endive in an oil and vinegar dressing might be nice—the tenderness of the lettuce contrasts with the crispness of endive. A rich Viennese torte would not be too much for dessert.

A full-bodied red wine from the Rhône or Italy goes with the stew, and so does beer.

4 pounds oxtails (3–4 pieces per person)	1 tablespoon Worcestershire sauce
8–10 cups water	2 cups coarsely sliced celery
2 cups tomato purée	1 cup coarsely chopped green pepper
4 medium onions, coarsely sliced	6 medium potatoes, halved
2 teaspoons salt	6 carrots, cut in 2-inch pieces, thick ends halved to make uniformly sized pieces
¼ teaspoon freshly ground black pepper	2 tablespoons flour
1 bay leaf	½ cup finely chopped parsley

Wash and drain the oxtail pieces. Place in a large uncovered pot on top of the stove. Add the water to cover and bring to an easy boil. Skim off the scum as it appears on the surface. Boil 15–20 minutes or so until no more scum appears. Stir in tomato purée. Add the onions; bring to a simmer.

Add the salt, pepper, bay leaf, and Worcestershire sauce. Continue to simmer, partially covered, for about 2 hours, or until the meat is nearly coming off the bones.

❀ Stew can be prepared in advance to this point, and refrigerated or frozen after cooling.

Add the celery, green pepper, potatoes, and carrots. Continue simmering for ½ to ¾ hour longer, or until vegetables are tender.

Remove the solids to a clean, lidded casserole or pile up in a shallow baking or serving dish that can be brought to the table. Keep warm in the oven. Tip pot and skim off fat from the liquid. Check seasoning and add salt and pepper if needed.

Make a smooth mixture of the flour and ¼ cup of cold water. Stir into the stew liquid. Cook 5 minutes more. For a thicker gravy, add more flour in small amounts, always well mixed with cold water, until desired thickness is reached. Pour the liquid over the meat and vegetables in the casserole or baking dish and bring to a simmer. The sauce should not completely cover everything. If there is any left over, serve it, piping hot, in a bowl on the side, or keep it for soup another time.

To serve at this time, cover the casserole with its lid, or cover the baking dish with foil and place in a 350° oven for 10–15 minutes to heat thoroughly. Serve sprinkled with parsley.   *6 servings*

RAGOÛT DE BOEUF BORDELAIS

Ragoûter is a French word, meaning to restore or excite the appetite, an appropriate description of this hearty beef stew, marinated in a rich mixture of wine and seasonings and then cooked in the same liquid with broth added. Because the stew comes from France's Bordeaux district, the wine used should be from there. Choose a regional from St. Émilion, Pomerol, or the Médoc.

Oysters on the half shell would be a wonderful first course, light and elegant, and an appropriate start for a splendid meal. Potatoes are the customary accompaniment; any other vegetables are hardly needed; the stew has its own. But a green salad would be good to follow, perhaps with walnut oil instead of olive oil in the dressing.

A cheese course and fresh fruit make a fine finish: a variety of goat cheeses would be the best, including Chabichou, a Bordeaux cheese; pears and apples go nicely with the cheeses.

The wine used in the stew can be served with it. A château-bottled red, perhaps a 5- or 6-year old St. Émilion or Graves would be more elegant, particularly with the fruit and cheese.

BEEF AND MARINADE

- 3 pounds cross rib or chuck fillet, cut in 2-inch cubes
- 1 cup dry red wine
- 2 cloves garlic, minced
- 2 teaspoons salt
- ½ teaspoon freshly ground black pepper
- 1 bay leaf
- ½ teaspoon thyme
- 2 tablespoons finely chopped parsley
- 2 or 3 whole cloves
- 1 tablespoon olive oil

Wipe the meat and trim off any big chunks of fat. Put the beef into a non-metallic bowl and add the marinade ingredients. Allow to stand, stirring occasionally, for 2–3 hours, or overnight in the refrigerator.

- 3 tablespoons olive oil, more if needed
- 2 cups beef broth, or enough to barely cover meat
- 12 small white onions
- 4 medium carrots, cut in 2-inch pieces (halve thick ends)
- ¼ pound mushrooms, coarsely chopped
- 2 tablespoons butter
- ½ pound green beans, cut in 2-inch pieces
- ½ cup boiling water with ¼ teaspoon salt
- ⅓ cup finely chopped parsley

Drain and reserve the liquid. Remove the pieces of beef, shaking and scraping off seasonings into the liquid. Put the beef pieces on paper towel as they are drained, and pat them dry with paper towel. They don't brown well if they are wet. Heat the oil in a heavy skillet and brown the meat thoroughly, removing the pieces to a lidded, flameproof casserole as they are done. Turn on oven to 325°.

Pour the marinade liquid into the casserole and add enough beef broth to barely cover the meat. Bring to a boil, reduce heat and simmer, uncovered, for about 15 minutes. Cover and place in the oven. Check in 10 minutes and adjust temperature to maintain simmer. Cook for 1½ to 2 hours, or until meat is barely tender.

Check seasoning, adding more salt and pepper if needed. Tip the pot and skim off fat. Remove the last bits by blotting with paper towel.

Peel the onions and cut small crosses in the root ends to help keep them from separating. Add the onions and carrots to the stew. Cook 30–45 minutes more, until vegetables are tender.

❋ Stew can be prepared ahead to this point, and refrigerated or frozen after cooling.

At serving time, reheat the stew and keep warm in a turned-off oven. Sauté the mushrooms lightly in 1 tablespoon of the butter. Cook the beans in a covered saucepan with the salted water and the remaining tablespoon of butter for about 10 minutes, or until beans are tender but still crisp. Drain beans and add, with mushrooms, to the stew. Serve sprinkled with the parsley. *6–8 servings*

TANGY BEEF

This beef stew, tangy with mustard and vinegar and spiced with cloves, evolved from attempts at developing recipes to strengthen the flavor in a simple beef stew.

Boiled potatoes are added to the ample sauce the stew provides. Green beans go with it nicely, either hot and buttered, or cold in a vinaigrette, with scallions. A dessert that carries through the spicy taste could be Gingerbread (recipe follows) with whipped or sour cream on top.

Beer or a dry red jug wine is a suggested beverage for the stew.

2 pounds beef chuck, cut in 1½-inch pieces	1 teaspoon thyme
	1 tablespoon Dijon mustard
2–3 tablespoons cooking oil	2 tablespoons red wine vinegar
2 medium onions, coarsely chopped	½ cup tomato sauce
	1 cup beef broth
2 garlic cloves, minced	1 tablespoon cornstarch
1½ teaspoons salt	6–8 medium potatoes, boiled, peeled, and halved
3 whole cloves, broken up	
¼ teaspoon freshly ground black pepper	

Pat the meat dry with paper towels; it won't brown if it is wet. Heat the oil in a large, heavy skillet. Brown the pieces of beef in the skillet, a few pieces at a time. As they are done, place them in a heavy, lidded flameproof casserole, with the heat turned on low under it.

Add the onions to the casserole and cook, stirring, until onions soften slightly. Add remaining ingredients, except the cornstarch and potatoes. Bring to a simmer, cover and cook, just maintaining the simmer, for 1¼ to 1½ hours, until beef is tender. Tip pot and skim off fat.

❋ Stew can be prepared ahead to this point.

To serve at this time, mix cornstarch with 2 tablespoons of water to make a smooth paste. Stir into the stew and add the potatoes. Simmer gently until stew thickens and potatoes are heated. Grind some pepper over the potatoes.

To serve at a later time, omit the cornstarch and potatoes, cool with lid askew, and refrigerate or freeze, after stew has come to room temperature, well covered. To reheat, bring to room temperature and heat slowly to a simmer on top of the stove, or in a preheated 325° oven for 30–45 minutes. Add the cornstarch and potatoes as directed above.   *4–6 servings*

GINGERBREAD

Gingerbread is a cake I like to serve after a stew. It is not too sweet, and it is not too heavy. It can be dressed up with a dollop of sour cream or whipped cream and makes a good companion for stewed or fresh fruit.

½ cup dark brown sugar, firmly packed
½ cup shortening
1 cup dark molasses
2 teaspoons baking soda
1 cup boiling water

2½ cups flour
½ teaspoon salt
1 teaspoon each ginger, cloves, cinnamon
¼ teaspoon nutmeg
2 eggs

In a large bowl, cream the sugar and shortening well. Add molasses. Dissolve the soda in the boiling water and add to the sugar mixture. Sift together the flour, salt, and all the spices and add in 3 batches to the liquid mixture, beating until smooth each time. Beat in the eggs, one at a time. Pour into a greased 12-x-8-x-2-inch pan. Bake in a preheated 350° oven for 45 minutes. Cake is done when a skewer comes out clean after being plunged into the center.   *for 12-X-8-X-2-inch pan*

BOEUF BOURGUIGNON

Over the years, as we have all become more sophisticated about food, we have come to regard some of the great old favorites as boring clichés. Good food is good food, however, and Boeuf Bourguignon, well made, is still splendid fare. This version has the Parisian touch of flaming the browned chunks of beef with Cognac, adding a special, subtle flavor.

A first course in Paris bistros used to be oeufs durs mayonnaise—hard-boiled eggs on a lettuce leaf, with mayonnaise and freshly ground black pepper. This is as appropriate now as it ever was. Boiled potatoes are the usual accompaniment, but rice or noodles are more than acceptable. Salad can be a simple one of lettuce; the cheese should be the best French cheese to be found. Dessert should be cool and light, such as sliced oranges in Kirsch, before Cognac.

A Burgundy wine is called for, not necessarily a grand one from one of the famous townships, with a vineyard name on the label. It can be a good wine from a lesser town where vineyard names on the label are not important—a Monthélie, Santenay, Savigny, Auxey-Duresses.

3 pounds boned shoulder or chuck fillet of beef, cut in 2-inch cubes	6–8 grindings of the pepper mill
2 tablespoons olive oil, more if needed	1 teaspoon thyme
	1 bay leaf
2 slices bacon, diced	⅓ cup finely chopped parsley
3 tablespoons flour	1½ cups dry red wine
¼ cup Cognac	1–2 cups beef broth
3 cloves garlic, chopped	1 pound small mushrooms, about 1 inch in diameter
2 teaspoons salt	24 small white onions
	2–3 tablespoons butter

Dry meat thoroughly on paper towels; it won't brown if it is wet.

In a heavy skillet, heat the oil and cook the bacon until it is lightly browned. Remove it with a slotted spoon to a heavy, lidded flameproof casserole. In the same skillet, brown the beef carefully on all sides, a few pieces at a time, removing them to the casserole as they are done. Turn on heat very low under the casserole.

Turn on oven to 325°. Sprinkle flour on the meat, toss gently, and cook until flour is absorbed.

In a small saucepan, warm the Cognac and ignite with a match. Pour it, flaming, into the casserole, standing well back and shaking the casserole for a few seconds. Stop the flame by putting the lid on for a moment.

Mash the garlic with the salt. Add to the casserole with the pepper, thyme, bay leaf, and half of the parsley.

Pour in the wine gradually. Add enough beef broth to barely cover meat. Bring to a simmer on top of the stove. Cover and place in the oven. Check after 15 minutes and adjust oven temperature to maintain simmer. Cook for about 1½ hours, or until meat is nearly tender. Add hot water if needed during cooking.

Tip the casserole and skim off fat. Check seasoning and add salt and pepper if needed.

The small mushrooms stay firmer. Wipe clean with damp paper towel and trim stems. If mushrooms are large, slice coarsely. Peel onions and make a small cross cut in each root end to help keep them from separating.

Lightly sauté the onions and mushrooms together in butter. Sprinkle with salt and pepper. Add to the stew. Cook ½ to ¾ hour longer, or until meat and onions are tender.

❊ Stew can be prepared ahead to this point. Allow to cool and refrigerate or freeze.

Serve sprinkled with the rest of the parsley.   *6–8 servings*

BEEF WITH SOUR CREAM

A favorite hot buffet item, popular for a family dinner too, this flavorful stew goes a long way, laden as it is with mushrooms. It is a good stew to have in one's repertoire, because it can be served so many different ways: on a large platter or shallow bowl, surrounded by noodles or rice; in a casserole with potatoes boiled and added; with a large bowl of buttered kasha; or just with crusty bread and a salad.

The stew is good any time of the year, and accompanying vegetables, salads, and fruits for dessert can reflect the season. Consommé is a particularly good first course—hot in winter, jellied in summer.

A light red Burgundy 3 or 4 years old, a Volnay or Beaune or Santenay, is good with the stew.

2 pounds top rib beef, cut in 1-inch pieces	⅓ cup finely chopped parsley
1 tablespoon cooking oil	Several grindings of the pepper mill
3 tablespoons butter	2 tablespoons flour
1 medium onion, finely chopped	½ cup dry red wine
2 garlic cloves	½ to 1 cup beef broth
1 teaspoon salt	½ to 1 cup sour cream
1 bay leaf	1 pound mushrooms, coarsely chopped
1 teaspoon thyme	

Turn on oven to 325°.

Dry meat on paper towel or it will not brown. Put oil and 1 tablespoon of the butter into a heavy, lidded saucepan or casserole. Over moderately high heat, cook and stir the beef until it loses its red color and the pieces are coated with fat. Add the onion and cook for 1–2 minutes more.

Mash the garlic with the salt until no large pieces remain. Stir into the casserole with the bay leaf, thyme, 2 tablespoons of the parsley, and the pepper. Sprinkle in the flour and stir until it is absorbed.

Gradually add the wine; bring to a simmer; add the broth to barely cover the beef, and bring to a simmer again. Cover and place in the oven, adjusting the temperature to just maintain the simmer. Cook for 1½ to 1¾ hours, or until beef is fork tender. Tip the pot and skim off fat. Check seasoning and add salt if needed.

❋ Stew can be prepared in advance to this point and refrigerated or frozen after cooling.

To serve bring stew to a simmer and slowly mix 1 cup of stew liquid into the ½ cup of sour cream. Stir this mixture into the stew. Add more sour cream as needed to make a creamy, but not too thin sauce. Heat without boiling.

In a heavy skillet, sauté the mushrooms in the remaining 2 tablespoons of butter. Sprinkle with salt and pepper, turn onto the stew, and scatter the rest of the parsley on top.   *6–8 servings*

BEEF STROGANOFF

As described in *Glorious Stew*, this dish may have been invented in Paris in the Gay Nineties and named after royalty or otherwise famous people. As originally made, with fillet of beef and prepared practically at the moment of serving, it is indeed an elegant affair. This version uses round steak, making it possible to cook the dish as a stew ahead of time. It keeps its savor nicely in a chafing dish as a buffet item, or it can be a fine main course for a family or party dinner.

Rich with sour cream and a hint of Sherry, the stew is served on noodles, with a topping of mushrooms. A first course might be anchovies on toast with icy vodka; salad could be a simple one of greens, and dessert ripe pears served with chilled Poire, the Swiss distillation of the Williams pear.

A light young red wine suits this dish—a Burgundy like Mercurey or Givry, an Etna from Sicily or a Chianti.

2 pounds round steak, cut ½-inch thick	2 tablespoons tomato paste
4 tablespoons butter	5–6 grindings of the pepper mill
2 tablespoons cooking oil	2 tablespoons Amontillado Sherry
2 medium onions, thinly sliced in rings	¾ cup sour cream
2 tablespoons flour	12 ounces noodles, uncooked
1½ to 2 cups beef broth	¾ pound mushrooms
1 teaspoon salt	Paprika
2 cloves garlic	¼ cup finely chopped parsley
½ teaspoon dry mustard	

Turn on oven to 325°.

Trim fat from steak. Cut the steak in strips 1 x 2½ inches, and dry the pieces on paper towel. They won't brown if they are wet.

Heat 2 tablespoons of the butter and the oil in a heavy skillet. Add the onions and cook until they are limp but not brown. With a slotted spoon, transfer the onions to a heavy, lidded casserole.

In the same skillet, adding more oil if needed, brown the beef strips, a few at a time. Transfer them to the casserole as they are done. Keep a very low flame under the casserole.

Sprinkle flour into the casserole and stir until flour is absorbed and disappears. Rinse skillet with a little broth and gradually add, with more broth, to the casserole. Add enough to barely cover the meat, stirring to incorporate flour and any bits stuck on the bottom of the pan.

Mash the salt and garlic together on a saucer. Add the dry mustard and the tomato paste to the mixture. Stir all into the stew. Sprinkle with pepper.

Bring to a simmer. Cover and place in the oven. Check in 10 minutes and adjust oven temperature to just maintain the simmer. Cook 1 to 1½ hours, or until fork tender. Tip casserole and skim off fat; check seasoning and add salt if needed.

❁ Stew can be prepared in advance to this point.

To serve at this time: stir in the Sherry and simmer 2–3 minutes. Add a little sauce from the stew to the sour cream and stir the mixture carefully into the stew. Heat but do not boil. Keep warm.

Cook noodles according to package directions, drain, and butter. Sauté mushrooms until lightly brown but still firm, sprinkling with salt and pepper. Put the noodles into a baking dish or on a serving platter and add the stew. Spread the mushrooms on top. Sprinkle with paprika and parsley.

For later serving, cool the stew and refrigerate or freeze. Upon reheating, add Sherry, sour cream, noodles and mushrooms as instructed above.

6 servings

Note: For a buffet, put stew and mushrooms in a chafing dish and serve noodles separately.

PUCHERO CRIOLLA

Puchero Criolla is a sort of New England boiled dinner, South American style. A striking feature is acorn squash, quartered and unpeeled, among its vegetables. Garbanzo beans are frequently found in South American dishes, but Mariusa Verbrugghe, who knows about these things, says that garbanzo beans are never put *in* a puchero. So here we make the beans a part of the meal by serving them in a small casserole along with the stew, as a side dish (recipe follows).

This is indeed a meal in itself, served in large soup plates with knives and forks provided as well as spoons. Or it can be served in two courses: the broth as first course, with glasses of chilled Manzanilla or Fino Sherry, followed by the meat and vegetables as the main course.

Stewed fruit with a sprinkle of shredded coconut, or ice cream with crumbled macaroons on top would be a good dessert.

Serve with a South American red wine or a California Zinfandel.

3 pounds boneless beef shank or shin, cut in 2- to 3-inch pieces	2 celery stalks with tops
2 pounds beef bones	3 sprigs parsley
3–4 quarts boiling water	2 carrots, halved lengthwise
1 tablespoon salt	2 leeks, or 2 medium onions, halved
6 whole peppercorns	2 small acorn squash
2 cloves garlic, chopped	6 medium potatoes
1 bay leaf	6 white turnips
	2 green peppers

Wash beef and bones and put them into a 6-quart deep kettle equipped with a lid. Pour boiling water into the kettle to cover the meat and bones thoroughly. Bring to a boil; boil gently for 10–15 minutes, skimming off scum as it appears. When no more scum is forming, turn down to a simmer.

Add the salt, peppercorns, garlic, bay leaf, celery stalks, parsley, carrots, and leeks. These are pot vegetables, to flavor the stock, and will be strained out.

Bring to a boil, reduce heat and simmer, partially covered, for 2 to 2½ hours, or until meat is just tender.

❀ Stew can be prepared in advance to this point.

Drain, reserving liquid. Discard vegetables and bones, after extracting marrow from the latter, if you like. (Marrow can be spread on toast and sprinkled with salt and pepper for a little hors d'oeuvre.) Skim off fat from liquid; check and correct seasoning to taste; put the beef back in; bring back to a simmer. Remove and set aside ½ cup liquid for bean casserole.

Wash the squash, potatoes, turnips, and peppers. Quarter the squash and remove seeds, but do not peel. Peel and quarter the potatoes. Peel and halve the turnips. Trim, seed, and coarsely chop the peppers. Add the vegetables to the stew, but add peppers 10 minutes later than the rest. Cover and simmer 20–30 minutes or until vegetables are just tender.

For serving at a later time, it is best to refrigerate or freeze the meat and stock without these last vegetables. Cool thoroughly first. When you reheat, remove hardened fat from the surface and bring slowly to a simmer on top of the stove. Add the vegetables as above, and cook the 20–30 minutes until they are done.

8 or more servings

GARBANZO BEAN CASSEROLE

½ small (about 1 pound) cabbage, cored, cut in 8 wedges
½ cup stew liquid
1 one-pound-four-ounce can garbanzo beans (chick peas), drained

½ pound chorizo, sliced
¼ teaspoon freshly ground black pepper

Make the casserole about ½ hour before the stew is done, just before adding the vegetables.

Place the cabbage in a 1½- to 2-quart lidded flameproof casserole. Add the liquid from the stew. Cover and simmer 5–10 minutes until cabbage is just tender. Add the garbanzos, sausage, and pepper. Bring to a boil, reduce heat to a simmer, cover, and cook for 10–15 minutes.

CARBONNADES FLAMANDES

This famous Flemish stew is cooked in beer and, like many European stews, uses equal weights of meat and onions. The onions cook down to make a rich sauce, which contains a little sugar to counteract any bitterness in the beer, and a touch of vinegar for a special flavor.

When available, a good companion for the carbonnades is endive. The leaves can be served with a dip for a first course, tossed with watercress for a salad course, or braised for a side dish with the stew. Boiled potatoes are added to the stew in this recipe. They could be served separately, warmed in butter and sprinkled with parsley. Dark bread is good with the carbonnades.

If appetites warrant, a cheese course could precede a dessert of Gingerbread (page 173) with applesauce or sour cream, or both.

Beer is the thing to drink with this stew.

3¼ **pounds boneless beef rump or chuck roast**
2 **slices bacon, diced**
3 **tablespoons cooking oil, more if needed**
3 **pounds medium onions, sliced (9–10 cups)**
1 **pint (2 cups) beer**
1 **cup beef broth**
1 **teaspoon brown sugar**
⅓ **cup finely chopped parsley**
1 **bay leaf**
½ **teaspoon thyme**

2 **teaspoons salt**
¼ **teaspoon freshly ground black pepper**
2 **tablespoons cornstarch mixed with 3 tablespoons tarragon vinegar, or with ⅛ teaspoon tarragon and 3 tablespoons cider vinegar**
6–8 **medium potatoes, boiled, halved, and peeled, or 12–14 whole new potatoes, boiled, unpeeled**

Trim outside fat from the roast and cut in ¾-inch slices and then into 2-×-4-inch pieces. Dry meat with paper towels; it won't brown if it is wet.

In a large heavy skillet, slowly cook the bacon bits until they are golden and barely crisp. With a slotted spoon, transfer the bacon to a heavy, lidded flameproof casserole.

Add the oil to the bacon fat in the skillet. Put in the onions and stir over low heat until onions are limp and golden but not brown. Remove them to the casserole with the slotted spoon.

In the same skillet, over moderate heat, brown the pieces of beef on both sides, a few pieces at a time. As they are done, place them in the casserole.

Turn on the oven to 325°. Add the beer and broth, and stir in the sugar, 2 tablespoons of the parsley, bay leaf, thyme, salt, and pepper. Bring to a boil.

Cover and cook in the oven 1½ to 2 hours, or until beef is fork tender. Check during cooking and turn heat down to 300° if stew is cooking too briskly.

Remove from the oven, degrease by tipping the pot and skimming off fat. Check seasoning and add salt if needed.

❋ Stew can be prepared in advance to this point. Cool to room temperature and refrigerate or freeze. To reheat, allow stew to come back to room temperature and bring slowly to a simmer on the top of the stove.

Carefully stir in the cornstarch mixture and cook until sauce thickens, about 5 minutes. Add hot potatoes and serve sprinkled with parsley.

6–8 servings

CARBONADA CRIOLLA

Serve this South American beef stew in a pumpkin—a kind of edible tureen—which looks marvelous and keeps the stew hot. The pumpkin is baked separately and the stew is added just before serving. Individual pumpkins could be used, which would take slightly less time to cook. Corn and squash are essential, and some of the pumpkin is scooped out with each serving. All the vegetables brighten the dark richness of the stew.

Pictures of this stew show the corn on the cob, cut into 2-inch pieces—very pretty but hard to eat in a stew. Use corn off the cob in this recipe. Some versions include fresh peach halves, which may sound strange but the taste is fresh and wonderful. Serve it this way when the pumpkins first come in, and with luck, some peaches may still be around.

A main course in itself, the stew needs only crusty French bread or corn sticks to go with it. A traditional dessert of the Argentine is creamed quince, Dulce de Membrillo, served with Bel Paese or Muenster cheese and glasses of Ruby or Tawny Port. But the Brazilian favorite, guava paste, is much easier to find; serve it with cream cheese and crackers.

A South American or California red jug wine is the suggested wine.

3 pounds lean beef chuck, cut in 1-inch pieces	2 cups beef broth, or enough to barely cover
¼ cup olive oil	2 cups yellow squash, cut in 1-inch cubes
2 medium onions, chopped	
2 cups chopped green pepper	2 cups green beans, cut in half
3 garlic cloves, minced	2 cups carrots, cut in ½-inch dice
2 teaspoons salt	1 pound tomatoes, peeled, seeded, chopped, or 1 one-pound can tomatoes, drained, chopped
3 or 4 grindings of the pepper mill	
1 bay leaf	
½ teaspoon thyme	2 cups fresh or frozen corn kernels, or canned kernels, drained
1 tablespoon tomato paste	
½ cup dry red wine	4 fresh peaches, peeled, halved, and pitted

Turn on oven to 325°.

Pat the meat dry on paper towels. It won't brown well if it is wet.

Heat the oil in a heavy skillet and brown the beef pieces, a few at a time. As they are browned, transfer them to a heavy flameproof casserole equipped with a lid.

Add the onions, peppers and garlic to the oil left in the skillet. Add a little more oil if necessary. Stir over moderate heat until onions are soft but not brown. Remove with a slotted spoon and add to the meat.

With low heat under the casserole, stir in the salt, pepper, bay leaf, thyme, and tomato paste. Add the wine, cover, and cook for 5 minutes.

Pour in the broth, stirring up brown bits from the bottom, and bring to a simmer. Cover and place in the oven. Check in 10 minutes and adjust temperature to just maintain the simmer. Cook for 1 to 1½ hours, or until beef is just tender.

Add all of the vegetables, except the corn, cover and cook for 20–30 minutes, or until vegetables are tender. Add the corn and peach halves, cover and cook 5 minutes more. Tip the pot and skim off fat. Check seasoning and add salt and pepper if needed.

❊ Stew can be prepared in advance to this point. Cool partially covered to avoid further cooking in its own heat. Refrigerate or freeze, covered.

To reheat, bring to room temperature and proceed as follows:

THE PUMPKIN

1 pumpkin, 9–10 inches in diameter	**Salt and pepper**
½ cup milk	**Parsley or watercress**

Cut a generous top off the pumpkin, remove seeds, and scrape out fibers, being careful not to make a hole in the bottom. Rinse the pumpkin with milk and sprinkle with salt and pepper. Place the pumpkin with its lid beside it on foil in a 350° oven. Cook about ¾ to 1 hour or until the flesh is tender but not too soft when pricked with a fork (the stew will cook it a little more).

Reheat the stew on the top of the stove; carefully ladle it into the pumpkin. Bring to the table with the lid on, surrounded by parsley or watercress.

Serve some of the pumpkin flesh when you are serving the stew, but be careful not to go through the wall of the pumpkin.

8 or more servings

POT-AU-FEU

Pot-au-feu, which means pot-on-the-fire, isn't a stew at all, it's a weekly French dinner. To us it is a big warm comforting boiled dinner. It can vary enormously. The pot can contain, besides vegetables, meat, chicken, and sausage, all of them or in any combination. This recipe has meat and sausage and some bones for extra flavor. It is a winter dish as a rule, so winter vegetables are used. Some of the vegetables are cooked with the stock to add flavor and are then strained out. A new batch is added at the end of the cooking to be served with the meat.

The stock can be served as a soup first, and the meat and vegetables presented, for the main course, on a platter—a handsome sight—two courses from one pot. Serve with gherkins, mustard, good coarse salt, a pepper mill, and horseradish.

If the soup is not served as a first course, this might be an occasion for Ratatouille (page 318) with good French bread to start the meal.

If there is no handy patisserie where an assortment of pastries can be purchased, dessert might be sliced oranges with a sprinkle of sugar and Kirsch.

A French or Italian red jug wine would be good to drink with the meal.

4 pounds rump, boneless chuck roast, or fresh brisket of beef	1 bay leaf
	4 parsley sprigs
2 pounds beef bones	1 teaspoon freshly ground pepper
1 veal knuckle, cracked	8 medium potatoes
1 large onion	4–8 leeks, 1 inch in diameter, white
3 cloves	part only (optional)
10 medium carrots	4 medium onions
8 medium white turnips	1 one-pound yellow turnip
2 teaspoons salt	1 Polish sausage, about 1 pound
1 teaspoon thyme	

Wash the meat and bones; trim outside fat from meat; place meat and bones in a large kettle.

Peel the onion, trim off ends, and stick in the cloves. Clean 2 of the carrots and 2 of the turnips and cut them in half. They are to flavor the stock and do not need to be peeled. They will be strained out later. Add them to the kettle. Cover completely with water.

Add the salt. Bring to a boil; reduce heat to a simmer. Skim off foam as it appears on the surface. After 10–15 minutes, or when no more skimming is necessary, add the rest of the seasonings.

Simmer very slowly, partially covered, for at least 2 hours, adding water occasionally if necessary to keep everything covered. When beef is fork tender, turn off heat and remove meat.

Drain stock through a colander, reserving the liquid and discarding the vegetables and bones. Put the liquid back in the pot. Skim off fat, and add salt and pepper to taste. Return the meat to the pot.

Scrape the remaining 8 carrots, cut in quarters lengthwise. Peel and halve the remaining 6 white turnips. Peel and halve the potatoes. Halve the leeks (if used) and wash thoroughly. Peel the onions and quarter them. Peel the yellow turnip and cut into ¾-inch cubes. (The idea is to have all the vegetables cooked in the same time. If the potatoes are large, they may need to be quartered; if the onions are large, cut them into eighths.) Add the vegetables to the kettle. Bring to a simmer, add the sausage, cover and cook 20–30 minutes, or until vegetables are tender.

To serve, remove meats and vegetables from the kettle and put them on a large warm platter. Carve and serve the meat and vegetables at the table, or keep vegetables warm, carve the meats, and return to the platter.

If the soup is to be served at this meal, reduce stock to intensify flavor, and check once more for salt and pepper. Also, skim off any more fat which might have come from the sausage. Serve the soup in mugs or bowls, while the meat and vegetables keep warm in the oven, loosely covered with foil. Or serve slices of meat with soup and vegetables in large shallow soup plates.

❋ For later serving, allow to cool thoroughly, partially covered, and refrigerate. Remove any hardened fat from surface. To reheat, bring slowly to a simmer and simmer just to heat through, not to cook further.

8–12 servings, depending on additions

SWEDISH BEEF STEW

Allspice, instead of the usual herb seasonings, gives this simple stew its subtly different taste. New potatoes, unpeeled, are cooked in the stew, which is enriched at the end with sour cream.

Beets, hot and buttered, or cold and pickled, are good with the stew, and Sweet-Sour Cucumbers (recipe follows), more a relish than a salad, is just right with it. Dark bread is called for, as well as any of those Scandinavian rye crisps, to have with Crema Danica and other cheeses from that part of the world, before or after the main course, with tiny chilled glasses of Aquavit. Dessert could be ice cream with Cassis poured over it.

Scandinavian beer is the drink for this meal.

2 tablespoons butter	¼ teaspoon allspice
2 tablespoons cooking oil	1 bay leaf
2 pounds boneless beef chuck, cut in 1-inch pieces	½ cup finely chopped parsley
2 medium onions, finely chopped	1½ cups beef broth
1 tablespoon flour	8 small new potatoes (2–3 inches in diameter), quartered, unpeeled
½ teaspoon salt	½ cup sour cream
⅛ teaspoon freshly ground black pepper	

Turn oven on to 325°.

Heat the butter and oil in a large heavy skillet. Pat the meat dry; it will brown better. When the butter stops foaming, put in the beef pieces, a few at a time, and brown them well on all sides. As they are browned, transfer them to a lidded flameproof casserole. Cook the onions in the remaining fat in the skillet until they are soft but not brown. Add more oil if needed.

Add the onions to the casserole. Sprinkle in flour and stir until no white shows. Add the salt, pepper, allspice, bay leaf, and half the parsley.

Pour off any fat left in the skillet, and add the broth. Stir to incorporate bits on the bottom of pan. Add to the casserole and bring to a boil.

Cover and place in the oven. Check in 10 minutes and adjust oven temperature to just maintain the simmer. Cook for 1 hour and 10 minutes. Remove the casserole from the oven and degrease the stew by skimming off the fat. Add the potatoes, sprinkle with salt and pepper, cover and return to the oven for 20 minutes, or until beef and potatoes are done.

❋ Stew can be prepared ahead to this point. Cool with lid askew to prevent further cooking. When cool, cover. Refrigerate: It will keep for 2 or 3 days. The stew does not freeze well because of the potatoes, and the potatoes cooking *in* the stew give it a special flavor.

To reheat, bring to room temperature, and place, covered, in a preheated 325° oven for 30–40 minutes, until heated through, or bring slowly to a simmer on the top of the stove.

To serve, carefully transfer the meat and potatoes to a hot platter or baking dish and keep warm. Cook the sauce remaining in the casserole for about 5 minutes on high heat. This reduces it slightly and intensifies the flavor. Beat in the sour cream. Heat but do not boil and pour over the meat and potatoes. Sprinkle with the rest of the parsley.   *4–6 servings*

SWEET-SOUR CUCUMBERS

2 medium cucumbers
  Salted water to cover (½
  teaspoon salt per cup)
⅔ cup cider vinegar
½ cup water
½ teaspoon salt

2 tablespoons sugar
¼ teaspoon freshly ground black
  pepper
1 tablespoon chopped fresh dill, or
  1 teaspoon dried

Scrub the cucumbers well and cut off the ends but do not peel them. Score with a fork, and slice very thin. Cover with the salted water and let them stand for 1 hour in the refrigerator.

Pour off salted water and add the mixture of vinegar, water, salt, sugar, pepper, and dill. Chill for 2 or 3 hours, stirring occasionally. Serve in small portions—it is more a relish than a salad.

WIENERSAFT GULYAS

In this Viennese-style Hungarian goulash the beef and onions are cooked in butter with paprika and caraway. And the Italian influence is noted in the tomato paste, garlic, and lemon rind. Serve with noodles, rice, or boiled potatoes, rye bread and a big leafy salad.

The method for starting this stew is rather unusual. The seasonings are mashed together and cooked briefly with the onions. The meat is then added and cooked just until it loses its raw red color. Because of the small amount of liquid used, the stew is cooked in the oven, rather than on top of the stove where it is likely to burn.

A Viennese dish is always a good reason to have something *mit Schlag.* If you don't want your whipped cream with pastry, have it with berries of the season.

A flowery white Austrian wine—a Loibner, Kremser, Gumpolds-kirchner, or Grinzinger—is good with most Viennese dishes.

2 pounds boneless beef chuck or rump, cut in 1½-inch pieces	2 tablespoons sweet Hungarian paprika
2 teaspoons marjoram	1 tablespoon tomato paste
2 teaspoons zest of lemon, finely chopped	2 tablespoons flour
1 teaspoon caraway seeds	1–2 cups hot water
1 clove garlic, minced	1 green pepper, cut in strips
1½ teaspoons salt	2 whole pimientos, cut in strips
5 tablespoons butter	10–12 black olives (preferably Greek)
2 pounds onions, chopped	

Turn on oven to 325°.

Wipe meat with paper towels. It is not to be browned but needs drying anyway.

Crush or mash together marjoram, lemon zest, caraway, garlic, and salt.

In a heavy, lidded flameproof casserole melt 4 tablespoons of the butter and stir in the mashed seasonings. Add the onions and cook gently until they have softened slightly. Sprinkle in the paprika and cook for about 1 minute. Stir in the tomato paste.

Add the beef, maintaining medium heat under the casserole. Stir to coat the pieces and cook until beef loses its raw red color. Sprinkle in the flour and stir until it is no longer white. Stir in 1 cup of the water and mix well. Add more water, if it is needed, to cover the bottom of the casserole with about 1 inch of liquid. The onions and meat will supply some liquid as they cook.

Bring to a simmer, cover and place in the oven. Reduce oven temperature to 300° or whatever temperature will maintain the simmer. Check in 10 minutes and adjust temperature if necessary. Cook for 1½–2 hours, or until beef is tender. Add hot water if needed during cooking, ½ cup at a time. The stew is supposed to be thick. When beef is tender, tip pot and skim off fat.

❄ Stew can be prepared in advance to this point, and refrigerated or frozen after cooling. To serve: Lightly sauté the green peppers in the remaining tablespoon of butter until tender but still firm. Scatter over the reheated stew with the pimientos and olives. *6 servings*

BEEF IN APPLE CIDER

Reminiscent of Germany's famous Sauerbraten, this stew has a pleasant sweet-sour-spicy quality. It is cooked in apple cider and wine vinegar and thickened with crumbs made of dried black pumpernickel bread. Serve with noodles or boiled potatoes. Buttered cabbage with a sprinkle of caraway seeds would be an appropriate German accompaniment; sliced black bread or dark rye is good too. Dessert could be a wickedly rich strudel.

Beer or a white wine with a touch of sweetness—a Sylvaner or Gewürtztraminer—would go well with the stew.

2¼ pounds stewing beef, cut in 1½-inch pieces	1 large onion, stuck with 3 whole cloves
2 slices bacon	1½ cups apple cider
1 tablespoon cooking oil	¾ cup red wine vinegar
2 teaspoons salt	1½ to 2 cups dried pumpernickel bread crumbs
¼ teaspoon freshly ground black pepper	Juice and grated zest of ½ lemon
1 teaspoon grated fresh ginger	¼ cup finely chopped parsley
2-inch piece of cinnamon	
1 bay leaf	

Wipe the meat with paper towel.

In a heavy saucepan or casserole, cook the bacon until it is crisp. Set aside on paper towel to drain. Pour off all but 1 tablespoon of fat from the pan. Add the oil. Add the meat, and stir over moderately high heat until the meat loses its red color.

Stir in salt, pepper, and ginger. Tuck in the piece of cinnamon, the bay leaf, and the onion.

Add the cider and vinegar, and crumble in the bacon. Bring to a boil. Reduce heat, cover, and simmer for 1½ to 2 hours, or until meat is tender, stirring occasionally. Discard the onion, bay leaf and stick of cinnamon.

❊ At this point the stew can be cooled and refrigerated or frozen for later serving.

To serve, remove fat from the top and check for salt. With the stew at a simmer, stir in crumbs a few at a time, until desired thickness is arrived at. Sprinkle with lemon juice, lemon rind, and parsley.

A Viennese suggestion for an accompaniment to Sauerbraten, also good with this stew, is hot stewed prunes, cooked with a strip of lemon rind and 2 or 3 cloves.

4–6 servings

SWISS STEAK

I wonder how many people, now of a certain age, remember their grandmothers pounding seasoned flour with the edge of a plate into beef for Swiss steak. This activity in the kitchen always meant delectable aromas, followed by a fine, hearty dinner.

Potatoes, mashed or boiled, and a winter vegetable, squash, carrots, or turnips, would accompany the stew. We may add a salad and serve rye or pumpernickel bread sometimes, instead of the usual French or Italian.

To carry through the nostalgia, dessert would be pie, probably apple, with a piece of sharp Cheddar cheese.

Serve beer or a hearty dry red jug wine.

Beef chuck roast, 2½ to 3 pounds with bone, boned and split into 2 steaks	1 teaspoon savory
	4 tablespoons cooking oil
	2 large onions, coarsely chopped
¼ cup flour	1 one-pound can Italian tomatoes, broken up with the hands
1 teaspoon salt	
½ teaspoon freshly ground black pepper	½ to 1 cup beef broth

Choose a piece of beef chuck about 2 inches thick. Even a supermarket butcher, if you ask him nicely, will usually debone and split a piece of meat for you. If not, it is reasonably simple to cut the meat into 2 steaks.

Mix the flour with the salt, pepper, and savory on a large plate or a platter. Turn the steaks in the seasoned flour and pound them with the edge of a plate, or a meat mallet, until they are thinner, ¼ to ½ inch, and all the flour has been incorporated. Cut the steaks into 4 or 6 pieces.

Heat 3 tablespoons of the oil in a heavy skillet and when a light haze appears, brown the pieces of beef, a few at a time. As they are browned, place them in a flameproof casserole.

Put the rest of the oil in the skillet and cook the onions for 2–3 minutes, until they soften slightly. Place them on the meat. Add the tomatoes.

Turn on oven to 325°. Rinse the skillet with ½ cup of broth, let it cook down slightly. If too much broth evaporates, add a little more.

Add the broth to the casserole, and bring to a boil. Cover and place in the oven. Check the stew after 10 minutes and adjust oven temperature, if necessary to maintain simmer. Cook for 1½ hours, or until meat is tender. Skim off fat before serving.

❀ The stew can be refrigerated or frozen after cooling.   *4–6 servings*

BOEUFA À LA HONGROISE

Paprika, tomatoes, and plenty of onions make this French stew "Hungarian-style" and hearty, but it is still basically French with the classic seasonings—thyme, bay leaf, and parsley. Serve with noodles or parslied potatoes, followed by a lettuce salad with cucumbers and scallions in it.

Oysters on the half shell would be a perfect first course, and after a tray of cheeses, dessert could be Pears in Red Wine (recipe follows).

The wine has to be up to the strong taste of the stew. Try a Zinfandel, a Rioja, or a Chianti.

3 pounds boneless beef shoulder, cut in 1- to 1½-inch pieces	1 cup tomato purée
3 tablespoons butter	1–2 cups beef broth
2 tablespoons oil	¼ teaspoon freshly ground black pepper
4 medium onions, coarsely chopped	½ teaspoon thyme
2 tablespoons Hungarian paprika	1 bay leaf
2 teaspoons salt	¼ cup finely chopped parsley
2 garlic cloves, chopped	1 green pepper, cut in strips
2 tablespoons flour	2 pimientos, cut in strips

Turn on oven to 325°.

Trim outside fat from beef. Dry on paper towels; it won't brown if it is wet.

In a heavy skillet, heat 2 tablespoons of the butter and the oil. Slowly cook the onions until they are transparent and slightly golden but not brown. With a slotted spoon, transfer them to a heavy, lidded flameproof casserole.

In the same skillet, brown the beef a few pieces at a time, using more oil if necessary. As the pieces are browned, transfer them to the casserole with the onions.

Turn heat on very low under the casserole, sprinkle in the paprika, stirring to blend. Mash the salt and garlic together and stir into the stew. Sprinkle in flour, a little at a time, stirring until no white shows.

Add tomatoe purée and stir to blend with the flour. Add beef broth until liquid barely covers meat. Stir to clear the bottom of the casserole. Add the pepper, thyme, bay leaf, and parsley. Bring to a simmer, cover, and place in the oven. Turn oven temperature down to just maintain the simmer. Check in 10 minutes and adjust temperature, if necessary. Cook for 1½ to 2 hours, or until beef is tender. Tip the casserole and skim off fat. Check seasoning and add salt if needed.

❀ Stew can be prepared in advance to this point.

To serve: Lightly sauté the green pepper strips in the remaining tablespoon of butter until they are tender but still bright green. Scatter them over the reheated stew. Strew pimiento strips over all.   *6–8 servings*

PEARS IN RED WINE

6–8 pears
  2 cups dry red wine
  1 cup sugar

4 whole cloves
1 two-inch stick cinnamon

Choose pears that are firm and not too ripe. Peel them carefully, leaving stems on.

In a lidded, flameproof casserole, large enough to hold the pears in 1 layer, put wine, sugar, cloves and cinnamon. Simmer for 5 minutes.

Put in the pears, turning to coat with liquid. Bring to a simmer, cover and place in a 350° oven for 30–40 minutes, depending on the size of the pears. They are done when they are tender but not overly soft. Turn them carefully and baste at least twice during cooking so the pears will color evenly.

Cool with the liquid in the smallest bowl that will hold them. Spoon the liquid over them and turn gently as they cool. Chill for about 1 hour. Serve in dessert dishes with some of the liquid.

YOGURT KHORESHE

Yogurt gives this meatball stew a freshness, and raisins supply that bit of sweetness that goes so well with curry. Rice with toasted almonds in it is an appropriate and delightful accompaniment, and can share the ample amount of sauce with the meatballs.

A big bowl of nuts in their shells would make a first course, or a nibble with drinks, and an unusual combination salad and dessert could be a Melon, Pear, and Cucumber Mélange (recipe follows).

Serve with beer, or hot or iced tea.

1½ pounds ground chuck beef	2 teaspoons curry powder
1 teaspoon salt	6 whole cloves, broken up
½ teaspoon pepper	1 teaspoon ground cardamom
½ teaspoon turmeric	1 cup beef broth
¼ to ½ cup ice water	½ cup raisins
2 tablespoons butter	1 cup plain yogurt
2 tablespoons oil	¼ cup finely chopped fresh parsley
1 medium onion, finely chopped	

Put the ground meat in a bowl and sprinkle over it the salt, pepper, and turmeric. Beat in ¼ cup of water, beating to spread the seasonings throughout and to make the mixture light and fluffy, capable of sticking together in balls. Use more water if necessary. Form into 1-inch balls.

Heat the butter and oil in a skillet, and when the foam subsides, put in the meatballs a few at a time to brown on all sides. As they are browned, remove them to a heavy, lidded flameproof casserole, wide and shallow, rather than deep.

Cook the onion in the skillet until it is transparent but not brown. Transfer to the casserole with a slotted spoon. Turn heat on very low under the casserole.

Mix the seasonings together; sprinkle over the meat and onions, and mix well.

Add the beef broth gradually, stirring to detach any bits on the bottom. Add the raisins. Bring to a simmer, cover and cook 35 minutes on low heat. Tip pot and skim off fat.

❀ Stew can be prepared ahead up to this point.

To serve, stir in the yogurt gradually, with the pan off the heat. Heat but do not boil, and sprinkle with parsley. *4 servings*

MELON, PEAR, AND CUCUMBER MÉLANGE

When you find a couple of perfect pears and a perfect cantaloupe or honeydew, or any melon except watermelon, this is a lovely first course. It can also be served as a salad with some dishes, particularly something with curry.

3 tablespoons lemon juice	1 teaspoon Dijon mustard
5 tablespoons salad oil	1 small cantaloupe, or ½ large one
1 teaspoon grated onion	1 large cucumber
1 teaspoon sugar	2 ripe pears
1 teaspoon salt	Freshly ground black pepper

Mix together everything but the fruit, and pepper. Peel and seed the cantaloupe. Cut into ¾-inch dice. Peel the cucumber, cut it in half lengthwise, scoop out the seeds and cut into ½-inch dice. Peel and core the pears and cut into ¾-inch dice.

Mix the fruit with the dressing and sprinkle with pepper. Chill for 1–2 hours before using.   *6 servings*

FIVE FRAGRANCES BEEF

Five fragrances powder, a wondrous blend of spices found in Chinese groceries, is strangely delicate in flavor—and essential for this stew. The recipe is adapted from *Jim Lee's Chinese Cookbook*, where it is a pot roast. We have cut up the beef, and suggest even smaller pieces if chopsticks are to be used.

Serve plain rice with this and Jim Lee's Chinese Broccoli (recipe follows) if it is the season; otherwise serve plain steamed green beans or Chinese Green Beans (page 153).

Seafood makes a hearty preface to this meal, chicken consommé a light one. An appropriate dessert is lemon or lime sherbet with cut-up preserved kumquats (available in jars) and Cream Sherry on it.

A chilled dry Sherry, the ultra-dry Manzanilla, slightly less dry Fino, or medium dry Amontillado is delicious with the stew, although tea or hot rice wine is closer to tradition.

2 tablespoons cooking oil	3 pounds boneless chuck, or top or
½ teaspoon sesame oil	bottom round, cut in 1½-inch
1 teaspoon salt	cubes (1-inch cubes for
3 slices peeled fresh ginger	chopsticks)
2 cloves garlic, crushed	8 scallions with crisp green
3 tablespoons sugar	Water
½ teaspoon cracked black pepper	2 tablespoons cornstarch, mixed
1 teaspoon five fragrances powder	with ¼ cup water
3 tablespoons white vinegar	2 tablespoons Amontillado Sherry
¼ cup soy sauce	

Heat a heavy, lidded casserole or Dutch oven and put in the oils. Add the salt, stir, and turn heat to medium. Add the ginger and garlic; stir-fry until golden, not brown.

Remove the pot from the heat, and stir in the sugar, pepper, five fragrances powder, vinegar, and soy sauce.

Trim off any outside fat from the meat and add meat to the casserole. Add 3 whole scallions (they will be strained out; no need to cut them up). Add water to barely cover the meat. Bring to a boil; reduce heat to a simmer. Cover and simmer for 1½ to 2 hours, or until beef is tender.

❀ Stew can be prepared in advance to this point, cooled, and refrigerated or frozen.

To reheat: remove hardened fat and bring to a simmer. Remove meat from liquid and place it in a clean casserole. Strain liquid into a saucepan. Bring to a simmer and add the cornstarch mixture to this liquid and cook 1–2 minutes until it thickens. Add the Sherry and pour over the meat in the clean casserole.

If liquid is too thin, add more cornstarch mixed with water, 1 teaspoon at a time, until it is the desired thickness. Cook 1–2 minutes after each addition. The sauce should not completely cover the meat. If there is an excess, serve it in a bowl, or save it to warm up with any leftover stew.

To serve, cut the green part of the remaining scallions across in ¼-inch slices to make little rings of green. Sprinkle over the stew.

6–8 servings

JIM LEE'S CHINESE BROCCOLI

Jim Lee calls this Jade-Green Broccoli, because the broccoli turns that bright green color when it is perfectly cooked.

1 large bunch broccoli (about 2 pounds)	½ cup water, or chicken broth
1 teaspoon sugar	¼ cup vegetable oil
1 tablespoon cornstarch	⅛ teaspoon salt
2 tablespoons soy sauce	1 clove garlic, minced
	2 tablespoons Sherry

Cut off 1 inch from broccoli stems, remove leaves, and peel off tough outer skin. Break off flowerets; split large ones to make them uniform in size. Wash the flowerets and stems. Cut the stems on a slant in ⅛-inch slices.

In a bowl, mix together the sugar, cornstarch, soy sauce, and water. Set aside.

Heat a large, lidded skillet, add the oil and salt. Turn heat to medium and add the garlic. When garlic is golden, add the broccoli. Turn up heat and fry for 2 minutes, stirring and turning the broccoli constantly.

Add the Sherry, cover and cook for 2 minutes.

Turn down heat, uncover skillet, and add the cornstarch mixture. Stir and cook until gravy has thickened and broccoli is a bright jade green.

6–8 servings

CARNE ALL' UNGHERESE

This is Hungarian goulash, Italian style. It is not a heavy stew, partly because of the zest of lemon in it. Served Hungarian style with noodles, the garnish of pimientos, green pepper, and black olives gives it the Italian touch.

A pleasant first course is asparagus or green beans, at room temperature, with a little good olive oil and a sprinkle of Parmesan cheese. Some Italian cheeses after a green salad would be good, and a cool Lemon Granita for dessert (recipe follows).

Red wine from Italy or Hungary would go with this stew.

2 pounds boneless beef shoulder or chuck, cut in 1-inch cubes	1 tablespoon Hungarian paprika
3 tablespoons olive oil	2 tablespoons tomato paste
2 medium onions, chopped	Zest of 1 lemon, minced
2 tablespoons flour	1½ to 2 cups beef broth
3 garlic cloves, chopped	1 green pepper, cut in strips
1 teaspoon salt	2 pimientos, cut in strips
1 teaspoon marjoram	10–12 pitted black olives

Dry meat on paper towels. It won't brown if it is wet.

Heat 2 tablespoons of the oil in a heavy skillet. Brown the meat in the skillet carefully, a few pieces at a time, transferring them to a flameproof casserole which has a lid as they are browned.

Turn the heat on low under the casserole and add the onions. Stir and cook until onions soften slightly. Sprinkle in flour and stir until it disappears.

Mash the garlic with the salt until no large chunks remain, and add to the casserole with the marjoram, paprika, tomato paste, and lemon zest.

Add beef broth gradually, stirring to clear the bottom of the pan. Bring to a simmer, cover and cook on low heat for 1½ to 2 hours, or until beef is tender. Check during cooking and add hot water in small amounts if liquid cooks down too much. When meat is tender, tip the casserole and skim off fat.

❊ Stew can be prepared in advance to this point.

To serve, lightly sauté the green pepper strips in the remaining tablespoon of oil, and scatter over the hot stew with the pimientos and olives.

6 servings

LEMON GRANITA

¾ cup sugar
3 cups water

1½ cups strained lemon juice

Mix the sugar and water in a saucepan and boil for 5 minutes. When this syrup cools, mix it with the lemon juice and pour into an 8- or 9-inch square baking or cake pan. Put in freezer. After about 1 hour, when the mixture has started to freeze, give it a stir, breaking it up. Do this once or twice as it freezes, so that it does not become one large ice cube. *6 servings*

SWEET AND SOUR MEATBALL STEW

Is there a family which does not have a recipe passed down from one generation to the next, its origins unknown—often reconstructed from memory? This recipe, with its surprising ingredient of cherry jam, came from a New Englander with a Swedish background and was called—the Armenian stew. It tastes good and is easy to prepare because the meatballs require no browning. By changing the size of the meatballs, you change the taste delightfully. The cooking time stays about the same.

Serve with pasta of some kind—buttered fettuccine, for instance, followed by a lettuce salad with crisp radishes, endive, cucumbers, celery, etc. Dessert could be sliced or sectioned oranges with sliced bananas, sprinkled with sugar and shredded coconut.

Beer is good with this or tea or wine—a rosé.

1½ pounds ground beef chuck	1½ tablespoons cherry jam
1 teaspoon salt	1 bay leaf
3–4 grindings of the pepper mill	1 teaspoon grated lemon rind
¼ to ½ cup ice water	Hot water if needed
1 eight-ounce can tomato sauce	Small sprigs of fresh parsley
Juice of 1 lemon	

Put the ground beef in a mixing bowl and sprinkle in the salt. Grind in the pepper and mix with your hands to spread the seasonings evenly. Beat in water gradually until the mixture is light and fluffy, but can still hold together. Form into 1-inch balls.

Mix together the tomato sauce, lemon juice, cherry jam, bay leaf, and lemon rind in a lidded saucepan or flameproof casserole, preferably a wide, shallow one.

Bring to a simmer and put in the meatballs, making sure they do not stick to the bottom. Cover and cook ¾ hour on very low heat, shaking the pot or stirring occasionally to keep from sticking. If the liquid cooks down too much, add small amounts of hot water. Degrease if necessary by tipping the pot and blotting up the fat with paper towel.

❀ Stew can be prepared in advance to this point.

Serve on or with pasta, and stick little sprigs of parsley in among the meatballs.

4 servings

COLLOPS

The early English word for slices of meat is *collops*, and versions of this stew surely delighted Chaucer. In this one, the slices are thin and cooked in a nicely seasoned sauce that includes a little anchovy and is thickened with bread crumbs. The dish is attractively presented on a platter, with toast triangles, lemon slices, a sprinkle of capers and parsley for extra flavor.

A rather moist accompaniment is called for with the stew—creamed onions, mashed yellow turnips perhaps—and a leafy green salad.

A first course could be toasted nuts and black olives, served with very dry Sherry, Fino, or the driest of all, Manzanilla. Toast the nuts—almonds, pecans, or walnuts—in a skillet with a little butter and a lot of salt. The collops are not too heavy, so a fine light cake or Orange Cake (page 109), with fresh fruit would not be too much for dessert.

Beer is good with the stew; try an English one—Bass or Whitbread, for instance.

3 pounds top round of beef, cut in ⅜-inch slices	Hot water if needed
½ teaspoon salt	1 onion, chopped
3–4 grinds of the pepper mill	6 flat anchovies, coarsely chopped
Large pinches of thyme, marjoram, savory	¼ cup dried bread crumbs
2 cups beef broth	Toast triangles
	1 thinly sliced lemon
	1 tablespoon capers
	¼ cup finely chopped parsley

Buy a 3-pound top round roast and either ask the butcher to slice it for you, or do it yourself if you have good sharp knives. Trim fat from the slices and pound them flat. Place them in a heavy saucepan or flameproof casserole equipped with a lid. Add the salt, pepper, thyme, marjoram, savory, broth, and onion. Cover and simmer for 1 to 1½ hours, or until beef is tender, adding a little hot water if needed.

Remove the slices of meat from the sauce and arrange them overlapping in a row on a warm platter or baking dish. Strain the sauce, skim off fat, and stir in the anchovies and bread crumbs. Simmer until slightly thickened. Check and add salt and pepper if needed. Pour the sauce over the meat.

❋ Stew can be prepared ahead to this point.

To serve, surround with toast triangles, arrange the slices of lemon over the top, and sprinkle with capers and parsley. *6–8 servings*

BOILED BEEF STEW

This is the most simple of stews, and, made beautiful with vegetables, it can grace a well-set table in attractive soup plates, or be the one-pot meal around a campfire. Just be sure there is enough salt, always important for boiled meat. For extra flavor, try adding a Polish sausage for the last ½ hour of cooking. Serve with gherkins, coarse salt, mustard, freshly ground pepper, and a Sour Cream and Horseradish Sauce (recipe follows).

Because it is a meal in itself—soup, meat, and vegetables—a first course is hardly necessary, perhaps only some crisp vegetables to go with drinks. A salad course is not needed either, or a cheese course. It might be the occasion for an easily made Chocolate Mousse though (recipe follows).

Beer goes with the stew, also a cold rosé, like a Tavel, or a Chianti.

3–4 pounds boned shank or shin of beef, cut in 2-inch pieces
2 pounds beef bones
Boiling water
4 onions, coarsely sliced
2 teaspoons salt
½ teaspoon freshly ground black pepper
1 bay leaf
2 tablespoons vinegar
1 cup coarsely chopped celery

6–8 medium potatoes, peeled and halved
1 small rutabaga (yellow turnip), quartered and sliced ½ inch thick
2 green peppers, coarsely chopped
2 cups fresh green peas, or 1 ten-ounce package frozen peas
½ cup finely chopped parsley

Trim off outside fat from meat. Wash meat and bones. Place meat and bones in a large kettle and pour in boiling water to cover them. Bring to a gentle boil and skim off foam as it appears on the surface. Skim for 15–20 minutes until no more scum is forming.

Add the onions, salt, pepper, bay leaf, and vinegar. More salt may be needed later when the other vegetables are added. The seasonings are added when foam no longer appears so they won't be skimmed off.

Adjust the heat to maintain a simmer. Cook, partially covered, for 2 to 2½ hours, or until meat is tender. Timing is hard to predict; keep checking. Skim off any fat that appears during cooking—it is easier to remove before the vegetables go in. Add water only if it is needed to keep the meat barely covered.

When the meat is tender, discard the bones and try to remove any last vestige of fat from the surface.

Add the celery, potatoes, turnip, and, after 10 minutes, the peppers. Bring to a boil again, and reduce heat to maintain a simmer. Cover and cook ½ to ¾ hour more, or until vegetables are tender. Check again for salt; potatoes absorb some. If needed, add by ½ teaspoons until broth is to your taste. If by any chance it is too salty, add water.

❄ Stew can be prepared ahead to this point. Cool with lid askew; when cool, refrigerate. Remove hardened fat. Stew can now be frozen. To reheat, bring to room temperature, and slowly bring to a simmer.

To serve, add the peas, cook for another 5 minutes or so, until peas are cooked and stew is just heated through.

Sprinkle with parsley and serve in deep bowls or soup plates, with knives and forks as well as spoons.   *6–8 servings*

SOUR CREAM AND HORSERADISH SAUCE
4 tablespoons horseradish, drained   **Salt and pepper to taste**
1 cup sour cream

Mix horseradish with sour cream. Add salt and pepper to taste.

The sauce can also be made with whipping cream instead of sour cream. Start with ½ cup, and add salt, pepper, and horseradish to taste.

CHOCOLATE MOUSSE

This incredibly easy mousse is a real find in our never-ending search for light, lovely desserts.

8 ounces semisweet chocolate   **6 eggs**
4 tablespoons water

Melt the chocolate with the water in a small saucepan, over low heat. Break the eggs, dropping the whites into a large mixing bowl, and the yolks into the melted chocolate, off the heat.

Mix the yolks and chocolate together. Beat the whites until they are stiff. Fold the chocolate mixture into the beaten egg whites and turn into a serving dish. Chill for at least 2 hours.   *6–8 servings*

PORTUGUESE TRIPE

It's a pity tripe is still considered an exotic meat. Many wonderful stews are made of it. This classic is from Oporto, whose citizens are so devoted to tripe they are called *tripeiros*. Both the recipe and the cooking time are long. The tripe takes a long time to cook to its proper tender chewiness; it then cooks still longer with other flavorful ingredients. Make this dish ahead because it is improved by a day or two in the refrigerator.

The various elements in this recipe are cooked separately and then assembled, a lot of work but worth it. The finished dish stays in the turned-off oven for about ½ hour with a towel over it. This is to simulate the final operation in Portugal. There, the stew waits for ½ hour or so by the fire, covered with a blanket, to absorb the steam and dry the stew more without further cooking.

This is a meal in a pot, needing only rice, good bread, and a melon for dessert.

Have lots of rough red wine to drink with the meal, and a bottle of old Port with the melon.

BEANS

1 cup dried white beans, Great Northern, navy, or baby lima	6 cups water
	1 teaspoon salt

Wash and pick over beans. Place in a lidded saucepan with the water. Bring to a boil, remove from the heat, and allow to stand for 1 hour, covered. Bring to a boil again, add salt and simmer until just tender. This can take from ½ to 1 hour longer; keep testing. Beans are done when the skin breaks and flutters when you blow on one.

TRIPE

2 pounds honeycomb tripe, cut in ½-×-2-inch strips	1 tablespoon salt
Tops from 1 bunch celery	3 quarts cold water
	2 tablespoons cider vinegar

Wash tripe thoroughly in cold water. Place in a large lidded pot or kettle. Cover with clean cold water, and bring to a boil. Boil 5 minutes, drain, and rinse with cold water.

Place again in the kettle with celery tops, salt, water, and vinegar.

Bring to a boil, cover partially, and simmer 3–4 hours, or until tripe is tender—the longer the better. Replace water as it boils away.

While tripe is cooking, make stock.

STOCK

2 pounds veal bones	2 cloves garlic, mashed
1 ham hock	3 sprigs parsley
3 celery stalks, broken in half	3–4 quarts water, or enough to cover
2 carrots, halved lengthwise	1 tablespoon salt
2 medium onions, quartered	¼ teaspoon pepper

Buy veal bones with a little meat on them. Buy a ham hock that is not all dried up, and be sure it does not smell rancid.

Wash the bones, hock, and vegetables. There is no need to peel the garlic or carrots because they will be strained out. Place everything except salt and pepper in a lidded pot or kettle with the water. Bring to a boil, boil gently for 10–15 minutes, skimming off scum as it appears. When foam stops rising, add salt and pepper. Partially cover and simmer very slowly for 2 hours.

Remove ham hocks, cool, peel, and remove ham from bones, chop across the grain, and reserve. Remove any meat from veal bones and reserve. Put the bones back in the pot and continue cooking for another hour. Strain, discard solids, and reserve stock.

When the tripe is tender, drain, discard vegetables and liquid.
Turn on oven to 300°.

TO FINISH

2 tablespoons olive oil	3 cups canned tomatoes, undrained, chopped
2 medium onions, finely chopped	½ pound chorizo, cut in ¼-inch slices
6 medium carrots, cut in ½-inch slices	¼ cup finely chopped parsley

In a 4-quart, lidded flameproof casserole, suitable for serving, heat the oil. Cook the onions until they are limp and transparent, but not brown. Add the carrots and tomatoes. Cook over moderate heat until the mixture is no longer watery. Add the chorizo. *Continued*

Add the reserved beans, the tripe, the ham, and any meat from the veal bones. Add about 2 cups of the stock, or enough to not quite cover the contents of the casserole. Stir gently to mix, cover and place in the oven. Cook for 1 hour, then remove lid and cook, stirring occasionally, for 40–60 minutes more. This allows you to get the stew moist enough. It should be thick and moist; if it gets too dry, add just enough stock to prevent burning or sticking.

Turn off the oven; place a clean dish towel over the casserole and replace the lid. Let it stand for ½ to ¾ hour in the oven. The towel absorbs the steam and keeps the stew at the proper state between too wet and too dry.

❋ Stew can be prepared in advance to this point. When cool, cover and refrigerate or freeze. Save the leftover stock. It will keep in the refrigerator for 4 or 5 days, and can be frozen. When reheating the stew, add a small amount of heated stock if needed to bring the stew to desired moistness.

Serve sprinkled with parsley.   *6–8 servings*

CORSICAN CHICK PEA CHILI

Last summer we visited an American friend in Corsica. Our host had been cooking fabulous meals for us, mostly French and Italian, when he was suddenly overcome with a fit of nostalgia, and a mad desire for chili. The customary pinto or kidney beans turned out to be unavailable, but there were chick peas. Undaunted, with a recipe from Pierre Franey's *More 60-Minute Gourmet* for inspiration and guidance, and seasonings chosen to get that remembered taste, he made this wonderful, full-flavored chili, and we have brought back the recipe—an American classic, reborn and revitalized abroad, now home.

Crusty bread and a big salad of assorted greens, followed by a tray of French cheeses and fresh fruit, completed the meal in Corsica. The same can be done with a flourish here.

Serve a thrist-quenching white wine like a Soave or reds like Valpolicella or Bardolino—or beer.

3 tablespoons cooking oil	1 teaspoon oregano
1 large onion, chopped	1 teaspoon thyme
1 large red or green pepper, cut in 1-inch squares	1 teaspoon basil
	1 bay leaf
2 cloves garlic, minced	3 tablespoons chili powder, or more if desired
1½ pounds lean ground beef	
3 tomatoes, cut in 1-inch pieces	3 tablespoons tomato paste
1 cup beef bouillon, or broth	1 teaspoon red pepper flakes
1 teaspoon salt	2 one-pound cans chick peas

Heat the oil in a large, heavy flameproof casserole. Put in the onion, red or green pepper, and garlic. Slowly cook until the onion is limp and transparent but not brown.

Add the beef and turn up the heat slightly. Cook, stirring and breaking up lumps with a wooden spoon, until the meat loses its color.

Add the tomatoes and beef bouillon. Simmer for 5 minutes. Stir in the salt, oregano, thyme, basil, bay leaf, chili powder, tomato paste, and red pepper flakes. Simmer for 15 minutes, or until meat is tender.

Stir in the chick peas and cook another 15 minutes.   *4–6 servings*

MANZO GAROFANATA

It smells like pickling time in the house when Manzo Garofanata is cooking. The spices of the East enrich this Roman stew, blending together to make a different and magic new taste. Pasta would go well with the stew—linguine with butter and Parmesan, for instance.

Start with antipasto, which could include the following items: salami, radishes, pickled peppers, anchovies on hard-boiled eggs, ripe and green olives, scallions, celery, strips of pimiento, and some Italian cheese—to name a few.

A salad is hardly necessary, but when tomatoes are at their best, a platter of them, sliced, garnished with a squeeze of lemon, salt and pepper, and fresh basil leaves would be perfect.

Fresh fruit and Amoretti cookies, and Strega or Fior d'Alpi with coffee would make a fine finish to this Italian meal.

One of the white wines from Sicily, generally dry and lemony, goes well with the stew. Red wine, a young Chianti or Valpolicella, would go with the antipasto as well as the stew.

2 pounds boneless beef shoulder or cross rib, cut in 1-inch cubes
3 tablespoons oil, more if needed
3 cloves garlic, chopped
1 teaspoon salt
6 whole cloves, broken up
¼ teaspoon freshly ground black pepper
¼ teaspoon cinnamon
⅛ teaspoon nutmeg
⅛ teaspoon allspice
2 tablespoons finely chopped parsley
½ cup dry red wine
3 large ripe tomatoes, peeled, quartered, or 1 one-pound can Italian tomatoes, undrained
2 cups celery, chopped
10–12 black olives
3 whole pimientos, chopped

Pat the beef pieces dry with paper towel; they won't brown if they are wet.

In a heavy skillet, heat the oil and brown the cubes of beef, a few at a time, removing them when they are done to a flameproof casserole that has a lid.

Mash the garlic and salt together on a saucer, using a strong fork. Stir into the casserole with the cloves, pepper, cinnamon, nutmeg, allspice, and parsley.

Stir in the wine and cook for 2–3 minutes. Add the tomatoes and cook, stirring to clear the bottom of the pan. Bring to a simmer, cover and cook for 1½–2 hours, until meat is fork tender. Check occasionally during cooking. If stew seems dry, add hot water, ½ cup at a time.

Skim off fat and check seasoning, add salt if needed.

❋ Stew can be prepared in advance to this point, and refrigerated or frozen after cooling. To serve: Remove ½ cup of liquid from the stew and put it in a saucepan with ½ cup of hot water and the celery. Cook, covered, on a low low flame until celery is tender, about 10–15 minutes. Add to the reheated stew.

Garnish with olives and pimientos. *4–6 servings*

8

Veal Stews

BLANQUETTE DE VEAU

This lovely stew is supposed to be as white as possible. The veal is blanched and does not brown in the butter, the pepper is white, and the mushrooms are the whitest, bleached whiter still with lemon juice. The stems of parsley are used because they color the stew less than leaves, and the whole wonderful thing is finished with egg yolks and cream.

With mushrooms and tiny white onions in it, the blanquette needs only rice and a green vegetable—snow peas, for instance. A first course could be shrimp tossed with lemon, chopped scallions and parsley, or Nova Scotia salmon with sour cream and capers. Endive and watercress is a suitably elegant salad, and a good goat cheese with fruit of the season would finish a memorable meal.

The wine can be red or white—young, dry and French.

3 pounds boneless veal shoulder, cut in 1½-inch pieces
Boiling water
2 teaspoons salt
½ teaspoon white pepper
4 tablespoons butter
⅓ cup chopped shallots
¼ cup flour
1 teaspoon thyme
1 bay leaf
6–8 stems of parsley, 6–8 parsley tops, chopped
18–24 tiny white onions
1 pound small white mushrooms
2 lemons, juice of 1, the other thinly sliced
3 egg yolks
½ cup heavy cream
Pinch of nutmeg

Wash veal, place in a large saucepan or kettle and pour boiling water over it to cover. Turn heat on high under the pan and agitate the veal with a wooden spoon until the pink disappears. Bring to a boil and allow to boil gently for 30 minutes, skimming off scum and grease as they appear. When scum is no longer appearing, add the salt and pepper.

Drain the meat and reserve the liquid. Melt the butter in a lidded flameproof casserole over a very low flame. Add the shallots and cook until they are limp and transparent but not brown. Add the pieces of veal, and stir to coat them with butter. Do not allow them to brown.

Sprinkle flour over the contents of the casserole and stir until it disappears. Add enough of the reserved liquid to barely cover the meat. Mix well. Leftover liquid can be reduced and used as stock another time.

Check the stew for salt and pepper, and add the thyme, the bay leaf, and the parsley stems tied together. Reserve the chopped parsley for garnish. Bring to a simmer, cover and simmer for 30 minutes, or until veal is almost tender.

While the stew is cooking, peel the onions and make small crosscuts on the root ends to keep them from separating. Clean the mushrooms with a damp paper towel; sprinkle with lemon juice to keep them white. Add the onions and mushrooms to the stew. Cover and cook for ½ to ¾ hour or more or until meat and vegetables are tender. Remove bay leaf and parsley stems.

❊ Stew can be prepared in advance to this point and refrigerated and frozen after cooling.

To serve: With the stew at a simmer, beat the egg yolks with the cream in a small bowl. Slowly add a few tablespoons of hot sauce from the stew, stirring constantly. Stir the mixture gradually into the stew. Do not let the stew boil after adding the eggs and cream.

Sprinkle with nutmeg, lay the lemon slices along the center of the stew, and sprinkle with the chopped parsley.   *6–8 servings*

LEMON VEAL

Veal and lemon make a wonderfully light stew, sparked with cayenne and Worcestershire sauce. Artichoke hearts are added as an enrichment, like the heavy cream. Serve it with rice or noodles.

The stew is light enough to be preceded by a pâté, or that entertaining array of good things called hors d'oeuvre variés. A list of the latter follows the stew recipe, in case you need some ideas.

Instead of a salad, a separate course of braised celery or asparagus with Hollandaise sauce would be excellent. After a selection of Italian cheeses—or with it—fresh fruit of the season would be refreshing.

White or red wine goes with this stew—a Chardonnay or a more expensive Pouilly-Fumé for white, or a Chianti or a fine Barolo for red.

3 pounds boneless veal shoulder, cut in 1½-inch pieces	1 bay leaf
1 tablespoon butter	1 clove garlic, minced
1 tablespoon cooking oil	2 teaspoons Worcestershire sauce
2 slices bacon, diced	2 lemons
½ teaspoon marjoram	1 ten-ounce package frozen
¼ teaspoon cayenne	artichoke hearts, cooked, or 1
1 teaspoon salt	sixteen-ounce can artichoke
1½ cups chicken broth (fat removed)	hearts, drained
	3 tablespoons flour
¼ cup dry Vermouth	½ to ¾ cup heavy cream
	¼ cup chopped fresh dill

Turn on oven to 325°.

Trim any fat from veal and dry with paper towel. The veal does not get browned but it needs to be dry to prevent splattering in the pan.

In a lidded flameproof casserole, melt the butter, add the oil, and slowly cook the bacon until it is golden brown. Add the meat, turning and cooking on moderate heat until the pieces lose their color but are not quite brown.

Stir in the marjoram, cayenne, and salt and continue cooking for 5 minutes.

Gradually add the broth and Vermouth. Add the bay leaf, garlic, Worcestershire sauce, and 1 of the lemons, cut into 6 quarter-inch slices. Bring to a boil, reduce heat to a simmer. Cover and place in the oven. Turn the oven temperature down to 300°, or whatever temperature will maintain the simmer. Check in 10 minutes and adjust temperature, if necessary. Cook for 1½ hours, or until veal is tender.

Tip the pot and skim off fat. Remove the bay leaf and the cooked lemon slices. Tuck in the artichoke hearts.

Make a smooth mixture of the flour and ½ cup of the cream. Stir carefully into the stew, and cook on low heat for a minute or two, until sauce thickens. Check and add salt if needed. Add the rest of the cream if you want a thinner sauce.

❊ The stew can be cooled and refrigerated or frozen at this point.

To serve: Garnish with the second lemon thinly sliced, placed in a row down the middle of the stew, and sprinkled with the dill.   *4–6 servings*

HORS D'OEUVRE VARIÉ

The French appetizer course is usually served in little matching oval or rectangular dishes, with a can of Portuguese sardines, or a can of tuna fish or some roe on a saucer. The labels are decorative and make for visual variety. French bread and sweet butter are the usual accompaniments. You can be very imaginative about the appetizers; a small amount is all that is needed of each, and as few as 2 different dishes can suffice but 3 or 4 are nice. Those little tastes are quite appetite-encouraging for what is to come.

Fresh mushrooms in oil and lemon dressing, with scallions and parsley
Julienne of pickled beets
Cooked green beans in a vinaigrette
Italian or Greek olives
Hard-boiled eggs with anchovy strips, or deviled eggs, quartered
Radishes
Sliced boiled potatoes and scallions in a vinaigrette
Grated carrot in a vinaigrette
Cucumbers with lemon and dill
Tiny shrimp with lemon and chives

OSSO BUCO

Milan gets the credit for Osso Buco, the justifiably famous dish. Rich and delightful, it is made of sections of veal shanks braised in wine and vegetables. *Gremolata,* a magic mixture of chopped fresh garlic, zest of lemon and parsley, strewn over the finished dish gives it a unique taste. Although it can be served with plain rice or pasta, Risotto alla Milanese is the perfect accompaniment (recipe follows). A salad of greens, including some arugula, would be good after or with the shanks, and Italian cheeses and fresh fruit of the season could round out a fine dinner.

A Valpolicella or a Bardolino is suggested for this meal, or a more elegant Valtellini.

4–6 pieces of veal shank, 2½ inches in size	¾ cup finely chopped parsley
2 tablespoons olive oil, more as needed	1 pound tomatoes, peeled, seeded, chopped
Salt and freshly ground black pepper	1 tablespoon chopped fresh basil, or 1 teaspoon dried
2 medium onions, finely chopped	½ cup dry white wine
2 stalks celery, finely chopped	1 tablespoon minced garlic
2 medium carrots, finely chopped	1 tablespoon minced zest of lemon

Turn oven on to 325°.

Wipe veal pieces with paper towel to remove any splinters and to dry for browning. They won't brown well if they are wet. Tie if necessary to hold meat around the bone.

Heat the oil in a heavy, shallow casserole that has a lid and is large enough to take the veal pieces on edge in one layer. Brown the shanks well on all sides, sprinkling with salt and pepper. Set aside on paper towel to drain.

Put the onions, celery, and carrots into the casserole and stir over low heat until the onions are limp and pale gold, but not brown. Add ¼ cup of the parsley, the tomatoes, basil and wine. Stir and cook for 1–2 minutes to clear the bottom of the casserole. Stand the veal pieces on edge in the casserole with sauce and vegetables between and around them. Bring to a boil, cover and place in the oven for 1 to 1½ hours, or until the veal is tender. Turn once during cooking. Taste and add salt and pepper if needed.

❀ Stew can be prepared in advance to this point and refrigerated or frozen after cooling.

To serve, remove veal to a platter and remove trussing strings. Keep warm. Skim fat from sauce, bring to a simmer, and pour over the shanks. Mix together the garlic, lemon zest, and the remaining parsley. Sprinkle over the top.

4–6 servings.

RISOTTO ALLA MILANESE

5 tablespoons butter
2 cups rice
1 small onion, finely chopped
½ to 1 teaspoon saffron threads
  (optional)

4 cups hot chicken broth
¼ to ½ cup freshly grated
  Parmesan cheese

Melt 3 tablespoons of the butter in a lidded saucepan. Add the rice and onion and cook slowly, stirring, until the onion is transparent and the rice opaque, and both are golden but not brown. Crumble the saffron, if used, into the hot broth. Add the broth to the rice and onions. Bring to a boil, stir once. Turn the heat down, cover and cook on low heat for 20–25 minutes.

Fluff with a fork, stir in remaining 2 tablespoons of the butter, and the Parmesan, little by little.

6–8 servings

STUFATINO

This simple, delicately flavored stew, a Florentine specialty, is usually made with slices of veal, cooked in wine and a little rosemary. Tomato paste gives color to the sauce, and bacon provides some of the fat for the browning of the meat.

Regular stewing veal, which is usually shoulder, can be substituted for the more expensive slices. The timing is about the same. As with all veal stews—any stew for that matter—cooking time can vary enormously, because of the unknown age of the meat, and the vagaries of stoves. Keep checking every 10–15 minutes, from the shortest time given—until meat is tender.

Parslied potatoes, a Risotto (page 217) or fettuccine with garlic and butter sauce would be a fine accompaniment, and a salad of garden lettuce could precede a cheese course of Italian cheeses—Fontina, Taleggio, Bel Paese, for example. Ripe pears with the cheese would make a nice light dessert. When pears are not at their best, apples with Gorgonzola makes a splendid alternative.

An Italian white wine is good with the stew, an Orvieto or a Soave. You might want to have a Chianti with the cheese.

2 pounds leg of veal, cut in ⅜-inch-thick slices	3 or 4 grindings of the pepper mill
1 tablespoon butter	¼ teaspoon crumbled rosemary
1 tablespoon cooking oil	2 tablespoons tomato paste
2 slices bacon, diced	1 cup dry white wine
1 medium onion, sliced	Hot water to barely cover
2 cloves garlic, chopped	¼ cup finely chopped parsley
1½ teaspoons salt	

Dry the slices for browning. They do not brown well if they are wet.

Heat the butter and oil in a heavy skillet. Add the bacon and cook on low heat, stirring with a wooden spoon, until bacon is lightly brown. Remove the bacon with a slotted spoon to a heavy, lidded flameproof casserole.

Brown the veal in the skillet, a few pieces at a time. Put them into the casserole as they are browned. Turn on heat very low under the casserole.

Cook the onions in the fat left in the skillet. Cook until the onions are limp and golden but not brown. Add them to the casserole.

Mash the garlic with the salt, using a strong fork. Add to the casserole with the pepper, rosemary, and tomato paste.

Stir in the wine and simmer the stew until the wine is reduced to half. Add hot water to barely cover the meat, and return to a simmer.

Cover the casserole and cook on low heat, just enough to maintain the simmer. Cook for 1 to 1½ hours, or until veal is tender. Tip pot and skim off any fat. Check and add salt and pepper if needed.

❋ Stew can be prepared in advance to this point, and refrigerated or frozen after cooling.

To serve, arrange veal slices in a warm baking dish or on a platter and pour the sauce over them. Sprinkle with parsley. If there is extra sauce, put it in a small bowl.

4–6 servings

VEAL STEW WITH PEAS

Like Veal and Green Peppers, this stew also has an Italian flavor. The taste is quite different though, because white wine and tomatoes supply the liquid, and the seasonings are thyme and sage. Bright green peas top the stew at the end, making a beautiful garnish, as well as providing a vegetable.

Pasta suits this stew. Try some of the odd shapes pasta comes in—little bows, corkscrews, or shells. Dress the pasta with 3 or 4 tablespoons of butter or olive oil, in which 2 smashed garlic cloves have steeped for 2–3 minutes, and serve with freshly grated Parmesan.

Salad could be tomatoes, red onion rings, green pepper rings, and black olives, with a dressing of lemon juice, olive oil, salt and pepper, and a pinch of oregano.

A good dessert for this meat is butter pecan ice cream, with a little Strega poured over it and sprinkled with macaroon crumbs.

White wine is best to drink with the stew—a Pinot Grigio or Sauvignon Blanc.

2 pounds stewing veal, cut in 1½-inch pieces	1½ teaspoons salt
2 tablespoons butter	¼ teaspoon freshly ground pepper
2 tablespoons cooking oil, more if needed	½ cup dry white wine
1 medium onion, finely chopped	1 cup tomatoes, peeled and chopped, or 1 cup canned tomatoes, undrained, chopped
2 garlic cloves, minced	2 cups fresh peas or 10-ounce package frozen peas
½ teaspoon thyme	
½ teaspoon sage	

Dry the veal on paper towels; it browns better when it is dry.

Heat the butter and oil in a heavy skillet and brown the veal pieces, a few at a time. As they are browned, transfer them to a heavy, lidded casserole with a low flame under it.

Add the onion and garlic to the meat. Stir and cook for about 5 minutes, until onions are slightly soft. Stir in the thyme, sage, salt and pepper. Add the wine and bring to a boil, stirring to blend everything, and to incorporate any bits stuck to the bottom.

Add the tomatoes and bring to a simmer. Cover and cook on very low heat, to just maintain the simmer, for 1 to 1½ hours, or until veal is tender. Check during cooking and add a little hot water if stew is in danger of sticking. Tip the pot and skim off any fat, and check the seasoning, adding salt and pepper if needed.

❄ Stew can be prepared in advance to this point and refrigerated or frozen after cooling.

Add the peas, cover and cook until peas are tender. Fresh peas will take about 15 minutes, so do not overcook the veal before adding them. Frozen peas need only about 5 minutes.   *4–6 servings*

VEAL PAPRIKASH

This rich and beautiful Hungarian-style stew is cooked in tomato purée, chicken broth, and a little vinegar. Onions and green peppers are cooked with the veal, and sour cream, stirred in at the end, puts the finishing touch to the flavor. Serve with fine noodles.

A first course could be cooked whole green beans, at room temperature, with a sprinkle of olive oil and Parmesan cheese. Salad could be leafy, the cheeses light, like Taleggio or Bel Paese, and for dessert, a tart or strudel, with chilled Poire or Kirsch and coffee.

The paprikash calls for a light red wine like Volnay or Santenay—good with the cheese too. If you prefer a white, serve a chilled Pouilly-Fumé, or a Chardonnay.

3 pounds boneless veal shoulder, cut in 1½-inch pieces	½ teaspoon thyme
2 tablespoons butter	1 bay leaf
2 tablespoons oil, more if needed	⅓ cup finely chopped parsley
4 medium onions, chopped	2 tablespoons flour
2 medium green peppers, chopped	1 cup tomato purée
1 garlic clove, minced	¼ cup tarragon vinegar
2 tablespoons Hungarian paprika	1–2 cups chicken broth
2 teaspoons salt	½ cup sour cream
¼ teaspoon white pepper	2 whole pimientos, coarsely chopped

Dry meat on paper towels. It browns better if it is not wet.

Heat the butter and oil in a heavy skillet. Add the onions, green peppers, and garlic and cook slowly until they are tender but not browned. Transfer them with a slotted spoon to a heavy, lidded, flameproof casserole.

In the skillet, using more oil if necessary, brown the veal pieces, a few at a time. As they are done, transfer them to the casserole. Turn the heat on very low under the casserole.

Add the paprika; stir to coat the meat evenly. Mix in the salt, pepper, thyme, bay leaf, and 2 tablespoons of the parsley. Stir in the flour, a small amount at a time. Stir with a wooden spoon until flour disappears.

Add the tomato purée. If you have no tarragon vinegar, add ¼ teaspoon tarragon and ¼ cup white wine or cider vinegar. Add chicken broth to barely cover the contents of the casserole, and stir to detach any bits stuck on the bottom of the pot.

Bring to a simmer, cover and cook on very low heat for 1 to 1½ hours, or until veal is tender. Check during cooking and stir frequently. Tip pot and skim off any fat on the surface. Taste and add salt and pepper if needed.

❀ Stew can be prepared ahead to this point and refrigerated or frozen after cooling.

To serve, remove ½ cup of liquid from the stew. Gradually stir it into the sour cream. Stir the mixture into the stew. Bring gently back to just below a simmer, but do not boil. Strew pimientos on top and sprinkle with the rest of the parsley. *6–8 servings*

ÉTUVÉE DE VEAU AU VIN BLANC

Cooking *à l'étuvée* means stewing slowly, with some liquid, in a tightly covered pot. In this recipe, veal is stewed in white wine and simple seasonings and crowned with mushrooms to make a handsome, delicious main course. Plain rice or parslied potatoes to take advantage of the good sauce, and fresh green peas or snow peas would be perfect in their season. In the spring, asparagus with lemon and butter and, later, broccoli are good choices for the green vegetable it needs.

For color, a beet and endive salad or a grated carrot salad would do the trick. For dessert, depending on the season, melons with Port in the hollows; a huge bowl of cherries; seedless green and red grapes on a large platter; strawberries, washed but not hulled, to be eaten one by one, dipped in a little pile of sugar on each plate.

A white wine from the Loire would go well with the stew—a Muscadet, Sancerre, or Pouilly-Fumé.

2 pounds boneless veal shoulder, cut in 1½-inch cubes	**2 cloves garlic, chopped**
3 tablespoons butter	**½ teaspoon thyme**
2 tablespoons cooking oil	**⅓ cup finely chopped parsley**
1½ cups dry white wine	**¼ teaspoon white pepper**
Hot water as needed	**2 tablespoons flour mixed with ¼ cup water**
1½ teaspoons salt	**¾ pound mushrooms**

Dry the veal on paper towels; it won't brown well if it is wet. Trim off any bits of fat.

Heat 2 tablespoons butter and the oil in a heavy skillet. Carefully brown the veal pieces, a few at a time, removing them as they are done to a heavy, lidded flameproof casserole. Turn heat on very low under the casserole.

Add the wine, bring to a simmer; add water if needed to barely cover the meat. Mash together the salt and garlic until no large chunks remain. Add to the casserole with the thyme, half the parsley and white pepper. Return to a simmer, cover and cook on low heat for 1 to 1¼ hours, or until veal is tender. Check seasoning and add salt and pepper if needed. Skim off any fat from the surface.

❀ Stew can be done ahead to this point, and when cool, refrigerated or frozen.

To serve, make a smooth mixture of flour and water and stir into simmering stew. Cook until it thickens.

Wipe mushrooms with damp paper towels and slice to make pieces more or less uniform in size. Sauté briefly in remaining 1 tablespoon of butter, sprinkling with salt and pepper. Spread mushrooms over stew and sprinkle with the rest of the parsley.   *4–6 servings*

VEAL BIRDS

Thin slices of beef, veal, pork, or poultry rolled around some kind of filling have a long tradition in many cuisines. There is a stunning number of choices for the filling, which not only taste wonderful but also make the meat go further.

These are *oiseaux sans têtes*, birds without heads; smaller versions are called *paupiettes*, meaning meat olives or corks. This filling is rather delicate—mushrooms and scallions with a lemon rind accent and finished with a creamy sauce. Instead of rice or potatoes, have a starchy green vegetable, like baby lima beans or peas, or acorn squash.

A good first course before the birds is avocado halves, with a dressing of oil, lemon, salt, pepper, and a few drops of garlic from the garlic press. A crunchy pastry would be a nice dessert.

Red or white wine goes with veal—a Petite Sirah for red, or a Chardonnay for white.

FILLING

2 slices bacon	¼ cup finely chopped parsley
1 tablespoon butter	½ teaspoon salt
¾ pound mushrooms, finely chopped	¼ teaspoon freshly ground black pepper
6 scallions with crisp green tops, chopped	1 teaspoon thyme
	1 tablespoon minced zest of lemon

Cook the bacon until it is golden and crisp in a wide, heavy skillet. Set aside on paper towel to drain. Pour off and reserve all but a film of fat from the skillet. Add the butter and the mushrooms, scallions, parsley, salt, pepper, and thyme. Cook and stir over medium heat until the pan is almost dry. Stir in the lemon zest and crumble in the bacon. Allow to cool.

BIRDS

8 slices veal for scaloppine, about 1¼ pounds	1 bay leaf
1 tablespoon cooking oil	2 sprigs parsley
1 tablespoon butter	½ to ¾ cup heavy cream
½ cup dry Vermouth	Salt and pepper
	Watercress

Pound, or have the butcher pound, the scaloppine to about ⅛-inch thickness.

Place ⅛ of the mushroom mixture on each of the veal slices. Roll up, tucking in the ends, and tie around the "waist," and then around the long way.

Heat the oil and butter and the reserved bacon fat in a shallow flameproof casserole or sauté pan. Brown the rolls on all sides. Pour off any fat left in the pan. Pour in the Vermouth and stir to clear the bottom of the pan. Add the bay leaf and parsley sprigs. Bring to a boil, reduce heat, cover and simmer for 1 hour.

Remove the rolls, take off the trussing string, and keep warm on a platter. Skim off any fat from the sauce and boil it down to strengthen the taste. Remove the bay leaf and parsley. Add ½ cup of the cream and cook, stirring to clear the bottom of the pan, for 1–2 minutes. Taste and add more salt, pepper and/or cream to taste. Pour over the rolls.

❀ Can be prepared in advance to this point. For later serving, cool the birds in their sauce and refrigerate or freeze.

To reheat, bring to room temperature and heat slowly on top of the stove, or in a preheated 325° oven, covered in both cases.

Serve with a generous garnish of watercress. *4 or 8 servings*

VEAL AND GREEN PEPPERS

Red wine and beef broth, rather than the more customary white wine and chicken broth, subtly strengthen the taste of this handsome stew. Tomato paste, oregano, and a touch of lemon rind mark it as Italian.

Noodles or rice goes with the stew, but mashed potatoes, un-Italian though they may be, are particularly good with it. A salad of greens with cucumbers, thinly sliced mushrooms, and scallions could follow. For dessert, lime or lemon sherbet with an orange liqueur like Triple Sec or Cointreau poured over it, and a tiny grating of lemon rind on top would make a fine finish to the meal.

The stew deserves a good red wine, like a St. Émilion from Bordeaux, or a Cabernet Sauvignon.

1 tablespoon olive oil	⅛ teaspoon crushed red pepper
2 slices bacon, diced	flakes, or to taste
2 pounds boneless stewing veal,	1 teaspoon oregano
cut in 1½-inch pieces	½ cup dry red wine
¼ cup finely chopped shallots	2 tablespoons flour
2 medium green peppers, coarsely	3 tablespoons tomato paste
chopped	1 cup beef broth
⅓ cup finely chopped parsley	Grated rind of 1 lemon
1½ teaspoons salt	

Put the olive oil and bacon into a heavy, lidded casserole and stir over low heat, separating the bits of bacon, until the bacon is golden. Wipe the veal pieces with paper towel so they will not splatter and add them to the casserole. Stir and cook over moderately high heat until the veal is coated with fat and loses its color. Add the shallots, green peppers, 2 tablespoons of the parsley, salt, red pepper, and oregano. Stir and cook on low heat for 4–5 minutes, until shallots soften.

Add the wine, stirring to clear the bottom of the pan, and bring to a boil.

Make a smooth mixture of the flour, tomato paste, and beef broth. Stir into the casserole and bring to a simmer. Cover and cook on low heat for 1 to 1¼ hours, or until veal is tender. Tip pot and skim off any fat from the surface and check the taste for salt and hot pepper.

❈ Stew can be prepared in advance to this point.

To serve at this time, sprinkle with the remaining parsley and the lemon rind.

4–6 servings

VEAL STEW WITH SHERRY

The mushrooms make this stew rather hearty, but its cornstarch-thickened sauce, with its slight translucency, has a kind of delicacy. Although there is Sherry in it, the stew is not particularly Spanish. A medium dry (Amontillado) Sherry would be good, though, with a first course of pecans, toasted in butter and salted, and anchovy-stuffed olives.

Rice or noodles and a green vegetable, or just a green salad, go with the stew. For dessert follow through on the Sherry theme by serving vanilla or butter pecan ice cream, with a sweet Sherry (Oloroso or Cream) poured over it.

A red wine from the Rioja, dry and light, suits the stew.

2 pounds stewing veal, cut in 1½-inch pieces
2 tablespoons cooking oil
2 slices bacon, diced
1 medium onion, finely chopped
1 clove garlic, minced
¼ cup Amontillado Sherry
1 teaspoon marjoram
Few drops of Tabasco sauce
1½ to 2 cups chicken broth
½ teaspoon salt
5 teaspoons cornstarch mixed with ¼ cup water
¾ pound mushrooms, sautéed in 1 tablespoon butter
¼ cup finely chopped parsley

Pat the veal dry with paper towels and remove any outside fat. Heat the oil in a heavy skillet, put in the bacon and cook until it is golden brown, separating the bits with a wooden spoon. Remove the bacon with a slotted spoon to a heavy lidded saucepan or casserole. Brown the veal, a few pieces at a time, in the skillet. Place the veal in the casserole as it is browned. Put the onion and garlic in the skillet and cook 2–3 minutes, until onion softens slightly. Add to the casserole.

Pour the Sherry over the veal and cook until the wine is almost evaporated. Stir in the marjoram, Tabasco, and chicken broth, enough to barely cover. Taste and add salt as needed. The amount of salt will depend on the saltiness of bacon and broth. Add more Tabasco, if desired.

Bring to a boil, reduce heat, cover and simmer for 1 to 1½ hours, or until tender. Tip pot and skim off any fat.

❀ Can be prepared ahead to this point, and refrigerated or frozen after cooling.

Stir cornstarch mixture into simmering stew. Cook 2 more minutes.

Sauté mushrooms lightly in 1 tablespoon of butter. Sprinkle with salt and pepper, and spread over the stew. Serve sprinkled with parsley.

4–6 servings

TERNERA AL JEREZ

This veal stew from Jerez, the Sherry-producing district of Spain, derives its distinctive taste from the very dry Sherry and cumin used in its preparation. Sherry is used in the marinade, which is discarded, and fresh Sherry is used for the cooking. This may seem rather extravagant; however, the water that dilutes the Sherry causes a cloudiness which makes the cooking liquid look very unappetizing.

Traditionally the stew is served with potatoes, home-fried in olive oil, and a salad of red and green sweet peppers and ripe olives. In tomato season, I prefer a salad of sliced tomatoes, green pepper rings, and thinly sliced red onions, perhaps with Boston lettuce. I put the olives into the stew at the end, with pimientos. Plain rice or noodles can be used instead of the potatoes, but crisp home-fries are wonderful with the stew.

A first course of chorizos, sliced and lightly sautéed, would be delicious with very cold Manzanilla, the driest of Sherries—the driest wine in the world. A Spanish melon or Caramel Custard (flan) (page 279) is a traditional dessert, served with Cream Sherry.

A red wine of Rioja would be good with the stew, or perhaps a Tavel rosé.

MARINADE AND VEAL

2 pounds boneless veal shoulder, cut in 1½-inch pieces
½ cup Fino Sherry
½ cup water
2 teaspoons olive oil

Trim any fat from veal and wipe with damp paper towels. Place veal in a non-metallic bowl and pour the Sherry, water, and olive oil over it. Let it stand for 2–3 hours, stirring occasionally.

1½ tablespoons olive oil
2 slices bacon, diced
2 medium onions, sliced
2 tablespoons flour
2 garlic cloves, chopped
1½ teaspoons salt
1 teaspoon cumin
3–4 grindings of the pepper mill
¾ cup Fino Sherry, brought to a boil
½ to 1 cup boiling water
2 whole pimientos, cut in strips
10–12 pitted black olives
¼ cup finely chopped parsley

Drain meat and discard marinade. Dry meat; it will not brown well if it is wet.

Put the oil into a heavy skillet with the bacon. Slowly cook the bacon, stirring and separating bits, until it renders its fat and is golden but not too brown. With a slotted spoon, transfer the bacon to a heavy, lidded flame-proof casserole.

Add the onions to the fat in the skillet and cook slowly until they are limp and golden, but not brown. Remove them with a slotted spoon and place in the casserole. Turn heat on low under the casserole.

Brown the veal pieces in the same skillet, a few at a time, transferring them as they are done to the casserole. Sprinkle flour on the meat and stir gently until flour disappears.

On a saucer, mash the garlic with the salt, using a strong fork. Stir into the casserole with the cumin and pepper.

Pour in the hot Sherry, stirring carefully to detach any bits stuck on the bottom. Add the boiling water, enough to barely cover the meat and onions. Bring to a simmer, cover and cook on very low heat for 1 to 1¼ hours, or until veal is just tender. Skim any fat from the surface, check for salt and pepper.

❀ Stew can be prepared ahead to this point. When cool, cover and refrigerate or freeze.

To serve, sprinkle with pimientos, olives, and parsley.   *4–6 servings*

VEAL AND CAPERS

The capers in this slightly creamy stew do not overwhelm the wonderful taste of veal. The taste is brought out by what seems to be a perfect balance of liquids and seasonings. Sliced water chestnuts give an interesting touch of crispness, and a little cayenne pepper supplies a subtle accent.

Serve with rice or noodles and a leafy salad. The stew is not too heavy for an easy home-made ice cream (recipe follows).

Red or white wine goes with the veal—a Rioja or a Côte du Rhône for red, or an Entre-Deux-Mers from Bordeaux for white.

2–3 tablespoons butter	½ cup dry white wine
¼ cup chopped shallots	1 cup chicken broth
2 pounds stewing veal, cut in 1½-inch pieces	¼ cup flour
	1 cup milk
1 teaspoon marjoram	1 eight-ounce can water chestnuts, drained, sliced
1 teaspoon salt	
¼ teaspoon white pepper	½ cup finely chopped parsley
⅛ teaspoon cayenne pepper	2 tablespoons capers, drained

Heat 2 tablespoons of the butter in a large, heavy saucepan or flameproof casserole. Put in the shallots and cook on low heat until the shallots have softened slightly.

Trim outside fat from the veal and pat dry with paper towels. Add to the shallots. Cook and stir over high heat to coat the veal with butter (add the other tablespoon if needed), and until the meat loses its color.

Stir in the marjoram, salt, white pepper, cayenne, and the wine. Bring to a simmer and add the chicken broth. Cover and cook on very low heat for 30–45 minutes, or until veal is tender.

Mix the flour with a small amount of the milk to make a smooth paste. Add the rest of the milk and stir into the stew. Cook until the sauce thickens, add the water chestnuts and cook another minute.

❊ The stew can be refrigerated or frozen, after thorough cooling.

Serve garnished with the parsley and capers.   *6 servings*

PEACH ICE CREAM

This delightfully simple dessert is good any time of the year, cool and fresh after a stew or a main-course soup.

1 pound frozen sliced peaches   **8 ounces heavy cream**
2 tablespoons sugar, or to taste

Prepare this in 2 batches in the food processor.

Break up half the peaches and put in the food processor with the metal blade installed. Add half the sugar and process while adding half the cream, through the chimney. Remove to a serving bowl and keep in the freezer until you finish the other half. Combine the batches and serve at once.

4–6 servings

Variation: To make this with strawberries, use 4 cups of berries. Wash and pat the berries dry. Spread them out on a tray in the freezer. When they are frozen, put them in a plastic bag and use as soon as possible.

9

Lamb Stews

LAMB PILAF

Pilaf is a rice dish found in the Middle East, Near East, and southern Asia.
It is made of well-seasoned rice to which are added meat, chicken, nuts,
fruit, in all sorts of combinations. This version has prunes and raisins with
a dice of lamb, but is not as sweet as might be expected.

Since it is mildly curried, there is an excuse for those little dishes of
condiments that make this kind of meal fun. Garden lettuce and thinly
sliced cucumbers make a cooling salad, and lime sherbet a refreshing dessert. A good first course, from further west, is chorizos, sliced and quickly
sautéed, to have with drinks, or some of the wine.

Light, not too dry wines go with the pilaf, a Mosel or Rheinpfalz
Kabinett, a Chenin Blanc or Johannisberger Riesling from California.

1½ pounds boneless lamb shoulder,
   cut in ¾-inch pieces
1 slice bacon, diced
1 tablespoon butter
1 tablespoon cooking oil, more if
   needed
2 medium onions, finely chopped
1 teaspoon salt
¼ teaspoon freshly ground black
   pepper

⅛ teaspoon crushed red pepper,
   or more, to taste
1 teaspoon turmeric
1 teaspoon curry powder
1 small bay leaf
2½ cups beef broth
8–10 pitted prunes, quartered
⅓ cup seedless raisins
2 lemons
1 cup rice
¼ cup finely chopped parsley

Trim fat from the lamb and pat dry with paper towels. It won't brown if it is wet.

In a lidded flameproof casserole, slowly cook the bacon in the butter and oil until it is golden brown. Push to the side of the casserole. Add the pieces of lamb, a few at a time, pushing them to the side as they brown. Use more oil if necessary, but remove any surplus left in the casserole after browning the meat.

Add the onions. Cook and stir gently until they are limp. Stir in the salt, pepper, red pepper, turmeric, curry powder, and bay leaf. Add 1 cup of the broth, cover and simmer on low heat for 25 minutes.

After 15 minutes turn on the oven to 325°.

When the stew has cooked for 25 minutes, add the prunes and raisins. Add 1 of the lemons cut into 6 slices.

Add the remaining 1½ cups of broth and bring to a simmer. Add the rice; bring to a simmer again. Stir once, cover and place in the oven. Cook for 45 minutes, or until lamb is tender and rice has swollen and absorbed the liquid. Check after 10 minutes and adjust oven temperature, if necessary, to keep the pilaf just at a simmer. Add a little hot water if it is too dry; cook uncovered for a few minutes if it is too wet. The dish should be moist but not wet.

❋ The pilaf can be made ahead to this point, and refrigerated or frozen, after thorough cooling.

To serve, remove cooked lemon slices as well as you can—or leave them in if they don't bother you. Cut the remaining lemon into thin slices and place on the stew. Sprinkle parsley over all.   *4–6 servings*

CONDIMENTS

In little side dishes serve: chutney; almonds lightly browned in butter; sweet pickles; chopped orange rind; crumbled bacon; guava jelly, etc.

LAMB STEW WITH APRICOTS

The idea of fruit in meat dishes is found in many cuisines, but some people will not tolerate so much as a raisin in their pilaf. The fear of sweetness is often unwarranted, because the fruit merely rounds out the taste, counteracting any little bitternesses in other ingredients, and any sweetness is often offset by lemon. This lamb stew is not too sweet, even before the lemon is added at the end, but it does have a unique taste and texture.

Versions of this stew appear in a French and an Armenian cookbook; there may be others. Since it is hard to pinpoint the ethnic origin, possible accompaniments are not limited. One suggestion for a meal designed around the stew is: rice with toasted slivered almonds stirred in; spinach with a pinch of nutmeg; a salad of blanched cauliflower in a vinaigrette, with chopped scallions. Greek pastries would not be too heavy for dessert.

The stew, rather than being sweet, is a little tart, which makes it hard to pick a wine. Best choice might be to serve spritzers—half white wine and half club soda, with a slice of lemon, and ice.

3 to 3½ pounds meaty lamb neck, cut up for stewing, with bones	3 cups water
2 tablespoons cooking oil	2 teaspoons salt
1 tablespoon butter	¼ teaspoon freshly ground black pepper
1 large onion, finely chopped	2 cups dried apricots
2 garlic cloves, minced	Juice of ½ lemon
1 teaspoon grated fresh ginger, or ½ teaspoon dried	¼ cup finely chopped parsley

Dry the lamb with paper towels; it won't brown if it is wet. Trim off any large pieces of outside fat.

In a heavy skillet, heat the oil and butter and brown the lamb pieces on all sides, a few at a time, and transfer them to a heavy, lidded flameproof casserole, with low heat under it after browning. Add the onion, garlic, and ginger. Stir briefly and cover for 1–2 minutes to soften the onion.

Pour in the water and stir in salt and pepper. Bring to a boil, reduce heat, cover and simmer for 1¼ hours. Add the apricots and cook for another 15–30 minutes, until lamb is almost falling off the bones, and apricots are nearly turned into a purée. Tip pot and skim off fat. Check and add salt if needed.

❀ Stew may be prepared in advance to this point.
Before serving, stir in the lemon juice and sprinkle with parsley.

6 servings

Note: Since apricots are expensive, bony lamb, less expensive than boned (even though you need a little more), is used here. I happen to like bony cuts, finding the meat sweeter, as claimed in the old saying.

To make the stew with boneless lamb, for a buffet, or for more elegance, buy 2 to 2¼ pounds of boneless shoulder lamb. Use less water, just enough to barely cover the meat; start with only 1 teaspoon of salt, adjust later. Otherwise follow the recipe as given.

ARNI PRASSA

The foamy finish of eggs and lemon distinguishes this subtly seasoned Greek stew. A great favorite from *Glorious Stew,* it was developed by Leon Lianides of the Coach House, a fine restaurant in New York's Greenwich Village. The stew can be served simply with hot pita or crusty bread, but rice is good with it too.

Olives and a bowl of toasted almonds, served with Raki, Pec, or Pernod, all of which are anise flavored and turn cloudy when mixed with water and ice, make a fine preface to the meal. Salad could be green, with Feta cheese in it or after it, and dessert, since the stew is light, might be rich.

A Beaujolais like Juliénas or Chiroubles, or a white wine like the one in the stew—a Chardonnay say, would be excellent with the stew.

3½ pounds boneless lamb shoulder, cut in 3-inch pieces	1 tablespoon finely chopped parsley
2 tablespoons cooking oil	1 cup water
2–4 tablespoons butter	1 cup dry white wine
2 medium onions, finely chopped	½ cup chicken broth
2 teaspoons salt	6–8 medium leeks
1 teaspoon pepper	1 teaspoon cornstarch
1 teaspoon finely chopped fresh dill	Juice of 2 lemons
	4 eggs

Trim fat from lamb and dry it with paper towels; it won't brown if it is wet. Heat the oil and 2 tablespoons of the butter in a heavy skillet. When the butter stops foaming, brown the meat, a few pieces at a time. As the meat browns, put it into a lidded flameproof 4-quart casserole. Add the onions to the casserole and cook slowly on medium heat until the onions are tender but not brown. Add a little butter if needed.

Turn on oven to 325°.

Stir in the salt, pepper, dill, and parsley. Add the liquids, bring to a simmer, cover and place in the oven. Reduce oven temperature to whatever will just maintain the simmer. Cook 50–60 minutes, or until almost tender. Tip the casserole and skim off fat.

Trim the leeks, removing the roots and the green tops down to the palest green, at the point where they become tender. Cut in 2-inch pieces, and allow them to stand in lukewarm salted water for a few minutes. Wash very thoroughly under running water, gently spreading the leaves to get out all dirt. Place them carefully on the stew. Spoon some of the liquid over them. Cover and return to the oven. Cook 20–30 minutes more, or until the leeks are tender but not overdone. Spoon liquid over the stew as it cooks, but do not stir—the leeks should not be disturbed. If liquid cooks down, add a little hot water, but only if there is danger of sticking.

✺ Stew can be prepared in advance to this point. Cool with lid askew, cover, and refrigerate or freeze. To reheat, bring to room temperature, place, partially covered (to avoid steaming the leeks), in a preheated 325° oven for 30–40 minutes, or until stew is warmed through.

To finish: With the stew hot but out of the oven and off the heat, mix the cornstarch with the lemon juice. Beat the eggs vigorously for about 4 minutes. Gradually add the cornstarch and lemon mixture, beating constantly for another 2 minutes. Slowly stir 1 cup of hot liquid from the stew into the egg mixture, still beating, until all the liquid is in, about 2 more minutes. Pour this mixture over the stew, shaking the casserole to mix through. Do not stir. Serve immediately. *4–6 servings*

LAMB AND BEAN KHORESHE

A khoreshe is a Persian stew, with a little meat and a lot of vegetables. This one has respectable amounts of lamb, green vegetables, and white beans, making it a substantial, delicious main course, almost a meal in itself. Khoreshes are traditionally flavored with sour juices, in this case lemon. The lemon gives a lightness unexpected in a bean dish.

Although it seems an excess of starch to us, the customary accompaniment to the khoreshe is rice; it is especially good with some almond slivers, toasted in butter, stirred in.

A first course could be Hummus, a chick pea spread (recipe follows), served with pita bread or sesame crackers. A salad of cucumbers, scallions, and oranges would be refreshing. Dessert could be persimmons and pomegranates with some Feta cheese.

The pitch-flavored wine of Greece, Retsina, might be served with the khoreshe, but Retsina is an acquired taste, so a California Hungarian Riesling, or an Italian Verdicchio is suggested. Beer is also good.

2 cups dried white beans, Great Northern, navy, pea	2 pounds boneless lamb shoulder, cut in 1-inch pieces
6 cups water	2 tablespoons oil
2 teaspoons salt	1¼ teaspoons salt
4 tablespoons butter	¾ teaspoon freshly ground black pepper
2 cups chopped parsley	1 teaspoon turmeric
2 bunches scallions, chopped	3 lemons
2 cups chopped spinach	Water to barely cover meat

Wash and pick over beans. Put with 6 cups of water into a saucepan that has a lid. Bring to a boil, boil 2 minutes. Remove from heat, cover, and allow to stand for 1 hour. Bring to a simmer and cook, partially covered, for 30 minutes. Add 2 teaspoons of salt. If beans are tender but not too soft at this point, drain and set aside. If they are not done, continue cooking, checking often, and drain when done.

Melt 2 tablespoons of the butter in a heavy, lidded flameproof casserole or Dutch oven. Add the parsley, scallions, and spinach. Cook gently until the vegetables are limp. Turn off heat.

Dry the lamb pieces with paper towel; they will not brown otherwise. In a heavy skillet, heat the rest of the butter and the oil and brown the lamb, a few pieces at a time. As they are browned, put them into the casserole with the vegetables.

Sprinkle the meat and vegetables with salt; stir in pepper and turmeric. Add the juice of 2 of the lemons and tuck in the quartered remains of 1 of them. Add water to barely cover the meat. Bring to a simmer, cover and cook on low heat for 1 to 1½ hours, or until meat is tender. Pick out and discard the pieces of lemon rind; tip the pot and skim off any fat.

Carefully stir in the beans. Cover and cook for about 10 minutes, or until beans are heated through, stirring occasionally.

❀ Stew can be refrigerated or frozen at this point.

Serve with the third lemon, cut in thin slices, on top.   *6–8 servings.*

HUMMUS (Chick Pea Spread)

This is a rather fresh, lemony version of the well-known dip or spread. A useful item to have in your repertoire, it can be served with pita bread, warmed or toasted, corn chips, or sesame crackers.

2 cups (one-pound can) chick peas	½ to ¾ cup vegetable or olive oil
1 tablespoon onion, minced	Juice of 1 lemon (about ¼ cup)
2 garlic cloves, minced	2 tablespoons finely chopped
1 teaspoon salt	parsley
⅛ teaspoon cayenne	A few grindings of the pepper mill

Drain the chick peas through a sieve. Wash them thoroughly by running cold water over them until the water runs clear. Spread them out on paper towel and pat them dry.

Place the chick peas, onion, garlic, salt, cayenne, ½ cup of the oil, and the lemon juice in the blender. Blend until you have a thick smooth purée, stopping occasionally to scrape down the sides. Add the rest of the oil gradually. Add more if needed to keep blender from stalling.

Chill or not, as you wish. At serving time, sprinkle with parsley and freshly ground black pepper.   *makes about 3 cups*

Variation: Some people like to use 1 teaspoon of sesame oil and reduce amount of other oil accordingly.

BLANQUETTE D'AGNEAU À L'ANCIENNE/LAMB AND MADEIRA

There is a kind of elegance to this beige-colored stew, served with a ring of toast triangles, its own good flavor enhanced with tiny onions and mushrooms cooked along with the lamb. Rice with some toasted almonds on top, or stirred in with butter, and asparagus, broccoli, or fresh peas, for a green vegetable, the choice depending on the season, would go very well with the stew.

A watercress and endive salad could precede a splendid cheese course of a Chèvre and a French cream cheese, like Boursault or Explorateur. Smoked salmon with capers would be a fine beginning for the meal, and some miracle of the French patisserie, like a dacquoise or a croquembouche, end it with a flourish.

For a less glorious, but still splendid dinner, and certainly a less expensive one, here are some suggestions: zucchini strips with a sprinkle of salt, pepper, lemon, and parsley, for a first course; a simple salad of Boston lettuce; no cheese course; and butter pecan ice cream with a topping of crumbled ginger snaps for dessert.

The wine could be a Côte du Rhône.

A fine old château-bottling from Bordeaux—at least 10 years old—brings out the subtlety of the dish. To make a special occasion of the dinner, you might serve Champagne with the salmon.

VELOUTÉ
This sauce goes into the stew later, but it should be made first.

2 tablespoons butter	1½ cups chicken broth
2 tablespoons flour	½ cup heavy cream, more if needed later

In a saucepan, melt the butter and blend in the flour. Stir in the broth and cook until it thickens. Add the cream and set aside.

2½ pounds boneless lamb shoulder, cut in 1½-inch pieces	½ cup Madeira
4 tablespoons butter	12–18 tiny white onions
2 tablespoons cooking oil, more if needed	¾ pound small button mushrooms, or larger ones sliced
1 teaspoon salt	6 slices bread with crusts removed
½ teaspoon white pepper	¼ cup finely chopped parsley

Trim fat from the meat and dry on paper towels. It does not brown as well when it is wet.

In a large, heavy enamelware or stainless steel skillet, heat 2 tablespoons of the butter and the oil. Brown the lamb well on all sides, a few pieces at a time, and transfer them to a heavy, lidded flameproof casserole. Turn the heat on low under the casserole and cook the meat, uncovered, for 15–20 minutes, sprinkling with salt and pepper. Shake the casserole occasionally to prevent sticking.

Pour leftover fat from the skillet and reserve it if there is enough to warrant saving. Rinse the pan with the Madeira, stirring to dislodge any particles. Add the velouté to the Madeira in the skillet and boil briskly for 5 minutes. Strain into the casserole, stirring with a wooden spoon to incorporate any brown on the bottom.

Bring to a simmer, cover and cook on low heat for 30–40 minutes, or until meat is almost tender.

Peel the onions and make a small crosscut in the root end to help prevent separating. Trim the stems of the mushrooms and wipe them clean with damp paper towels.

In a clean skillet, briefly sauté the onions and mushrooms in the remaining 2 tablespoons of butter. Add to the casserole. Cook 30–40 minutes more, or until meat and onions are tender. Check for salt.

❀ Stew can be prepared ahead to this point, and refrigerated or frozen after cooling.

To serve, turn into a clean casserole or baking dish. Toast the bread and cut each piece into 4 triangles. Arrange around the edge of the dish, points up, and sprinkle the stew with parsley.   *6–8 servings*

NAVARIN PRINTANIER

Spring is the time for this lovely French lamb stew, as its name implies. When the garden and the markets offer fresh young vegetables—tiny carrots, potatoes, and onions, white turnips and new green beans, and the lamb is spring lamb—it is *navarin* time.

Only the purest purist, however, would forgo the pleasure of the stew just because it wasn't spring. Older and larger vegetables can be cut up, as long as they are of the best quality.

Radishes, complete with their leafy tops, make a pleasant nibble with pre-dinner drinks. Cut off the roots, trim the leaves down to 1–2 inches above the radish, clean around the stems and serve in a large bowl to eat with French bread and sweet butter.

Salad, if any, should be garden lettuce with a simple oil and vinegar dressing. Cheese and fruit of the season make a fine finish. In France the spring fruit would likely be wild strawberries with cream followed by Green Chartreuse and coffee.

Red wine suits the navarin, a St. Émilion or Graves, or a light Côte de Beaune, like Savigny or Santenay.

3 pounds boneless lamb shoulder, cut in 1½-inch pieces	½ cup dry white wine
2 tablespoons butter	2 cups beef broth, or enough to barely cover
2 tablespoons cooking oil	12 small new potatoes in skins, or 6 medium regular potatoes, peeled and halved
2 teaspoons sugar	
2 tablespoons flour	
1 teaspoon salt	12–16 baby carrots, scraped, or 6–8 medium carrots, cut in 2-inch pieces
¼ teaspoon white pepper	
2 garlic cloves, minced	
¼ teaspoon crumbled rosemary	6 white turnips, peeled, halved
¼ teaspoon thyme	12–18 small white onions
1 bay leaf	½ pound fresh green beans
2 tablespoons finely chopped parsley	

Turn on oven to 325°.

Trim fat from lamb and dry the pieces for browning, on paper towels. The meat browns better when it is not wet.

In a heavy skillet, heat the butter and oil, and carefully brown the lamb, a few pieces at a time. As they are done, transfer them to a heavy, lidded flameproof casserole, large enough to hold the meat and the vegetables. Turn on heat to medium under the casserole, and sprinkle the sugar on the meat. Stir and cook until sugar browns nicely. The sugar will color but not sweeten the stew if it is dark brown but not burned. Reduce heat to low under the casserole.

Sprinkle flour on the lamb, a little at a time, turning and stirring to spread it through the meat. Continue stirring until flour is browned and disappears.

Add salt, pepper, garlic, rosemary, thyme, bay leaf, and parsley. Add the wine, stirring to incorporate the flour and seasonings, and to dislodge bits stuck to the bottom of the casserole. Add beef broth to barely cover the meat. Bring to a simmer, cover and place in the oven. After 10 minutes check and adjust oven temperature to maintain simmer. Cook for 1 hour. Tip pot and skim off any fat from the surface. Taste and add salt and pepper if needed.

❀ Stew can be prepared in advance to this point and refrigerated or frozen after cooling.

Prepare the vegetables. If the potatoes are new, scrub but do not peel. If they are very small, leave them whole. Cut slightly larger ones in half. Peel and halve older potatoes. Trim and scrape baby carrots. If they are larger, cut them across in 2 and split the thick ends to make them all equal in size. Trim, peel and halve the turnips. Pour boiling water over the tiny onions, drain, dip in cold water and slip off skins. Make a small crosscut in the root end to help them cook more evenly and be less likely to separate.

Put the vegetables carefully into the stew, sprinkling with a little salt and pepper. Cover and put back in the oven for ½ to ¾ hour longer, or until meat and vegetables are tender.

Cook beans in a large amount of salted boiling water for 10–12 minutes, or until they are just tender, but still crisp, and bright green. Scatter over the stew—they supply all the garnish you need.   *6–8 servings*

ABBACCHIO ALLA ROMANO

Romans do interesting things with lamb when they cook it in a casserole. This recipe, adapted to our older lamb (an *abbacchio* is a very young lamb), has sage and rosemary, anchovies and wine, and vinegar, with cooked green beans, crisp-tender and bright green, added at the end.

Fettuccine, preferably home-made and wickedly buttery, is a fine accompaniment, and one you would be likely to have with a stew like this in Rome. Other thin pastas, with olive oil and garlic, would also be good with it, and so would a risotto.

A first course could be salami, olives, and celery; salad, made with arugula; and dessert, a typically Italian one like Zabaglione (recipe follows), or pastries with custard fillings.

White or red wine goes with the stew—Soave or Frascati for white, and a Chianti or Nebbiolo for red.

2 pounds boneless shoulder lamb, cut in 1½-inch pieces	1 tablespoon flour
¼ cup olive oil	½ cup dry white wine
2 cloves garlic, minced	½ cup wine vinegar
1 teaspoon salt	½ cup water
Several grindings of the pepper mill	3 anchovy fillets, chopped
½ teaspoon rosemary, crumbled	½ pound fresh green beans, cut in 2-inch pieces, cooked
½ teaspoon sage	¼ cup finely chopped parsley

Turn on oven to 325°.

Dry meat on paper towels. It won't brown if it is wet.

In a heavy skillet heat the oil. When a haze appears over the oil, brown the lamb pieces thoroughly, a few pieces at a time. As they are browned, transfer them to a heavy lidded flameproof casserole.

Stir in the garlic, salt, pepper, rosemary, and sage, mixing well. Sprinkle flour over the stew, stirring until it disappears. Stir in liquids and bring to a simmer. Cover and place in the oven. Reduce heat to a temperature that will maintain the simmer. Check in 10 minutes and adjust temperature if necessary. Cook for 1 to 1½ hours, or until lamb is tender.

Tip the casserole and skim off fat. Stir in the anchovies, and taste for salt and pepper.

❁ The stew can be made ahead to this point. Refrigerate and freeze after cooling.

To serve, stir the beans into the stew carefully and put back in the oven for 5–10 minutes, or on a low burner, to heat the beans. Do not cook long enough for beans to lose their bright green. Serve sprinkled with parsley. *4–6 servings*

ZABAGLIONE

In principle, Zabaglione is a custard made of an equal number of egg yolks and tablespoons of Marsala and sugar. One egg white is included here for extra fluffiness.

5 egg yolks, plus 1 whole egg   **6 tablespoons Marsala**
6 tablespoons sugar

In the top part of a double boiler, away from the heat, beat the eggs and sugar until pale and almost fluffy.

Put the pan over simmering water in the bottom of the double boiler, but not touching the water. Continue beating, adding the Marsala gradually. Beat until the mixture is hot and thick, thick enough to hold its shape in a spoon. This may take as long as 10 minutes. Spoon into dessert dishes or parfait glasses and serve immediately. *4–6 servings*

Note: This can be made with Cream Sherry instead of Marsala, making it Spanish, and equally good.

Abbacchio means lamb, baby lamb, which comes to Italian markets in the spring. New York restaurateur Romeo Salta uses our lamb any time of the year to make this interesting dish from the Lazio town of Ciociara. The meat is braised in Cognac with some ham, preferably prosciutto; bright, crisply cooked green beans are added at the end because they go so well with the stew's rosemary seasoning. This dish cooks in very little liquid— and therefore needs attention.

A thin pasta like fettuccine, just buttered, would go well with the stew, or matchstick potatoes. If endives are in the market, for a first course, serve the leaves and sliced radishes, with a little olive oil and a sprinkle of Parmesan.

Salad could be leafy and green, dessert, a range of Italian cheeses and fruit of the season.

Abbacchio calls for a good red Chianti Riserva or Bardolino Superiore.

3 pounds shoulder lamb, cut in 1-inch cubes	½ teaspoon rosemary, crumbled
2 tablespoons oil	½ teaspoon freshly ground black pepper
3 tablespoons butter	½ to 1 teaspoon salt
¼ pound prosciutto or cooked ham, cut in ¼-inch julienne	½ cup Cognac
	Boiling water as needed
2 cloves garlic, minced	½ pound fresh green beans

Turn on oven to 325°.

Dry lamb on paper towels. It won't brown if it is wet.

In a heavy skillet, heat the oil and 2 tablespoons of the butter; brown the lamb carefully, a few pieces at a time, transferring them to a heavy, lidded flameproof casserole as they are done. Turn on heat very low under the casserole. Add the ham and cook 5 minutes uncovered.

Stir in the garlic, allowing it to cook for 1–2 minutes, but not to brown. Stir in the rosemary and pepper. Add salt carefully if ham is very salty.

Add the Cognac and bring to a simmer. Cover the casserole and place in the oven. Turn the oven down to 300°, or whatever temperature will just maintain the simmer. Check in 10 minutes and adjust temperature if necessary. Cook 1 to 1½ hours, until lamb is tender. Check frequently. If the liquid cooks away, add boiling water in ½-cup amounts if needed. Turn the stew into a clean casserole or baking dish.

❀ Stew can be prepared in advance to this point.

Trim the ends of the beans but leave them whole if they are small; cut in 2-inch pieces if they are large. Cook the beans in a covered saucepan with ½ cup salted water and the remaining tablespoon of butter. Cook for 10–12 minutes, shaking the pan occasionally. Beans should be tender, but still crisp and bright green. Stir the beans into the simmering stew.

6–8 servings

JAVANESE LAMB STEW

Many of the seasonings in this stew are used in making curry powder, but the taste, though quite strong, is not overly hot. Turmeric is the seasoning that gives the handsome yellow color to the stew and the Lemon Rice (recipe follows) that goes with it. Serve with a good bottled chutney.

A big tossed salad with crisp raw vegetables, apples, and nuts in it could precede or come after the main course. Fresh fruit or a cool lime or lemon sherbet would make a fine dessert.

To drink with the stew, a Côte du Rhône is suggested, or one of the reds from Eastern Europe—Hungary or Yugoslavia—or beer.

2½ pounds boneless lamb shoulder, cut in 1-inch pieces
3 garlic cloves
2 teaspoons salt
⅛ teaspoon cayenne pepper
2 teaspoons turmeric
2 teaspoons cumin
2 teaspoons ground coriander
1 teaspoon ground ginger
2 teaspoons poppy seeds
1 teaspoon ground cardamom
½ cup cider vinegar
½ cup water
2 teaspoons cornstarch, mixed with a little water
2 hard-boiled eggs, whites chopped, yolks crumbled
½ cup finely chopped parsley

Trim any outside fat from the meat. Put the trimmed meat into a non-metallic, ovenware pot or casserole that has a lid—preferably enameled ironware.

With a mortar and pestle, grind together the garlic, salt, cayenne, turmeric, cumin, coriander, ginger, poppy seeds, and cardamom. Add this mixture to the meat in the casserole, and mix well with the hands to coat all the pieces.

Pour the vinegar into the casserole and stir. Allow to stand for ½ to 1 hour, stirring occasionally.

Stir in the water, cover the pot and place in a cold oven. Turn the oven on to 350°. Cook for 1½ to 2 hours, until lamb is tender. Tip pot and skim off fat.

❀ Stew can be prepared in advance to this point, and refrigerated or frozen.

With the casserole on a burner, bring to a simmer and stir in the cornstarch mixture. Cook until stew thickens.

Serve in a large, shallow bowl or platter surrounded by the rice. Sprinkle egg on the stew, and parsley over stew and rice.   *6–8 servings*

LEMON RICE

<table>
<tr><td>2 tablespoons butter</td><td>1 teaspoon turmeric</td></tr>
<tr><td>2 tablespoons cooking oil</td><td>4–5 cups cooked rice</td></tr>
<tr><td>1 teaspoon salt</td><td>Juice of 1 lemon, strained</td></tr>
<tr><td>1 teaspoon mustard seeds</td><td>¼ cup seedless raisins (optional)</td></tr>
</table>

In a heavy saucepan, heat the butter and oil. Add the salt, mustard seeds, and turmeric. Stir and cook on low heat until the mustard seeds jump. Add the rice and stir until all is blended and heated through. Add the lemon juice and mix again.

If raisins are used, soak them in boiling water to cover for about 10 minutes. Drain and add them to the rice at the end.

A bowl of plain yogurt can be served as a sauce for the rice and stew.

LAMB CURRY

This is a ridiculously long recipe because we list the ingredients that go into curry, rather than use the packaged powder. Indian women mix and grind fresh spices every day to suit the dish they are making. This mixture is made with easily available spices and is not too hot or too strong in taste. It can be made hotter by the addition of red pepper flakes, which are offered in a small bowl with other condiments.

A curried dish is great for a party because of all the condiments (a list of suggestions follows). Guests help themselves from an array of small bowls, adding to their curry, served with a mound of steamy rice. Salad should be leafy and lemony—the best of greens and a dressing made with lemon instead of vinegar, or fruit vinegars.

Curried dishes seem exotic, and an exotic introduction to the meal, like cold lobster or crab with mayonnaise, would be appropriate. But almost as good is a bowl of cashews, lightly browned in butter, and well salted. For dessert, a large bowl or platter of persimmons, pomegranates, mangoes, and grapes—all or some—is a crowning touch.

Pimm's Cup or gin and tonic, a nice English touch, can be served all through the meal—or serve tea, hot or iced, or beer.

MARINADE

2–3 cups buttermilk	1 teaspoon cooking oil
3 cloves garlic	

Pour the buttermilk into a large, non-metallic bowl. Crush the garlic cloves with the flat of a heavy knife. Add, with the oil, to the buttermilk.

4 pounds boneless lamb shoulder, cut in 1½-inch pieces	4 teaspoons turmeric
5 tablespoons clarified butter (page 40)	1½ teaspoons ground cardamom
4 medium onions, chopped	6 whole cloves, broken
3 cloves garlic, chopped	1 teaspoon crushed red pepper flakes
1 tablespoon salt	¼ teaspoon cayenne
2 teaspoons ground dried ginger	½ teaspoon black pepper
3½ teaspoons ground cumin	2 tablespoons ground almonds
3½ teaspoons ground coriander	2 teaspoons poppy seeds
2 four-inch sticks cinnamon, broken in half	1 bay leaf
	2 tablespoons flour
	½ cup heavy cream

Wipe the meat with damp paper towels and trim off big pieces of outside fat.

Put the lamb pieces into the marinade and allow to stand for 1–2 hours, stirring occasionally.

Heat the butter in a heavy, lidded flameproof casserole and add the onions. Cook slowly until the onions are limp and transparent. Mash the garlic with the salt and add to the onions.

Add all of the following ingredients except flour and heavy cream. In order not to get mixed up, line up the spice containers with a piece of wax paper in front of each. Put the measured ingredient on its wax paper and stir it into the casserole, stirring and blending it with the onions. When all have been added, cook for 2 minutes.

Turn oven on to 300°.

Drain the lamb well; discard the garlic; reserve the marinade, which will be a little pink, and measure it. Add buttermilk to bring quantity back to 2 cups.

Add the lamb to the casserole, stirring to mix it well with the spices, onions, and butter, but not to brown. Add the buttermilk; stir to dislodge any bits stuck to the bottom. Bring to a simmer, cover, and place in the oven. Cook for 1¼ to 1½ hours, or until lamb is tender.

Cool to room temperature and refrigerate overnight for flavors to meld and for fat to harden on the top.

❋ After cooling, stew can be refrigerated for a few days or frozen.

When you are ready for the stew, the next day, or up to 3 days later, remove the hardened fat and bring stew to a simmer. With a slotted spoon, remove the meat from the sauce to a clean, smaller casserole or baking dish. Keep warm. Discard cinnamon sticks and bay leaf.

Cook the sauce in the original casserole briskly for 2–3 minutes and reduce it slightly to strengthen the flavor. Make a smooth mixture of the flour and cream and stir into the sauce. Cook for another 2–3 minutes, until sauce thickens. Pour over the meat.   *8–10 servings*

Continued

CONDIMENTS

Finely chopped parsley
Chutney
Raisins
Shredded coconut
Slivered almonds, toasted
Finely chopped sweet pickles
Minced zest of orange and lemon
Crushed red pepper flakes

Offer all these, or just some of them, in small bowls. The parsley, chutney and almonds are the most essential, for color, taste, and texture; the red pepper flakes for hotness. But tell people to try the curry as is, before adding more pepper flakes.

BALKAN LAMB STEW WITH ZUCCHINI

A large pot is needed for this stew, which is made with the sweet meat on lamb neck bones, bulkier than boneless, plus zucchini, and a mixture of mint and yogurt added at the end.

Rice goes well with this stew, particularly a pilaf with almonds. A leafy green salad with the Greek touch of crumbled Feta cheese in it could go with, or follow, the stew.

The first course could be the famous lemony Avgolemono soup, page 151. Fresh fruit of the season would be just right for dessert.

A full, dry white wine is good with this—a Chardonnay or Sauvignon Blanc; so is beer.

2½ to 3 pounds meaty lamb neck for stewing, with bones	2 garlic cloves, minced
2 tablespoons cooking oil	1 one-pound can tomatoes, crushed
2 teaspoons salt	½ cup beef broth
¼ teaspoon black pepper	3 medium zucchini, cut in ¾-inch slices
1 teaspoon oregano	2 tablespoons butter
1 tablespoon crumbled dried mint, or 3 tablespoons chopped fresh mint	Additional salt, pepper and oregano
	¾ to 1 cup plain yogurt

Pat the lamb pieces dry with paper towel so they brown more readily. Heat the oil in a large pot or casserole that has a lid. Put in the lamb and stir over moderately high heat until the lamb loses its color.

Stir in salt, pepper, oregano, 1 teaspoon of the mint, and the garlic. Add the tomatoes and broth. Bring to a simmer. Cover and simmer on top of the stove, or in a preheated 300°– 325° oven, for 1¼–1½ hours, or until lamb is tender.

❀ Stew can be prepared ahead to this point. Refrigerate or freeze after cooling.

To serve, lightly sauté the zucchini in the butter, sprinkling with salt, pepper and oregano. Add to the stew.

Mix the remaining mint with the yogurt and spread over simmering stew. Do not cook any more. Serve as soon as possible.   *6 servings*

IRISH STEW

Irish stew, with its lovely old-fashioned taste of lamb, leeks, cabbage, onions, and the all-important thickening with potatoes, deserves more honor and respect than it gets. This recipe is a famous version from New York's St. Regis Hotel, where it has been enjoyed for years and is remarkably similar to the one my grandmother used to make.

The potatoes in the stew are only for thickening, so boiled potatoes are served with it and green beans or carrots and peas. An Irish beginning for the meal could be smoked trout or salmon. An endive and watercress salad would be good, followed by Irish Cheddar or Camembert. A really splendid apple pie could top off the meal.

A dry white wine—a Chardonnay or Meursault—would go well with the stew. A light red Bordeaux from Graves or the Haut-Médoc would go with the stew and the cheese.

3 pounds boneless lamb shoulder, cut in 1½-inch pieces	1 small head of cabbage
8–10 cups water	1 cup sliced leeks, white part only (3 or 4 leeks, 1 inch in diameter, or the equivalent)
2 teaspoons salt, or 1 teaspoon per quart of water	For each 4 cups of liquid, 1 cup mashed potatoes, or 1 cup instant potato flakes
½ teaspoon white pepper	Dash of Worcestershire sauce
1 bay leaf	¼ cup finely chopped parsley
2 large onions, sliced	

Wash and drain the meat. Place in a 4-quart lidded pot on top of the stove. Cover with cold water and bring to a gentle boil. Skim off the scum as it forms on the surface and keep on skimming as long as it appears, for 10–15 minutes.

When no more scum appears, add the salt, pepper, and bay leaf. Reduce heat to the merest simmer. Simmer, partially covered, until meat is tender, about 1 hour.

Transfer the meat to a slightly smaller, clean casserole or 9-X-12-inch baking dish and keep warm.

Check the seasoning in the liquid. Add salt and pepper if needed. Add the onions. Trim and core the cabbage; cut into ½-inch slices and cut the slices across at 2-inch intervals. Split the leeks lengthwise and wash thoroughly between the leaves before slicing across. Add cabbage and leeks to the liquid.

Cover and cook 10–15 minutes, or until vegetables are tender. Stir in the potatoes and cook until smooth. Check seasoning again; potatoes absorb salt. Stir in the Worcestershire sauce, and pour the vegetables and sauce over the meat.

Cover the casserole, or wrap the baking dish with foil, and heat in a 350° oven for about 10 minutes.

❀ For later serving, allow to cool, partially covered, before covering to refrigerate. To freeze, it is better to omit the vegetables until the stew is being reheated.

Serve sprinkled with parsley.   *6–8 servings*

FRUIT AND NUT KHORESHE

This Persian-style stew of lamb, dried fruit, nuts, and split peas is wonderfully different and rather exotic. The small amount of curry is just enough to flavor the stew without making it hot. The nuts remain crunchy and the dried fruit does not make it too sweet. Yogurt, stirred in, or served separately, adds a sharpness and completes the taste.

Plain rice and hot pita bread go with the stew, and spinach—in a salad or hot and buttered—is a good vegetable accompaniment. Lemon or lime sherbet would make a fresh cool dessert. Honeydew melon, or cantaloupe, with Port in the hollow would be nice if available.

Beer or an Amontillado Sherry would be good to drink with the khoreshe, or for wine—a dry white jug wine.

2 cups mixed dried fruit	1 teaspoon salt
1 cup chopped blanched almonds or walnuts	½ teaspoon freshly ground black pepper
1 pound boneless lamb shoulder, cut in 1-inch pieces	1 tablespoon curry powder
3 tablespoons cooking oil	¼ cup yellow split peas
1 large onion, coarsely grated or finely processed	2 cups hot water
	1 cup plain yogurt
	Mint sprigs (optional)

Cut dried fruit into somewhat uniform pieces. Halve and pit prunes. Cover with hot water and set aside.

Toast the nuts in a dry skillet and set aside.

Dry the meat on paper towels; it browns better if it is not wet. Heat the oil in a wide, heavy, flameproof casserole with a lid, and brown the meat on all sides. Add the onion, salt, pepper, and curry powder. Stir and cook for 1–2 minutes. Add the split peas and water. Bring to a simmer, cover and cook on low heat for 30 minutes.

Drain the fruit and add to the stew. Add the nuts. Cover and simmer for 30 minutes more, or until lamb is tender. Stir occasionally.

The khoreshe should be moist but not watery, and not dry. Cook, uncovered, for a few minutes if it is too wet, and add a small amount of water if it is too dry. Add salt if needed.

Serve with yogurt and, if possible, a sprig of mint.   *4–6 servings*

LAMB SHANKS

In this recipe the shanks are braised in the classic French way, in wine, with bay leaf, parsley, and thyme. The sauce is rich with cream and capers. The shanks can be served in many different ways, making a different kind of meal with each choice of accompaniments. Some suggestions are: mashed potatoes, asparagus, and a beet and endive salad; kasha, green beans, and a cucumber and yogurt salad; parsley potatoes, puréed broccoli, and a green salad.

The shanks do not make a meal too heavy for a substantial dessert, but fruit of the season is always good—a mixture of berries; fresh pears; peaches or plums; or a platter of assorted melon slices.

Serve with a Côtes du Rhône or a Rioja.

2 tablespoons cooking oil	½ cup finely chopped parsley
4 lamb shanks, about 1 pound each	1 bay leaf
1 small onion, finely chopped	½ cup dry red wine
2 garlic cloves, minced	1 tablespoon flour
Salt and white pepper	½ to ¾ cup heavy cream
1 teaspoon thyme	2 tablespoons drained capers

Heat the oil in a heavy, flameproof casserole or pot that has a lid. Use a pan that will take the shanks in one layer. Dry the shanks; they will brown better. When there is a slight haze over the oil, brown the shanks on all sides. Pour off any excess oil.

Add the onion and garlic. On low heat stir and turn the shanks until the onions soften slightly. Sprinkle with salt, pepper, the thyme, ¼ cup of the parsley, and tuck in the bay leaf.

Add the wine and turn the shanks to spread the seasonings evenly. Bring to a simmer, cover, and cook on low heat for 1¼ to 1½ hours, or until shanks are tender. Turn at least once during cooking, and add hot water if liquid cooks down too much.

Take out the shanks and keep warm on a platter. Tip the pot and skim off fat. Blot with paper towel to get the last drops. If there is a lot more liquid than you started with, cook it down a little, to strengthen the taste.

Make a smooth mixture of the flour and ½ cup of cream. Stir into the casserole liquid and cook until it thickens. Add more cream if you want more sauce. Taste and add salt and pepper if needed. Pour over the shanks.

❀ Stew can be prepared in advance to this point.

Garnish with the capers and remaining parsley.   *4 servings*

MINTED LAMB STEW

Shoulder lamb chops can be very meaty and are often on sale. Make this stew when you find four nice chops and want to do something interesting with them. The taste is Middle Eastern, with mint and yogurt, nuts and raisins, and rice cooked with the meat.

Hot pita bread and zucchini in some form, sautéed or raw in salad, go with the stew. Cucumber sticks, with a squeeze of lemon and a sprinkle of salt, pepper, and chopped fresh dill make a pleasant first course. For dessert, stewed dried fruit would be good in the winter, fresh fruit other times of the year.

White wine from Portugal, a Vinho Verde, or a white from Sicily would be good.

4 shoulder lamb chops, about 1½ pounds	1½ cups chicken broth
2 tablespoons butter	½ cup dry white wine
1 large onion, finely chopped	Juice of ½ lemon
2 garlic cloves, minced	1 bay leaf
1½ teaspoons salt	¾ cup rice
¼ teaspoon white pepper	⅓ cup raisins
2 teaspoons crumbled dried mint	¼ cup chopped walnuts
	½ cup plain yogurt

Pat chops dry with paper towels. Cut off large outside pieces of fat, and cut chops into 1-inch pieces, including large bones. Trim off small bones. You may need a cleaver to chop a large bone (the anatomy of shoulder chops is unpredictable).

In a heavy, lidded flameproof casserole heat the butter and put in the lamb. Stir over moderately high heat, until the lamb loses its color. Add the onion and garlic and continue cooking until onions soften. Stir in the salt, pepper, and mint.

Pour in the broth and wine, add the lemon juice and bay leaf. Bring to a simmer, cover and cook on low heat for 30 minutes. Stir in the rice, bring back to a simmer, cover and cook 20–30 minutes more on the low heat, until lamb and rice are tender.

Stir in raisins and nuts, cover and cook another 1–2 minutes.

❀ Stew can be prepared in advance to this point. When cool, cover and refrigerate or freeze.

Stir in yogurt, heat but do not boil.   *4–5 servings*

LAMB, BEANS AND SPINACH

A large pot is needed to accommodate this big hearty stew made with white beans and the sweet meat on lamb neck bones. Space is needed for the bulk of raw spinach, cooked on the stew at the end to make a handsome bright green topping. Rosemary and garlic are the main seasonings.

A first course could be celery root rémoulade or asparagus in season. For color, salad could be one of beets and onion rings, or tomatoes with fresh basil leaves, when *they* are in season.

Serve with a Côtes du Rhône, a Chianti, or a Petite Sirah.

BEANS

1 pound dried white beans, Great Northern or navy	6 cups water 2 teaspoons salt

Wash and pick over the beans. Place in a saucepan with the water and bring to a boil. Remove from the heat, cover and allow to stand for an hour. Bring to a simmer, cover and cook on low heat for ½ hour. Add the salt, cover and cook for another 15 minutes to ½ hour, or until beans are tender but not too soft. Drain and add to the stew as directed.

2 tablespoons olive oil	¼ teaspoon white pepper
4 pounds meaty lamb neck, with bones	2 cups beef broth
	1½ cups water
3 garlic cloves, chopped	10–12 ounces fresh spinach, chopped
2½ teaspoons salt	
¾ teaspoon rosemary, crumbled	Juice of 1 lemon

Heat the oil in a large, heavy saucepan or casserole and put in the lamb, which has been patted dry and checked for splinters. Stir over moderately high heat until the meat loses its color and browns in spots.

Mash the garlic with the salt until it is a paste. Add, with rosemary and pepper to the meat. Add broth and water. Bring to a boil, reduce heat and simmer, covered, for 1½ to 2 hours, or until meat is tender. Carefully stir in the beans and bring back to a simmer.

❊ Stew can be prepared in advance to this point. In fact the stew improves with standing.

Lay the spinach on top. Cover and cook for 5–10 minutes, until spinach is cooked. Sprinkle with lemon juice. *6–8 servings*

10

Pork and Sausage Stews

PORK AND RED CABBAGE

This slightly sweet-sour and spicy stew—somewhat German in style—lends itself to being the star of a variety of dinners. The starchy accompaniment can be boiled potatoes, plain and buttered, or in a creamy white sauce; or buttered noodles, with a sprinkle of poppy seeds or caraway seeds. Salad can be cooked sliced beets with red onion rings in oil and vinegar, or raw spinach with radishes—a beautiful color combination.

In place of the potatoes or noodles, serve a bean salad—kidney, black, or garbanzos, in oil and vinegar with chopped scallions. This combines the starch and salad requirements, but don't make the salad too sharp—use less vinegar than usual.

Whatever the combination, serve a good rye or other dark bread with the meal. And for a meal that is hearty but not all that heavy, a rich strudel would not be too much for dessert.

Serve with a Rhine wine or a Sylvaner from California or Alsace, or beer.

2 pounds boneless loin end pork, cut in 1-inch pieces	2 tablespoons brown sugar
1 tablespoon cooking oil	⅓ cup water
2 slices bacon, diced	⅓ cup red wine vinegar
1 teaspoon salt	⅛ teaspoon each cinnamon, cloves
¼ teaspoon pepper	¼ teaspoon cayenne
1 tart apple, peeled, cored, grated	6 cups red cabbage, coarsely shredded
1 large onion, finely chopped	

Dry pork pieces with paper towel so they won't sputter in the fat.

Put the oil and bacon into a large, heavy casserole that has a lid, and cook on low heat, stirring to separate the bits, until the bacon is golden. Add the pork, and cook on moderately high heat until the pork loses its color and has a few brown spots. Sprinkle with salt and pepper.

Add the apple and onion and cook on lower heat for about 5 minutes, until onion and apple soften. Stir in the remaining ingredients. Bring to a simmer, cover and cook on low heat for 1 to 1¼ hours, or until pork is tender. *6 servings*

SWEET AND PUNGENT PORK

Although this stew is made with large chunks of pork, rather than shreds or thin slices in a proper Chinese version, and takes more than 1 hour to cook, it has the wonderful taste of the famous Chinese dish.

Fresh ginger is essential; store-bought sweet gherkins will do, but Jim Lee's home-made pickles are better (a recipe follows).

Serve the stew with rice and soy sauce, and possibly offer the diners chopsticks. First course and dessert choices can be American, or anything you think would taste good—even French or Italian bread. A dessert which has been enjoyed with it is Gingerbread (page 173), topped with tart apple-sauce and whipped cream and sprinkled with grated lemon rind.

The sweet-sour taste fights with wine, but the battle is an interesting one. Try a sparkling Vouvray or one of the Italian sparkling wines, like Asti Spumante.

2 pounds boneless pork shoulder, or rib end, or loin end, cut in 1½-inch cubes	2 cups tomato juice
2–4 tablespoons cooking oil	⅓ cup cider vinegar
1¼ teaspoons salt	⅓ cup juice from 2 cups sweet gherkins, or from your own Chinese pickles
4 medium carrots, cut in ¾-inch diagonal slices	¼ cup granulated sugar
2 medium onions, each cut in 8 wedges	2 cups sweet gherkins, or your own pickles
1½ inches of fresh ginger, peeled and thinly sliced across the grain	2 green peppers, seeded and cut in 1-inch squares
	4 teaspoons cornstarch

Turn on oven to 325°.

Dry the meat on paper towels for browning. Heat the oil in a heavy skillet or wok, and brown the pieces of pork well on all sides, a few at a time. As they are done, transfer them to a lidded flameproof casserole, preferably enameled ironware.

Cover and place in the oven and cook for 50–60 minutes, or until the pork is almost tender. Stir in ¾ teaspoon of the salt.

While the meat is cooking, prepare the sauce, which will be combined later with the meat.

Place the carrots, onions, and ginger in a 1½- to 2-quart lidded saucepan, preferably enamelware or stainless steel. Add the tomato juice. Cover and simmer on top of the stove for 45 minutes. Add vinegar and juice from the pickles. Cook 15 minutes more or until carrots are cooked, but still firm. This seems like a long time to cook the vegetables, but cooking in tomato juice takes longer than in water. Add the sugar and the remaining ½ teaspoon salt.

At this point, the meat in the oven and the sauce and vegetables will each have cooked about 1 hour. Pour off fat from the pork, or remove it with a bulb baster. Combine meat, sauce, and vegetables in the casserole. Cover and place in the oven. Cook 20–30 minutes, or until pork is tender.

Add the pickles and green peppers and cook 10 more minutes in the oven. Remove ½ cup of the sauce, cool, and blend with the cornstarch. Add to the casserole. Cook on top of the stove until sauce thickens.   *6 servings*

JIM LEE'S CHINESE PICKLES

These pickles can be used after standing in the refrigerator for 1 week. They will keep in the refrigerator for a year.

4 carrots	3 quarts boiling water
3 bunches red radishes, or 1 bunch white radishes	2 cups sugar
1 medium head cauliflower	2 cups white vinegar
2 medium green peppers	1 teaspoon salt
2 hot chili peppers	1 cup water

Wash vegetables, peel carrots and white radishes (if used). Discard cauliflower stems. Remove seeds from peppers. Cut all vegetables into bite size.

Put all the vegetables into boiling water; turn off heat at once. Allow to stand 2 minutes. Drain off water and spread the vegetables in 1 layer to cool and dry. When vegetables are cool, pack them at random in a glass jar or plastic container.

Put the rest of the ingredients into a saucepan; bring to a boil. Remove from stove to cool. Pour this marinating liquid over the vegetables until they are completely covered. Cap the container and refrigerate. Let stand for 1 week before using.

With beautiful bright green sprouts on top, and other vegetables cooked in it, this stew is a main course in itself.

Hot consommé or some other light soup would make a good first course. Salad should have endive in some form (Belgian, you know). It could be in leaves, with watercress, or sliced across, with julienne beets, or slivered, with Boston or garden lettuce.

After the salad, a small cheese tray could have Edam or Gouda and Brie or Camembert, and dessert could be an easy one, Triple Sec Pears (recipe follows).

Since there is beer in the stew, beer would be good to drink with it. For wine, try a light red like a Beaujolais, or a white like a Riesling.

3 pounds boneless pork shoulder, loin end or rib end	1 pint beer
1 tablespoon cooking oil, more if needed	1½ cups beef broth
2 teaspoons salt	4 medium carrots, cut in ¼-inch slices
½ teaspoon freshly ground black pepper	4 medium potatoes, cut in ½-inch slices
1 teaspoon rosemary, crushed	4 medium onions, quartered
3 tablespoons flour	1 pound fresh Brussels sprouts, or 2 ten-ounce packages frozen

Turn on oven to 325°.

Trim large pieces of fat from the pork and dry it with paper towels; it won't brown if it is wet.

In a heavy skillet, brown the pork, a few pieces at a time. Even after trimming the pork may still render enough fat to do the browning. If not, add some oil. As the pieces are browned, transfer them to a heavy, lidded, flameproof casserole. Turn heat on low under the casserole.

Stir in the salt, pepper, rosemary, and flour. Stir to mix well and until no white shows.

Add the liquids and stir to dislodge any bits stuck to the bottom. Bring to a simmer, cover and place in the oven. Reduce oven temperature to 300°, or whatever temperature will just maintain the simmer. Check in 10 minutes and adjust temperature accordingly. Cook 45 minutes. Tip the casserole and skim off fat.

Add the vegetables, except the sprouts, cover the casserole and return to the oven for 30–40 minutes, or until pork and vegetables are tender.

❀ Stew can be prepared in advance to this point. When cool refrigerate or freeze.

If fresh sprouts are used, and do use them if you can, peel off any bad outer leaves, trim stems, wash thoroughly, and make a small cut in the stem end for more even cooking. Place in a saucepan with 1 cup boiling water and ¼ teaspoon salt. Cover and cook about 5 minutes, or until sprouts are just tender and still bright green. If frozen sprouts are used, cook according to package directions. In either case, do not overcook. Cover the stew with the sprouts; they are all the garnish you need. *6–8 servings*

TRIPLE SEC PEARS

6–8 ripe pears	1 teaspoon sugar per pear
1 teaspoon lemon juice per pear	½ cup sour cream
1 teaspoon Triple Sec per pear	Grated orange rind

Peel, core, and cube pears. As each pear is done, put it in a large bowl and stir with a teaspoon of lemon juice. Add Triple Sec and sugar for each pear and allow to stand for 1 hour. Stir in sour cream. Serve from a pretty bowl, or in individual dishes or parfait glasses with a grating of orange rind.

6–8 servings

HOT GREEN CHILI STEW

The spiciness of the pork stew is easily controlled by the number of jalapeño chilies used. This well-seasoned stew adds a special flavor to the beans in it. Canned beans do very well, but dried beans can be cooked so that they are not too soft. Both are given in the recipe. The juice of a lime is squeezed in at the end, giving an added piquancy.

Corn chips with Cheddar cheese and strips of red and green sweet peppers with Margaritas would be good before the stew. A simple lettuce and tomato salad with red onion rings would complement the stew, and ice cream with a few drops of Tequila on each serving would be a cool finish for the meal.

Serve with beer, or a hearty red wine like a Premiat from Rumania.

2¼ pounds boneless pork, shoulder, loin end or rib end, cut in 1½-inch pieces
1 tablespoon cooking oil
1 large onion, chopped
2 garlic cloves, minced
2 teaspoons oregano
1 teaspoon cumin
2 cups peeled tomatoes, crushed (fresh or canned)

½ to 1 cup beef broth
2 teaspoons salt
¼ teaspoon freshly ground black pepper
1–4 fresh or canned jalapeños (see note)
3 cans red kidney or pinto beans, or 2 cups dried beans
Juice of 1 lime

Trim large pieces of fat from pork. Dry pork on paper towel for browning.

Heat the oil in a large, heavy skillet. Cook the pork to render the fat in it and to brown it. Cook a few pieces at a time, and transfer them as they are browned to a heavy, lidded casserole with heat on low under it.

Add the onion and garlic to the meat and cook until onions have softened slightly. Stir in the oregano, cumin, and tomatoes. Add enough broth to barely cover the meat and onions. Add the salt and pepper and the jalapeños, bring to a simmer, cover and cook on low heat for 1 to 1¼ hours, or until pork is just tender. Skim off fat.

Carefully stir in the beans and cook another 15–20 minutes until stew is piping hot (in temperature). Squeeze lime juice over stew.

DRIED BEANS
2 cups red kidney or pinto beans
6 cups water

2 teaspoons salt

Wash and pick over beans. Place them in a saucepan with water and bring to a boil. Remove from the heat and allow to stand for 1 hour. Bring to a simmer, cover and simmer for ½ hour. Add salt, cover and cook for another 15–30 minutes, or until beans are tender but not too soft. Timing is hard to predict—keep checking. Drain and add to the stew as directed.

❀ Stew can be refrigerated for 2 or 3 days or frozen after cooling.

6–8 servings

Note: Fresh jalapeños are the very hot green chilies, about 1½ inches at the top, about 2–3 inches long, with rounded, not pointed ends. Using rubber gloves and keeping hands away from the face, trim off stem end, split down one side, and remove seeds. Chop in ½-inch pieces and add to the stew. Chop canned jalapeños as they come. Use the minimum if you are not used to that kind of hot spiciness.

PORK AND RED CHILI STEW

The stew has a wonderful taste of chili, without undue hotness. In fact, those inured to hotness in their food may find it bland, though pleasantly so. The dried ancho chilies used here are the roughly heart-shaped ones, about 3 inches across at their widest point. Soaked and puréed, with added seasonings, they make the liquid in which the pork pieces cook. It is hard to believe those crinkly black dried chilies will end up as a gorgeous red purée.

Serve with kidney or pinto beans, and rice; crusty bread or tortillas; and grated Cheddar cheese to sprinkle on top. A generous handful of watercress on the plate nestled next to the stew is a different but colorful accent.

This is one occasion when iceberg lettuce and firm, off-season tomatoes are just right. Topped with scallions or red onions, and an oil and vinegar dressing with a pinch of sugar in it, they make a nice crisp accent for the stew.

Dessert could be chocolate—chocolate cake or Chocolate Mousse, (page 205), or Chocolate Almond Mousse (page 91).

Serve beer or a dry red jug wine.

8 dried ancho chilies, about 4 ounces	3 garlic cloves, minced
2 cups water	2 tablespoons flour
2 tablespoons vegetable oil	2 teaspoons salt
2 pounds boneless rib end or loin end pork, cut in 1-inch pieces	2 teaspoons cumin
	1 teaspoon oregano
2 medium onions, coarsely chopped	2 tablespoons vinegar
	Watercress or parsley sprigs

Break stems off chilies and remove seeds. Use rubber gloves and keep hands away from face and eyes. Put chilies in a bowl with hot water to cover, and allow them to soak for 15 minutes. This cleans the outside and softens the flesh somewhat. Drain chilies and put in the blender. Add 1 cup of the water and blend briefly. Add the other cup of water gradually and keep blending until you have a smooth liquid, a little thinner than cream. Add a little more water if it is too thick. Leave in the blender while you prepare the pork.

Heat the oil in a heavy, lidded saucepan or flameproof casserole. Pat the pork pieces dry with paper towel and remove any large pieces of outside fat. When a slight haze appears over the oil, add the pork. Cook over moderately high heat until the pork loses its color and browns in spots. Stir in the onions and garlic and cook until the onions soften.

Sprinkle in the flour. Stir until it disappears. Add salt, cumin, oregano, and vinegar. Reduce heat and strain the puréed chilies through a sieve into the casserole. Stir to clear the bottom of the pan and to mix everything thoroughly. Bring to a boil, cover and simmer for 1 to 1¼ hours.

Check occasionally and stir. Add hot water in small amounts if stew gets dry or sticks.

Tip the pot and skim off fat. Check seasoning and add salt if needed.

❋ Stew can be prepared in advance to this point, and can be refrigerated or frozen after cooling.

Serve with generous batches of watercress or parsley on the side.

4–6 servings

PORK AND GREEN CHILI STEW

There are as many recipes for this Southwestern stew as there are makers, and each one defends his own. Most agree that onions and potatoes should be included, but carrots and garlic, used in this version, are not always added. Sometimes the stew is thickened with flour; this one is not.

The Spanish, Mexican, and Indian origins of New Mexican cuisine offer a great variety of food and drinks for an interesting meal: corn chips with dip (recipe follows); avocado in a purée, as a cold soup or in salad; corn, on the cob or in a soufflé; beans, puréed or vinaigrette or refried; a dessert of mangoes, guava paste, or something chocolate.

A good red wine like Cabernet Sauvignon tastes fine with this stew; so does beer.

1½ pounds boneless pork shoulder or loin end, cut in 1-inch pieces	**1 quart water**
1 large onion, chopped	**8–12 green chilies, seeded, cut in ½-inch pieces (see note)**
1 garlic clove, chopped	**4 carrots, cut in ½-inch slices**
1 teaspoon salt	**5 medium potatoes, cut in ¾-inch pieces**
1 teaspoon oregano	

Put the pork and onions into a heavy saucepan or casserole with no fat. Cook and stir over moderate heat until onion softens and pork loses its pink and almost browns. There should be some juices in the pan from the onion and from the pork.

Mash the garlic with the salt until it makes a paste and no large pieces remain. Stir into the onion and pork mixture with the oregano. Add the water gradually and bring to a boil. Reduce heat to a simmer and cook, partially covered, for 1¼ hours, or until pork is barely tender. Replace water if it cooks away.

Put in the chilies, carrots, and potatoes and sprinkle with the remaining ¾ teaspoon of salt. Cover and cook on low heat for 20 minutes, or until vegetables and pork are tender.

❀ The stew can be cooled and refrigerated or frozen when it is finished.

4–5 servings

Note: Use the chilies about 1 inch in diameter at the top, tapering to a point, about 6 inches long. It is essential to wear rubber gloves to handle the chilies and to keep hands away from the face. Cut off the stem end and split down one side. Remove seeds and cut into ½-inch pieces.

DIP FOR CORN CHIPS

1 tablespoon olive oil	1 cup tomatoes, peeled, finely
½ cup minced onion	chopped
1 clove garlic, minced	Salt and pepper to taste
½ teaspoon oregano	Tabasco to taste
½ teaspoon cumin	Juice of ½ lime

Put the oil, onion, and garlic into a small saucepan, preferably enameled. Cook and stir on low heat until onion softens, but not until it browns. Add other ingredients except the lime juice. Cook for 15 minutes, stirring occasionally. When sauce has cooled, stir in lime juice. Serve at room temperature.

about 1 cup

Pork and Sausage Stews   273

PERUVIAN PORK AND SWEET POTATOES

This interesting stew from South America has orange and lemon juice added to the liquid produced in the cooking to make a marvelous sauce. An essential ingredient, *achiote,* also called *annatto,* a spice dear to Peruvians, imparts a lovely flavor and orange color. The seeds can be found in markets that sell Mexican, Puerto Rican, and South American food. The subtle taste they give marks this as a dish from another country.

Sweet potatoes and corn add to the stew's basic orange and supply vegetables; a salad of bright greens and crisp cucumbers provide another color note.

The meal could start with corn chips and Hummus (page 241), or Seviche (page 165), and Margaritas.

Dessert could be creamed quince (Dulce de Membrillo, available at the Latin American market) and Bel Paese or Muenster cheese, or the more easily available guava jelly with cream cheese. Another choice, Avocado Dessert (recipe follows) is simplicity itself.

Beer, Sherry, or Sangría (page 111) are all good to drink with this meal.

2 pounds boneless pork loin end, cut in 1-inch pieces	2–3 tablespoons cooking oil
1 tablespoon annatto (achiote) seeds, ground in blender or with mortar and pestle	½ cup water
	Juice of 1 lemon
	½ cup orange juice
1 teaspoon cumin	2 tablespoons cornstarch
½ teaspoon freshly ground black pepper	4–6 medium sweet potatoes, boiled, peeled, cut in ½-inch slices
1½ teaspoons salt	1 eight-ounce can corn Niblets, drained, or 10-ounce package frozen corn Niblets, cooked
2 garlic cloves, chopped	
⅓ cup white or cider vinegar	

Trim large pieces of fat from the pork and put meat in a large, non-metallic bowl with the ground annatto seeds, cumin, and pepper. Mix the salt and garlic together and mash with a fork until no chunks remain. Add to the bowl and add the vinegar. Stir to mix well, cover and allow to marinate for 2–3 hours, or overnight in the refrigerator if it is more convenient. Stir occasionally.

Remove the pork from the marinade, reserving the liquid. Shake and scrape the bits of seasonings left on the pieces into the marinade, and dry the pieces on paper towel.

Heat the oil in a large heavy skillet. When a haze appears, brown the pork pieces, a few at a time, transferring them as they are done to a large, lidded saucepan or flameproof casserole. The vessel should be large enough to accommodate the sweet potatoes that go in later.

Add the reserved marinade liquid and the water. Stir and bring to a simmer. Cover and cook on low heat for 45 minutes, or until pork is tender. Skim off fat.

✻ The stew can be prepared in advance to this point.

To serve, make a smooth mixture of the lemon juice, orange juice, and cornstarch. Stir into the simmering stew and cook until stew thickens. Arrange the sweet potatoes on top. Strain the corn and add it. Cover and cook on low heat for 5–10 minutes, until the vegetables are hot.

4–6 servings

AVOCADO DESSERT

This is an easy dessert, but it should not be prepared too far ahead or it will discolor, in spite of the lime juice. Have the avocados and parfait glasses or dessert dishes well chilled.

Try to buy the very dark green, rough-skinned avocados rather than the smooth, bright green, glossy ones.

Allow 1 medium or ½ large avocado per person.

2 or 3 large, ripe avocados, peeled, seeded, and coarsely chopped
¼ or ⅓ cup fresh lime juice (2–4 limes)

6 or 8 tablespoons sugar
1 small lime cut in 4 or 6 wedges

Put the avocados, lime juice, and sugar into a blender or food processor. Blend or process until smooth. Put into chilled glasses or bowls and garnish with lime wedges.

4–6 servings

PORK AND RUTABAGA STEW

Rosemary enhances the flavor of the pork, and a little ginger gives this delightful creamy stew a touch of piquancy.

The rutabaga is cooked in it, making the stew almost a meal in itself, with just good bread and a salad. However, mashed potatoes and a green vegetable, such as broccoli, go so well with pork that a fine substantial meal can be made by adding them—thereby stretching the meal to serve more people. The first course could be a simple consommé, with a slice of lemon.

Apples in some form would make an appropriate dessert—Baked Apples (recipe follows), applesauce with ginger snaps, or even an apple strudel.

White or red wines go well with this stew—a Soave or Sauvignon Blanc, a Chianti or Zinfandel.

2¼ pounds boneless pork loin, rib end, or shoulder, cut in 1½-inch pieces	¼ teaspoon white pepper
	¾ teaspoon rosemary, crumbled
	½ teaspoon dried ginger, or 1 teaspoon grated fresh ginger
2 tablespoons cooking oil	3 cups rutabaga, cut in ¾-inch cubes
2 medium onions, chopped	
2 garlic cloves, minced	½ cup heavy cream
½ cup dry white wine	2 tablespoons flour
1 cup beef broth	¼ cup finely chopped parsley
1½ teaspoons salt	

Trim any large pieces of outside fat from the pork.

Heat the oil in a wide, heavy saucepan or casserole with a lid. Add the meat and stir on moderately high heat until the pork loses its color. Stir in the onions and garlic and continue to cook and stir until onions soften.

Pour in the wine, stirring to clear the bottom of the pan, and cook over high heat for 1–2 minutes until liquid boils down about a third.

Add the beef broth, 1 teaspoon of the salt, pepper, rosemary, and ginger. Bring to a boil, reduce heat, cover and simmer for 45 minutes.

Add the rutabaga, sprinkle with the rest of the salt. Cover and cook for another 20 minutes, or until meat is tender and the rutabaga tender but not too soft.

Add the cream gradually to the flour to make a smooth mixture. Stir into the simmering stew and cook until it thickens.

❋ For later serving, cool and refrigerate or freeze. Serve sprinkled with parsley.

4–6 servings

BAKED APPLES

One forgets how good a baked apple can be—and how easy it is to produce this not-too-sweet dessert to top off a fine dinner.

1 apple per person	**cloves or allspice**
1 tablespoon brown sugar per apple	**1 tablespoon butter per apple**
Cinnamon or nutmeg or ground	**Water**

Wash and core the apples without cutting through the bottom. Mix the sugar with your favorite spice to taste. Fill the apple cavities with the sugar and spice. Top each one with butter. Place in a baking dish with ½ inch of water in it. Bake in a 350° oven for 30–40 minutes, or until tender. Baste occasionally with juices from the pan.

Serve hot or cold or room temperature, with a piece of sharp Cheddar cheese or a dollop of whipped or sour cream. *1 apple per person*

CHOUCROUTE GARNIE

A great party dish, this big platter of sauerkraut, smoked meats, and potatoes is easily stretched with another sausage, a couple of frankfurters, more potatoes. Serve it with rye bread, good Dijon mustard, and pickles.

A large pot is needed to accommodate everything, particularly the potatoes, cooked and put in to heat through and take on flavor.

Instead of a salad and cheese course, make dessert rich and special—pecan pie, a lemon meringue pie or Caramel Custard (recipe follows)—or for something a little less rich, a spicy Baked Apple (page 277) with a dollop of whipped cream.

The choucroute is an Alsatian dish, so you might seek out an Alsatian wine, but beer is really good.

4 slices bacon, diced	2½ cups dry white wine, or 2 cups
2 medium onions, chopped	wine plus ½ cup chicken broth
2 cloves garlic, minced	(more broth if needed)
3 pounds sauerkraut, bulk or	2–3 pounds smoked pork shoulder
packaged in plastic	1 pound Polish sausage
1½ teaspoons caraway seeds	2 knackwursts
15 whole black peppercorns	6–8 medium potatoes, boiled,
12 juniper berries, or 2	peeled
tablespoons gin	

In a large, lidded flameproof casserole, slowly cook the bacon until it has rendered its fat and is golden brown. Add the onions and garlic; cook on low heat until the onions are limp but not brown. Drain sauerkraut and squeeze out liquid by hand. Add to casserole. Cook 5 minutes, stirring. Stir in caraway, peppercorns, juniper berries, and wine. Cover and simmer for ½ hour.

In a heavy skillet, starting on the side with the most fat, brown the pork all over to render some of its fat. After blotting on paper towel, put the meat down into the sauerkraut. Bring to a simmer, cover and cook for 1¼ to 1½ hours, or until meat is tender. Add a little more chicken broth if sauerkraut becomes dry during cooking.

When the meat is just tender, put in the Polish sausage and cook another 15 minutes. Add the knackwursts and the potatoes and cook another 15 minutes, or until potatoes are warmed through. Salt and pepper the potatoes as you put them in.

To serve, carve the meats, drain the sauerkraut, and serve on a large platter with the potatoes.

❊ Choucroute can be frozen, but the potatoes are a better texture if they are added when the dish is being reheated.   *6–8 servings*

CARAMEL CUSTARD

This famous dessert, called *crème renversée* in French because it is served upside down, is wonderfully light after a stew, but still satisfying. The caramel on the bottom of the mold becomes a sauce on the top when the custard is turned out. Serve chilled or at room temperature.

½ cup sugar	5 whole eggs
Juice of ½ lemon	¾ cup sugar
4 egg yolks	3¾ cups hot milk
	1 teaspoon vanilla

Turn on oven to 325°.

Put ½ cup of the sugar and the lemon juice into a skillet and heat, stirring, until sugar has melted and turned caramel colored. Pour into a 6-cup mold, tilting the mold to coat the bottom completely.

Beat the egg yolks and eggs in a mixing bowl with a wire whisk. Gradually beat in the remaining ¾ cup of sugar, and when the mixture is light and foamy, beat in the hot milk and vanilla. Pour into the caramelized mold.

Set the mold in a pan of hot water and place in the lower third of the oven. Regulate the heat during cooking so the water in the pan never simmers, to ensure a smooth custard. Cook for 1 hour, or until a knife plunged into the center comes out clean. Cool and chill.

To unmold, run a knife around the edge, put a plate upside down over the mold and reverse the two to turn out the custard.   *6 servings*

PORK AND BEANS

When beans, molasses, and salt pork are on hand, here's a really good recipe. The 8–9 hours called for in the old recipes seemed excessive so I cut it down to under 5 hours, which seems to be enough.

The beans are great to have with frankfurters or hamburgers and with a corn roast. Cole slaw goes with it and cake and ice cream seem to be the inevitable dessert.

4 cups dried white pea beans	2 teaspoons salt
3 quarts water	1 teaspoon pepper
1 medium onion	2 tablespoons dark brown sugar
¾ pound salt pork	5 teaspoons dry mustard
½ cup dark molasses	

Wash and pick over beans. Cover with the water in a large kettle or saucepan that has a lid. Bring to a boil, remove from heat and allow to stand, covered, for 1 hour.

Bring to a simmer, and cook, partially covered, until beans are just tender. This can take from 30 minutes to 1 hour, or more. Keep checking. Beans are done when the skin breaks and flutters when you blow on it. Drain beans. Set aside the cooking water. Turn on oven to 250°.

Put the onion in the center of the bean pot and pour the beans in over it. Rinse the salt pork and cut it into 4 pieces. Score the pieces across without cutting through. Tuck the pieces into the beans, leaving ¼ inch above the surface—the rind side if there is one, otherwise the fattier side.

Measure the molasses into a metal or Pyrex measuring cup and add the salt, pepper, sugar, and mustard. Pour in enough hot bean water to make a smooth mixture and pour over the beans. Heat the rest of the bean water to a rolling boil and pour enough over the beans to just cover.

Cover the pot with its lid and place in the oven. Cook for 4 hours, without stirring. Check about every ½ hour; if beans are not covered with liquid, add boiling bean water or boiling plain water to just cover them.

After 4 hours of cooking, uncover and cook for ½ to ¾ hour, or until salt pork is golden and beans have browned lightly. Liquid should be below the surface at this point. Remove from the oven and if beans are not to be served right away, cool with the lid on so beans won't dry out.

To serve, either remove the onion, now very soft, or stir it in.

10 or more servings

PORK AND LIMA BEAN STEW

Sage, savory, and ginger flavor this simple pork stew, cooked in beef broth and Sherry. Lima beans are added at the end, because they make the stew more substantial and have an affinity for the pork and its seasonings. Hubbard or acorn squash would make a good accompanying vegetable, for the color they add and for their slight sweetness, which also suits pork.

Broccoli goes with pork too; it could be served as a first course or at room temperature as a salad, with thinned mayonnaise on it (thin mayonnaise with water). Serve the stew with rye or crusty bread, and follow it with apples in some form, Baked (page 277) or in Fruit Crisp (page 283).

Serve with beer, or red or white French jug wine.

2 pounds boneless stewing pork, shoulder, loin end or rib end, cut in 1-inch pieces
2 tablespoons cooking oil
2 medium onions, chopped
2 garlic cloves, minced
¼ cup Amontillado Sherry
1¼ cups beef broth
1½ teaspoons salt
¼ teaspoon white pepper

¾ teaspoon sage
¾ teaspoon savory
1 teaspoon grated fresh ginger, or ½ teaspoon dried
2 tablespoons flour
2 cups cooked fresh baby lima beans, or 1 ten-ounce package frozen, cooked
¼ cup finely chopped parsley

Trim off large outside pieces of fat from pork and dry on paper towel. It browns better if it is not wet.

Heat the oil in a large heavy skillet, and when a light haze appears, put in the pork pieces, a few at a time, and brown lightly. Transfer as they are browned to a heavy, lidded saucepan or flameproof casserole. Add the onions and garlic to the meat in the casserole and cook over moderately high heat, stirring, for 3–5 minutes, until onions soften slightly.

Add the Sherry and bring to a boil. Add 1 cup of the broth and return to a boil. Stir in salt, pepper, sage, savory, and ginger. Reduce heat, cover and simmer for 50–60 minutes, or until pork is tender. Skim off.

❀ At this point stew can be cooled and refrigerated or frozen.

To serve: Make a smooth mixture of flour and the remaining ¼ cup of broth. Stir into simmering stew and cook for 1–2 minutes until sauce thickens. Add lima beans and cook another 2–3 minutes, until beans are just heated through. Serve sprinkled with parsley.   *4–6 servings*

BRITTANY PORK STEW

The Calvados marks this as a Brittany affair inspired by a recipe for a terrine of pork, found in an old French cookbook—pork cooked with Calvados, peppercorns, and garlic. I transformed it into a stew with some chicken broth, a little thickening, and some squash to add body. Use meaty barbecue pork, cut into 2-inch pieces, and Hubbard squash, for a tasty dish. Put in at the end, the squash cooks just for 10–12 minutes and becomes completely soft, almost like a purée. Instead of serving as a vegetable, it gives the sauce extra body and a most beautiful color.

Brown rice or noodles and a watercress salad with some grapefruit in it for a touch of piquancy go with the stew. Dessert could be Brie or Camembert cheese and apples, or a warm Fruit Crisp (recipe follows), in this case made with apples. A little Calvados with coffee would be nice.

Serve with a not-too-dry white wine, such as a Sylvaner or Gewürztraminer.

2½ pounds meaty rib end pork for barbecue, cut in 2-inch pieces	1½ cups chicken broth (fat removed)
1 tablespoon cooking oil	1 medium Hubbard squash, cut in ½-inch cubes (about 4 cups)
1 tablespoon butter	2 tablespoons flour
⅓ cup Calvados	4 scallions with green tops, cut across at ¼-inch intervals
3 garlic cloves, minced	
1 teaspoon salt	
1 teaspoon black and white peppercorns, cracked	

Pat meat dry with paper towels. It browns better if it is not wet. Trim off large pieces of outside fat.

Heat oil and butter in a large, heavy skillet. When butter stops foaming, brown the meat, a few pieces at a time. Transfer the pieces as they are browned to paper towel to drain, and then into a lidded saucepan or flameproof casserole over low heat.

Pour in Calvados. Stir and cook down to half.

Add garlic, salt, peppercorns, and 1¼ cups of the chicken broth. Bring to a boil. Reduce heat, cover and simmer for 30 minutes.

Cut the squash in half lengthwise. Remove seeds; cut across in ½-inch slices; peel and cut into ½-inch cubes. Add to the stew. Cover and cook for another 10–15 minutes, or until pork is tender and squash has disintegrated. Tip the pot and skim off fat.

❋ Stew can be prepared in advance to this point.

At serving time, make a smooth mixture of the flour and remaining ¼ cup of broth. Bring stew to a simmer and stir in flour mixture. Cook until sauce thickens.

Serve sprinkled with scallions.   *4 servings*

FRUIT CRISP

Here is one of those old favorites, as delicious now as it ever was. Easy to prepare, it can be ready to put into the oven ½ hour before dessert time and served hot, with or without whipped cream.

2 cups sliced, peeled apples or pears, or blueberries	**½ cup brown sugar**
	⅓ cup flour
⅓ stick butter	**½ teaspoon salt**

Grease a pie tin and place fruit in it.

Combine butter, sugar, flour, and salt to make a crumbly mixture. Sprinkle over the fruit.

Bake in a preheated 350° oven for 30 minutes, or until bubbly and crisp on top.   *4–6 servings*

PORTUGUESE SAUSAGE STEW

Like many simple Portuguese dishes, this starts with a lot of onions slowly cooked in oil. Chorizos (Spanish sausages) go in to heat and to color the onions red, and the dish is finished with green peas. It's as simple as that. The chorizos, which can be found in Spanish and Portuguese markets, are essential for their special taste and the paprika in them that colors the stew. Serve the stew with rice or boiled potatoes and crusty bread.

Clams or oysters on the half shell are a good first course. After the stew serve a marvelous salad of oranges, cucumbers, and scallions with Boston lettuce (recipe follows) in an oil and vinegar dressing.

Frozen Banana Dessert, processed with a fresh fruit of the season (recipe follows), is a cool, refreshing end to the meal.

Serve with a Portuguese Vinho Verde, red or white, or a California Petite Sirah.

2 tablespoons cooking oil
4 medium onions, thinly sliced
3 garlic cloves, minced
1 large bay leaf
¾ teaspoon salt
¼ teaspoon freshly ground black pepper
½ pound chorizos, cut in ⅛-inch slices
1 ten-ounce package frozen peas

Heat the oil in a large, heavy saucepan or casserole that has a lid. Put in the onions and garlic and cook on low heat, stirring constantly, until onions are transparent and golden, but not brown. Add the bay leaf, ½ teaspoon of the salt, and the pepper.

Stir in the chorizos, cover and cook on very low flame until the oil takes on red color from the sausages. Stir occasionally.

Thaw the peas enough to separate them, and add them to the stew. Sprinkle with the remaining ¼ teaspoon salt. Cover and cook for 1–2 minutes. Stir, cover and cook a few minutes more, until peas are just done.

4 servings

ORANGE, CUCUMBER, AND SCALLION SALAD

2–3 navel oranges
1 cucumber
6 small scallions

Oil and vinegar dressing
Boston lettuce
Chopped parsley

Peel oranges so that not a vestige of white is left on them. Slice in thin rounds and remove seeds. Score a well-scrubbed cucumber with a fork and slice thinly. Chop scallions, crisp green tops and all. Toss with oil and vinegar dressing. Place in a salad bowl on a bed of tender Boston lettuce. Sprinkle with parsley.

FROZEN BANANA DESSERT

2 frozen bananas
2 ripe peaches, peeled and seeded,
  or 2 ripe pears, peeled and cored

1 teaspoon honey

Frozen bananas are a good thing to have in the freezer for a fast, refreshing dessert. Peel ripe bananas and wrap each one at once in plastic, before it goes brown, and freeze it. Cut frozen bananas into 1-inch pieces and place in the food processor with the metal blade in place. Cut up peaches, and add to the banana. Add honey and process until smooth. Serve at once.

4 servings

WHITE BEAN AND SAUSAGE STEW

Hot Italian sausage flavors the beans and cabbage in this stew. Spinach, with a squeeze of lemon, tops it off. It sounds like a heavy winter dish, but it has a lightness that makes it suitable year round—possibly because there are no tomatoes in it and the cabbage is lightly cooked. Cooking time, once the beans are done, is short. The dried beans used here have to soak for 1 hour. If you are able to find a satisfactory canned white bean, with no sauce, by all means use it.

A salad of sliced tomatoes, red onions, and green peppers goes well with the stew, especially with a little lemon in the dressing, and a few black olives scattered over.

A platter of assorted melon slices, when there are a variety on the market, makes a beautiful and cool dessert.

Red or white wine goes with the stew—an Italian red, Nebbiolo, or white, Trebbiano.

1 pound dried white beans, Great Northern or navy	¾ teaspoon sage
6 cups water	1 cup beef broth
2 teaspoons salt	1 small cabbage, cored, coarsely shredded
1½ pounds hot Italian sausage	Salt and pepper
2 tablespoons olive oil	½ to ¾ pound fresh spinach, chopped
2 medium onions, chopped	Juice of ½ lemon
2 garlic cloves, minced	

Wash and pick over beans, discarding bad ones. Place in a saucepan with the water and salt, and bring to a boil. Turn off heat, cover and allow to stand for 1 hour. Bring to a simmer, cover and cook on low heat until beans are tender but not too soft. This can take from ½ hour to over 1 hour. The time is infuriatingly hard to predict; keep checking. When the beans are done, drain and set aside.

Prick the sausages and put them in a heavy skillet with a few tablespoons of water. Cook until the water cooks away and the sausages brown lightly. Remove them to a paper towel to drain.

In a large, heavy, lidded saucepan or flameproof casserole big enough to accommodate the bulky cabbage and spinach before they cook down, heat the oil and cook the onions and garlic on low heat until the onions are soft, but not brown. Stir in the sage and beef broth.

Bring to a boil and put in the cabbage, sprinkling with salt and pepper. Cover and cook for 5–10 minutes, or until cabbage is cooked but still a little crisp.

Put the sausages back in the pot, cut into 1-inch pieces or left whole, as you wish. Reduce the heat and carefully stir in the beans. Cover and cook on low heat for 10–15 minutes, to heat the beans and sausages through.

❀ Stew can be prepared ahead to this point and refrigerated or frozen after thorough cooling.

Spread the spinach on the contents of the casserole, sprinkle with salt and pepper, cover and cook for 3–5 minutes, or until spinach is a bright, dark green and just cooked.

Squeeze the lemon over the spinach, and serve piping hot.   *6 servings*

SAUSAGE AND EGGPLANT STEW

This flavorful combination of eggplant, sausage, and tomatoes is a versatile dish. Accompanied by a big bowl of piping hot rice, it is a fine buffet main course; as a sauce for spaghetti, it will serve even more than eight; with potatoes and a green vegetable, it makes a regular meat and potato dinner.

However it is served, crisp Italian bread and a salad are called for. Red onion rings, thinly sliced raw zucchini, a lot of chopped parsley, and chopped pimientos, in an oil and vinegar dressing, would make a fine salad.

Serve with an Italian Chianti, California Zinfandel, or Spanish Rioja.

1 eggplant (about 1 pound)	¼ teaspoon fennel seeds, crushed
4 tablespoons cooking oil	¼ teaspoon freshly ground black
4 tablespoons olive oil	pepper
1½ teaspoons salt	1 teaspoon dried basil, or 1
1½ pounds Italian sausage, hot or	tablespoon chopped fresh basil
sweet	2 bay leaves
3 medium onions, chopped	½ teaspoon thyme
2 garlic cloves, minced	Freshly ground Parmesan cheese
3½ cups Italian canned tomatoes	
(one-pound, twelve-ounce can),	
chopped	

Trim off the ends of the eggplant, but do not peel. Cut into ½-inch cubes.

Heat 3 tablespoons of the vegetable oil and 3 tablespoons of the olive oil in a heavy skillet. When a haze appears over the oil, put in the eggplant cubes and cook quickly, stirring, until the pieces are brown in spots. Sprinkle with ½ teaspoon of the salt. Set aside on paper towel to drain.

Prick the sausages with a fork and put into the same skillet with ¼ inch of water. Cook until water evaporates, and then until sausages are browned. Drain them well on paper towel, cut into 1½-inch pieces and place in a lidded, flameproof casserole.

Put the rest of the oil into the skillet with the onions and garlic. Cook until the onions are limp and transparent but not brown. Remove from the skillet with a slotted spoon and add to the sausage in the casserole. Add the tomatoes, fennel, pepper, basil, bay leaves, and thyme.

Bring to a boil, reduce heat, cover and simmer for 30 minutes. Skim off any excess oil on the surface. If there is just a bit here and there, stir it in.

❀ Stew can be refrigerated for 2 or 3 days, or frozen, after cooling.

Serve the Parmesan cheese separately in a small bowl.   *6–8 servings*

SAUSAGE, BLACK BEAN, AND VEGETABLE CASSEROLE

When it is fresh corn time and you want a change from a hot dogs or hamburgers menu on the patio, this is a possibility. It does not take long to cook, and does not need to be served boiling hot.

Even with all the vegetables in the casserole, a salad is not redundant: a big leafy salad, with fresh tomatoes, cucumbers, and other summer bounty from the garden. Local fruit is the obvious dessert, either fresh, in Frozen Banana Dessert (page 285) or Peach Ice Cream (page 233), made in the food processor, or for lucky owners of ice cream machines, ice cream made of the fruit of the moment.

Summer isn't the only time for this casserole. Accompanied by the vegetables and fruit on the market at the time—from asparagus in the spring to beautiful baked squash in the winter, from the first of the berries to the last of the melons—it is hearty fare in any season.

A red jug wine, Italian, Spanish, or American, would go with the casserole.

1 pound Italian sausages, hot or sweet, or both
2 tablespoons olive oil
2 medium green peppers, coarsely chopped
2 medium red onions, cut in ¼-inch rings
3 garlic cloves, minced
1 medium zucchini, cut in ¼-inch slices

2 cups tomatoes, peeled, chopped, or 1 one-pound can Italian tomatoes, undrained, chopped
1 teaspoon salt
½ teaspoon pepper
½ teaspoon fennel seeds, crushed
1 teaspoon oregano
2 one-pound cans black beans, drained

Choose a deep heavy skillet or sauté pan or a wide casserole for this, one with enough room to accommodate the vegetables before they shrink down with cooking. Prick the sausages and put them in with ½ inch of water. Cook until the water evaporates and then until the sausages brown. Set them aside on paper towel to drain. Pour off all but a film of fat from cooking the sausages and put in the olive oil. Put in the green peppers, onions, garlic, and zucchini, and stir over medium heat until vegetables are tender but not too soft. Add the tomatoes and seasonings. Bring to a simmer. Cut sausages into 1-inch pieces and stir gently, with beans, into vegetables. Taste and add salt and pepper if needed. Cook until heated through.

❀ The stew can be refrigerated and frozen after thorough cooling.

6–8 servings

MAIALE AFFOGATO

The name of this delightful Italian stew means drowned pork. It is cooked, though hardly drowned, in white wine and chicken broth, with garlic and rosemary, and richly topped with a mixture of tomatoes and green peppers.

Spaghetti with a simple garlic and butter or garlic and olive oil sauce is a fine accompaniment—and Italian bread, of course. An appetizer, depending on the season and the pocketbook, could be clams on the half shell or steamed mussels or cold asparagus in a vinaigrette.

A salad is hardly needed; serve rather a tray of Italian cheeses. Fresh fruit or a fruit tart would be a satisfying dessert with Strega and coffee.

With the stew, a white wine like Soave or Orvieto would be good, with the cheese, a light red.

3 tablespoons olive oil	1½ cups dry white wine
2 garlic cloves, crushed	1 cup chicken broth
3 pounds lean boneless pork, shoulder, loin end or rib end	3 medium green peppers, cut in 1-inch squares
2 medium carrots, minced	1 pound tomatoes, peeled, seeded, chopped, or 1 one-pound can
2 teaspoons salt	tomatoes, drained and chopped,
¼ teaspoon white pepper	liquid reserved
½ teaspoon crushed dried rosemary, or 1 tablespoon chopped fresh	Salt and pepper Sprigs of Italian parsley

Heat 2 tablespoons of the oil in a heavy, lidded flameproof casserole. Cook the garlic in the oil until it is golden but not brown, then discard it.

Trim outside pieces of fat from the pork. Wipe the pork with damp paper towel. Stir the pork into the olive oil in the casserole. Cook, stirring, for 5 minutes, not to brown, just to coat with oil and let meat lose its color.

Stir in the carrots. Sprinkle in the salt, pepper, and rosemary. Add the wine and broth, stir and bring to a simmer. Cover and cook on low heat for 1 to 1½ hours, or until pork is tender. Skim off fat and check for salt.

❀ Stew can be prepared in advance to this point.

In a skillet, heat the remaining 1 tablespoon of oil and lightly sauté the green peppers. Stir the tomatoes into the peppers, sprinkle with salt and pepper and turn onto the stew. Cover and cook 15 minutes longer. If more liquid is needed add the reserved tomato liquid.

To serve, tuck sprigs of parsley here and there.   *6–8 servings*

11

Chicken, Duck, and Rabbit Stews

INDIAN CHICKEN

Chicken pieces are marinated in a blend of subtle Indian spices and yogurt before being baked with the marinade and rice. It is served with a simple, fresh salad of thinly sliced tomatoes, green pepper rings and sweet onion rings and a dressing of lemon juice, coarse salt, and freshly ground black pepper. When tomatoes are not in season, a salad of spinach, dressed with oil, lime or lemon juice, and a lot of Poupon mustard in it is good.

Some kind of cheese pastries could make a first course or hors d'oeuvre with drinks. Spinach and Cheese Puffs for instance (page 53). To finish the meal with a flair, try melon with Port poured in its hollow, or butter pecan ice cream with Oloroso Sherry on it.

With the chicken, a white wine would go well—Pinot Grigio or Sauvignon Blanc—or beer.

2 frying chickens, 2½ pounds each, cut up
2 teaspoons salt
1½ teaspoons cumin
1 teaspoon ground ginger, or 1 tablespoon minced fresh ginger
1 teaspoon ground coriander
¼ cup strained lemon juice
½ teaspoon dried red pepper flakes

3 garlic cloves, chopped
1 cup plain yogurt
1½ cups raw rice, mixed with 1 teaspoon salt
1 four-ounce jar pimientos, or roasted peppers, coarsely chopped
½ cup finely chopped parsley

Trim any large chunks of fat from chickens and wipe with paper towels. In a large, non-metallic pot or casserole, preferably enameled ironware, with a lid, mix the salt, cumin, ginger, coriander, and lemon juice. Put in the chicken pieces, and using your hands, turn the pieces in the mixture until all are coated.

Put the red pepper flakes, garlic, and ¼ cup of the yogurt into the blender. Blend on high speed for about 30 seconds, scrape down, and blend again, adding the rest of the yogurt.

Turn the chicken again and pour in the yogurt mixture. Stir to coat the pieces. Cover and allow to stand for 2–4 hours, at room temperature.

Preheat the oven to 325°.

Arrange the chicken pieces skin side up in the casserole, cover and place in the oven. Cook for ½ hour.

Open the casserole and carefully stir in the rice with its salt. Cover and continue to cook for 30 minutes, or until chicken thighs show no pink when pricked and rice is cooked.

Fluff up the rice and chicken, and scatter pimientos or red peppers over the top. Sprinkle with parsley. *6–8 servings*

GOLDEN INDIAN CHICKEN

Turmeric gives this chicken the golden yellow of a curried dish. It has some of the seasonings that go into that magic mixture called curry, but not the extreme hotness—more red pepper flakes can be added for a hotter sauce.

Serve the chicken with rice and a cool green salad with crisp cucumbers, green pepper strips, and radishes in it. Pita bread, buttered in the pocket, cut into quarters, and heated in the oven, would offer a change from French or Italian bread.

A first course could be a bowl of assorted nuts, served with Amontillado Sherry, and dessert, stewed dried apricots with rich, buttery cookies.

A slightly sweet wine like an American Chenin Blanc could go with the chicken; iced tea or beer are always good with a curried dish.

1 three-pound chicken, cut in
　serving pieces
2 tablespoons cooking oil
⅓ cup minced shallots
2 tablespoons flour
1 teaspoon salt
1 teaspoon cumin
2 teaspoons minced fresh ginger,
　or ½ teaspoon dried
½ teaspoon ground coriander
½ teaspoon ground cardamom
1 teaspoon turmeric
⅛ teaspoon dried red pepper flakes
¼ cup strained lime juice (2 or 3
　limes), or lemon juice
½ cup chicken broth
　Pimiento-stuffed olives
¼ cup finely chopped parsley

Dry chicken pieces on paper towel, and remove any big chunks of fat. Heat the oil in a heavy skillet and brown the chicken pieces lightly, a few at a time. Transfer the browned chicken to a heavy, lidded casserole. Add the shallots and stir over low heat for 1–2 minutes.

Mix together the flour, salt, cumin, ginger, coriander, cardamon, turmeric, and red pepper flakes. Sprinkle over the chicken and shallots, continuing to stir over low heat, until mixed throughout.

Add the lime juice and broth, stirring to clear the bottom of the pan. Bring to a simmer, cover and cook on very low heat for 30–45 minutes, or until tender.

Tip the pot and skim off fat.

❀ Stew can be frozen. It might need more lime juice upon reheating. Serve sprinkled with olives and parsley.　　　　　　　　　*4 servings*

CHICKEN TARRAGON

The French always roast chicken with fresh tarragon in the cavity, giving the dish a full tarragon flavor. In this recipe, using cut-up chicken, you can see how subtly the herb can flavor a dish. Needless to say, lovers of tarragon can use more.

Clarified butter is used here—unclarified butter is apt to burn by the time two chickens have been browned. Using half butter and half oil keeps the butter from burning, but for the real taste of butter, clarifying is the answer.

The chicken is excellent with rice and quickly cooked peas and cauliflower. A crisp salad of endive and watercress or of spinach could be followed by a selection of goat cheeses served with crusty bread. Dessert could be a dacquoise or fruit tart if there is a good bakery around, or for a sharper note, fresh pineapple and cookies.

A light and flowery white wine from the Loire, such as a Pouilly-Fumé or Sancerre, or a Chenin Blanc or Grey Riesling from California would be appropriate, with perhaps a Côtes du Rhône with the cheese.

2 frying chickens, disjointed	⅓ cup finely chopped parsley
4–5 tablespoons clarified butter	1 bay leaf
¼ cup chopped shallots	2 tablespoons flour
1 teaspoon salt	½ cup dry Vermouth
4–5 grindings of pepper mill	Hot chicken broth, as needed
½ teaspoon dried tarragon	½ cup heavy cream
½ teaspoon thyme	

Dry the chicken pieces on paper towel. They won't brown if they are wet.

If possible, in order to have the chicken spread out in one layer rather than piled up, cook in a large, heavy skillet or sauté pan or a wide shallow flameproof casserole, with a lid.

Clarify ¼ pound butter (leftover can be saved for another time) by heating in a small saucepan on low heat until it foams, but not long enough to brown. Let it settle, skim off the foam, and pour the clear butter off the sediment in the bottom. Discard the sediment, it is those milky solids that make the butter burn quickly.

Heat 2 tablespoons of the butter in the pan and brown the chicken pieces on all sides. Push them to the side of the pan as they are browned; add more butter as needed.

Add the shallots and cook with the chicken until they soften. Reduce heat under the pan.

Sprinkle in the salt, pepper, tarragon, thyme, 2 tablespoons of the parsley, and tuck in the bay leaf. Stir carefully.

Sprinkle in the flour and stir until it disappears.

Add the Vermouth, scraping the pan to loosen any bits stuck to the bottom. Bring to a simmer, cover and adjust heat to maintain a simmer. Check occasionally and add hot broth if more liquid is needed. Cook for 20–25 minutes, until breasts are done. Remove breasts and keep warm. Cook the rest for 25 minutes more, or until tender. Put the breasts back to warm up, then allow the liquid to cook down to about ½ cup.

Remove chicken to a hot baking dish. Skim fat off liquid in the pan, stir in cream, bring to a boil and pour over chicken.

❈ Stew can be prepared in advance to this point, cooled, covered well with foil, and refrigerated or frozen.

Serve sprinkled with remaining parsley. *6 servings*

CHICKEN PAPRIKASH

Paprika is the Hungarian touch in this beautiful chicken stew, but try to get really good paprika in bulk, at a spice store, or in a can at a specialty food store. It comes sweet or hot—use the one you like best, or mix them.

Deviled eggs, with plenty of mustard in them, make a good first course (recipe follows); noodles, boiled potatoes, or dumplings go with the chicken; salad could be fresh spinach, and dessert—the best of all fruit salads, good any time of the year—oranges and bananas.

To drink with this, try a Cabernet Sauvignon from Hungary, Yugoslavia, or Rumania.

3 tablespoons butter
2 tablespoons cooking oil
3 medium onions, thinly sliced
2 2½-pound frying chickens, disjointed, breasts split
2 tablespoons sweet Hungarian paprika
1 teaspoon caraway seeds, crushed
1 teaspoon salt
5–6 grindings of the pepper mill
1½ cups chicken broth
½ cup dry white wine
2 tablespoons tomato paste
½ to 1 cup sour cream
2 medium green peppers, cut in ½-×-2-inch strips

In a heavy skillet, heat 2 tablespoons of the butter and the oil. Add the onions and cook on low heat until they are golden but not brown. Transfer them with a slotted spoon to a lidded flameproof casserole.

Dry the chicken pieces on paper towel; they brown better when they are not wet. In the same skillet, with more oil if needed, brown the chicken pieces on all sides. As they are browned, transfer them to the casserole.

Sprinkle in the paprika, caraway, salt, and pepper. Stir carefully to spread throughout.

Add the broth. Make a smooth mixture of the wine and tomato paste and add to the casserole. Bring to a simmer, cover and cook on low heat for 30–40 minutes, or until chicken is tender. Tip the pot and skim off fat.

❀ Stew can be prepared in advance to this point and frozen after cooling.

To serve, transfer chicken to a platter or baking dish and keep warm. Cook down the liquid in the casserole by about ⅓ to intensify the taste. Stir in ½ cup of the sour cream, taste and add more if it won't overwhelm the taste of the sauce. Pour over chicken.

Lightly sauté the green pepper in the remaining 1 tablespoon butter. Sprinkle over the chicken.

6–8 servings

DEVILED EGGS

Everybody knows how to make deviled eggs, I am sure, but here are a few tips, some of which might be new and useful.

To avoid the green around the yolk, start the eggs in cold water. Bring to a boil, turn off the heat, cover the pan and let the eggs stand for 20 minutes. Lightly crack the pointed ends and plunge the eggs into ice water and let them stay there until they are cold. This also helps them peel better. Eggs that are 1 week to 10 days old are supposed to peel more easily; I always cook a couple extra, just in case.

Don't use too much mayonnaise, and mix some Dijon mustard with it.

Instead of mayonnaise and Dijon mustard, moisten the yolks with a very small amount of cider vinegar and mix in some dry mustard.

Finely chopped parsley and scallions add a little bulk, look pretty, and add enormously to the taste.

When adding salt and pepper to taste, use freshly ground black pepper and lots of it.

MEDITERRANEAN CHICKEN

This elegant chicken with its smooth and slightly piquant sauce, with mushrooms and green olives, is adapted from a recipe developed for his Coach House restaurant in New York City by Leon Lianides. The smooth sauce is the result of straining the sauce. The sauce is wonderful unstrained too, but in that case the tomatoes and garlic should be peeled and finely chopped.

The recipe looks formidably long, but is not difficult. Read it through before deciding against it on the basis of its length.

Plain rice is probably the best accompaniment for the chicken, with crusty bread, a lettuce and watercress salad, and some goat cheese or a mild Fontina to follow. Dessert could be ice cream with a dash of Strega and a sprinkling of macaroon crumbs.

A crisp white wine like a Chardonnay or a Pouilly-Fumé complements the stew.

4 tablespoons olive oil	2 -inch piece of orange rind
½ cup finely chopped onion	1 teaspoon salt
1 cup chopped leeks, white part only	4–5 grindings of the pepper mill
	A good pinch of saffron
2 pounds (4 cups) fresh ripe tomatoes, coarsely chopped	4 leg and thigh sections of chicken, disjointed
3 garlic cloves, unpeeled	2 whole chicken breasts, split
2 small chili peppers, seeded, chopped, or ⅛ teaspoon crushed red pepper flakes	2 tablespoons butter
	½ pound small white mushrooms
2 cups chicken broth	4 tablespoons lemon juice
2 cups dry white wine	½ cup small pitted green olives
½ teaspoon each, thyme, basil, oregano, dill	Tabasco

In a large, heavy, lidded flameproof pot, preferably enameled ironware, heat 2 tablespoons of the olive oil. Slowly cook the onions and leeks, turning with a wooden spoon until they are soft, but not brown.

Add the tomatoes and garlic, cover pot, and cook on low heat 10 minutes for tomatoes to render their juice. Add chili peppers. The sauce will be strained, hence the peeling of garlic and tomatoes is unnecessary.

Gradually add the chicken broth, then the wine, and bring to a simmer. Add the thyme, basil, oregano, dill, orange peel, salt, and pepper. Simmer, uncovered, 45 minutes.

Strain the sauce into a large bowl. Allow to cool slightly and degrease; the oil forms a film that is easy to remove.

Return the sauce to the original pot; bring to a boil. Boil vigorously to reduce to one third. Taste and add salt and pepper if needed, and add the saffron.

Dry the chicken on paper towels; it won't brown well if it is wet.

In a heavy skillet, heat the remaining 2 tablespoons of oil and the butter, and brown the legs and thighs lightly. Add to the simmering sauce. Cover and cook for 15 minutes on low heat. Brown the breasts and add them. Sprinkle mushrooms with 2 tablespoons of the lemon juice, sauté them lightly in the skillet and add to the chicken. Cook for another 15–20 minutes until chicken is tender, but not overcooked. Add the olives.

❀ Stew can be prepared in advance to this point and frozen after cooling.

To serve, stir in remaining lemon juice and a few drops of Tabasco, to taste.   *6–8 servings*

COQ AU VIN ROUGE

This famous French chicken stew is flamed with Cognac, cooked in red wine and stock, and finished with mushrooms. This recipe calls for a cut-up roasting chicken and stock.

Parslied potatoes, mashed potatoes, or rice and a green vegetable go with the chicken. When there are good melons around, cubes of the fruit wrapped in paper thin prosciutto make a first course; at other times use thin slices of ham wrapped around slivers of sharp Cheddar, with a sprig of watercress. A simple salad of mixed greens could precede a tray of interesting cheeses, and dessert could be a French pastry before coffee and Cognac.

An estate-bottled Burgundy is traditional with this dish, but a regional with a town name—a Volnay or Beaune—would serve almost as well.

1 five-pound roasting chicken	½ teaspoon thyme
3 tablespoons butter	1 bay leaf
1 tablespoon cooking oil, more if needed	⅓ cup finely chopped parsley
	2 cloves garlic, minced
2 slices lean bacon, diced	2 cups dry red wine
2 tablespoons flour	Chicken stock to barely cover
¼ cup Cognac	(about 2 cups)
1 teaspoon salt	¾ pound button mushrooms, or
¼ teaspoon freshly ground black pepper	larger ones sliced

Cut the chicken into serving pieces, or have the butcher do it. Dry the pieces on paper towel; they brown better when they are not wet.

Put 2 tablespoons of butter and oil into a deep, lidded 12-inch skillet or electric frying pan. Add the bacon and cook on low heat, stirring and separating the bits, until bacon is just golden. Remove with a slotted spoon and reserve.

Brown the chicken pieces carefully, a few at a time, pushing them to the side of the pan as they are done. Use more oil if needed. Turn heat very low. Spread out the chicken in the pan. Sprinkle flour on the chicken and turn to distribute it evenly.

Warm the Cognac in a small saucepan. Hold a match over it and carefully ignite. Pour the flaming Cognac over the chicken, standing well back. Shake the skillet for a few seconds until flame subsides.

Sprinkle the chicken with salt and pepper on all sides. Add the thyme, bay leaf, 2 tablespoons of the parsley, the garlic, and the reserved bacon bits.

Spoon off any fat from the skillet. Add a little of the wine to clear the pan. Add the rest of the wine and bring to a boil, stirring. Add the stock to barely cover, and bring to a simmer. Cover and cook on very low heat 25–30 minutes. If any pieces of chicken are done, remove them, particularly the breasts. Cook another 10–15 minutes or until all the chicken is done.

Place the cooked chicken in a baking dish and keep warm. Cook the liquid in the skillet on fairly high heat for about 10 minutes to reduce it to around half. Remove bay leaf, tip pan, and skim off fat. If sauce is too thin, thicken it with flour mixed into a thin paste with cold water (1 tablespoon flour at a time). Taste and add salt and pepper if needed, and pour over chicken.

❋ Stew can be prepared in advance to this point. Cool, and cover to freeze.

To serve, lightly sauté the mushrooms in the remaining tablespoon of butter, sprinkling with salt and pepper. Scatter over the chicken and sprinkle parsley over all. *4–6 servings*

BRUNSWICK STEW

Brunswick County, Virginia, and Brunswick County, North Carolina, both lay claim to the invention of this stew. Only the most ardent devotees continue this argument. More importantly, Brunswick stew is a glorious mush of vegetables, mainly succotash, with chicken, veal, and ham.

Wonderful when first made, the stew is, some say, even better warmed up. A first course of oysters or clams on the half shell would be excellent; salad is hardly needed, but a fine dessert is called for—pecan pie, or green apple pie with Calvados in or with coffee, could do it.

To drink with the stew try cider, cold and hard, or beer.

1 ham hock (see note)	1½ pounds tomatoes, peeled,
1 three-inch piece of veal shank	seeded, chopped, or 1 one-
Giblets and neck of three- to	pound-thirteen-ounce can
four-pound chicken	tomatoes, drained, chopped
2 cups chicken broth	2 cups fresh baby lima beans, or
Water to cover	1 ten-ounce package frozen
Tops from 3 celery stalks	baby lima beans
2 teaspoons salt	2 cups corn off the cob, or 1 ten-
1 teaspoon freshly ground black	ounce package frozen Niblets
pepper	¼ teaspoon crushed red pepper
1 three to four-pound roasting	flakes
chicken, cut up	1 tablespoon Worcestershire
2 medium onions, chopped	sauce
4 medium potatoes, cut in 1-inch	¼ cup Amontillado Sherry
dice	

Pour 2 quarts of water into a 5- to 6-quart kettle and note the water level in the pot. This is the amount of stock you will need; doing this now saves measuring later. Pour out the water and start the recipe.

Wash ham hock, veal shank, chicken neck and giblets; place in the kettle. Reserve the chicken.

Add chicken broth and water to cover completely.

Bring to a boil; reduce to a simmer; skim off scum as it appears. When scum stops appearing, add the celery, salt, and pepper. Simmer for 1¼ to 1½ hours or until ham and veal are almost coming off the bones. Add water, if necessary, during cooking to keep everything covered.

Add the chicken pieces, bring back to a simmer and skim as needed.

Simmer 30–40 minutes until chicken is ready to come off the bones. Drain everything through a colander into another large pot, reserving the stock.

Pick out the hock, shank, and chicken; remove skin and bones; leave meat in large bite-size pieces. Strain the stock and skim off fat. Turn up heat and boil vigorously if necessary to reduce stock to 2 quarts (see beginning of recipe). Put all the meat in the stock.

Put in the onions, potatoes, and tomatoes. Bring to a simmer and cook 20 minutes. Add lima beans; bring to a simmer and cook 10 minutes. Add corn; cook about 5 minutes more. Stir occasionally during addition of vegetables to prevent sticking.

Stir in red pepper (use more or less, as desired), Worcestershire sauce, and Sherry. Check seasoning and add salt and pepper to taste.

Keep stirring over very low heat until stew is a glorious mush, about 5 minutes.

Turn into a clean 4-quart casserole or tureen for serving.

Stew may be prepared in advance.

❀ The stew improves with standing, and can be refrigerated for 2 or 3 days. *6–8 servings*

Note: Choose a ham hock that doesn't look too dried out and doesn't smell rancid.

PLAIN OLD CHICKEN AND DUMPLINGS

The rich chickeny taste of an older bird that cooks for a long time is achieved here by cooking a roaster in chicken stock, preferably home-made (page 31). With its vegetables and dumplings it makes a fine, old-fashioned meal, like Sunday dinner at Grandma's.

Carrying out the theme, the meal could start with olives and celery, and end with lemon meringue pie, or apple pie and ice cream.

At my Grandma's, the beverage would be tea, hot or iced, depending on the time of year. Nowadays we have wine, white or red, Chardonnay for white, and Côtes du Rhône for red.

1 four- to five-pound roasting chicken, cut in 8 pieces, with giblets	1 teaspoon salt
	½ teaspoon freshly ground black pepper
2 quarts chicken stock	5 tablespoons flour
6 medium carrots, cut in ½-inch slices	Biscuit mix
	½ to 1 cup half-and-half cream
4 medium onions, quartered	¼ cup finely chopped parsley

Place the chicken pieces in a heavy, lidded 4-quart flameproof casserole. Pour in the stock, bring to a simmer, cook for about 10 minutes, skimming off foam and fat as they appear. Cover and cook on very low heat for 30 minutes.

Add the carrots, onions, salt, and pepper. Cover and continue to simmer for 20–30 minutes, or until chicken and vegetables are tender.

❀ Stew may be prepared in advance to this point. When cool, refrigerate or freeze.

Mix the flour with about ½ cup of water to make a smooth paste. Stir into stew and cook until sauce thickens, 2–3 minutes. Check and correct seasoning—flour makes it taste less salty.

Make dumplings according to biscuit package directions, but use half-and-half instead of milk. Dumplings should be dropped on stew that is not completely covered with liquid. If there is too much liquid, remove some until dumplings are cooked, then return it. If you have a favorite dumpling recipe, use it instead of this.

Serve from the pot, sprinkled with parsley.   *6 servings*

CHICKEN CACCIATORE

The popularity of this dish may be based on its pleasant-sounding name and romantic meaning—chicken stewed the hunter's way—which give no hints about what it contains. This version has been devised on the assumption that it would be simple, and most likely have wine and tomatoes.

Serve the chicken with a Risotto (page 217), or pasta with garlic butter and Parmesan cheese. Salad could be broccoli flowerets and raw mushrooms marinated in a vinaigrette. Some soft Italian cheeses and ripe apples and pears would make a good dessert.

Chianti or Valpolicella are suggested for the wines.

¼ cup olive oil
2 frying chickens, cut up
3 medium onions, coarsely
  chopped
2 garlic cloves, minced
1 large green pepper, coarsely
  chopped
1 teaspoon salt
¼ teaspoon freshly ground black
  pepper

1 tablespoon chopped fresh basil,
  or 1 teaspoon dried
½ teaspoon oregano
1 bay leaf
½ cup dry red wine
2 cups tomatoes, peeled and
  chopped, or 1 one-pound can
  Italian tomatoes, undrained,
  chopped

Heat the olive oil in a large, deep skillet, or wide shallow, flameproof casserole, with a lid. Brown the chicken pieces on all sides, a few at a time. As the pieces are browned, remove them with tongs and set aside on a plate. Blot with paper towel.

In the oil left in the pan, cook the onions, garlic, and green pepper, on low heat, until the onions are limp and pale gold, but not brown.

Return the chicken to the pan, sprinkle in the salt, pepper, basil, oregano, and tuck in the bay leaf.

Add the wine and cook until wine has boiled down slightly. Add the tomatoes, stir to spread seasonings throughout. Bring to a boil, reduce heat, cover and simmer for 40–60 minutes, until chicken is fork tender. Tip pan and skim off fat. Check seasoning and add salt and pepper if needed.

❄ For later serving, turn into a vessel that stew can be refrigerated or frozen in. Refrigerate or freeze after cooling.   *6–8 servings*

FRICASSEE OF CHICKEN

To keep this fricassee as wonderfully light and creamy in color as possible, the chicken is not browned, but merely turned in butter. This recipe also includes a step found in some old French recipes, that of blanching the chicken by letting it stand in tepid water for 1 hour. Even the mushrooms are blanched with a little lemon juice. The seasonings—thyme, parsley, bay leaf—are classic French, and so is the finish—egg yolks, cream, and lemon juice.

Rice or parslied potatoes, and snow peas or sugar peas go with the stew. A pâté or cold shrimp for a first course and goat cheese after a watercress and endive salad would be good. Fresh fruit with a touch of liqueur could be dessert.

A good fricassee calls for a delicate wine. If it is a red you prefer, try a 4- or 5-year-old Burgundy from Beaune or Chambolle-Musigny, for a white, a 3-year-old white Graves or a California Sauvignon Blanc.

2 frying chickens, cut up	⅛ teaspoon cayenne
Juice of 1 medium lemon	Bouquet garni (½ teaspoon
5 tablespoons butter	thyme, 1 bay leaf, 3 parsley
2 stalks celery, finely chopped	sprigs)
1 medium onion, finely chopped	½ pound button mushrooms
4 tablespoons flour	½ to 1 cup heavy cream
1½ cups chicken broth	2 egg yolks
1 cup dry white wine	Parsley and pimiento
Salt and white pepper to taste	

Put the chicken pieces in a glass or porcelain bowl and cover with tepid water, and 1 teaspoon of lemon juice. Let stand 1 hour. This bleaches the chicken a little and, more importantly, gets rid of some of the blood, which would darken the stew.

Melt 4 tablespoons of the butter in a heavy, lidded 4-quart flameproof casserole. Put in the celery and onion and stir over low heat until they have softened but have not browned. Dry the chicken pieces on paper towels and add to the pan. Turn the chicken to coat with butter and vegetables, but not to brown. Cook about 5 minutes. Flesh will stiffen.

Sprinkle the flour on the chicken, 1 tablespoon at a time. Turn with a wooden spoon to distribute evenly. Cook until flour disappears.

Add the broth and wine, stirring to incorporate all the flour and clear the bottom of the pan. Add water if needed to barely cover the chicken. Add the salt and pepper to taste, and the cayenne. Tie up the bouquet garni in a little cheesecloth bag if you care about the pure creaminess of the stew, otherwise just put the herbs in and remove the bay leaf and parsley before serving. Bring to a simmer, cover and cook on very low heat for 20 minutes.

Blanch the mushrooms by cooking them in boiling water with the remaining tablespoon of butter, and 2 teaspoons of the lemon juice, for 5 minutes (if large mushrooms are used, cut in ¼-inch slices). Drain and add to the stew. The mushrooms can be prepared beforehand and set aside.

Bring stew to a simmer again, cover and cook 15–20 minutes more, or until chicken is tender.

Tip pot and skim off fat. Remove cheesecloth bag or bay leaf and parsley sprigs.

❋ Stew may be prepared in advance to this point.

Remove the chicken and mushrooms to a warm deep platter, serving dish, or clean casserole. Keep warm.

Taste the sauce and either adjust with salt and pepper or boil down to intensify the flavor and thicken slightly.

Mix the ½ cup of cream with the egg yolks, beating well. Add about 1 cup of hot sauce to the mixture, beating it in 1 tablespoon at a time. Add more cream if you want a thinner sauce.

Stir in the rest of the lemon juice. Pour over the chicken, and serve sprinkled with the parsley and chopped pimientos.   *6–8 servings*

CURRIED CHICKEN

This beautifully golden curried chicken has a puréed sauce that is smooth and thick—and it can be sieved to make it even smoother.

Like all curries, this one is served with rice and condiments. Condiments can be simply bowls of chutney and slivered almonds or a marvelous array of small bowls containing a variety of good things for diners to help themselves to (page 254). A salad of cucumbers and scallions with oil and vinegar or a yogurt dressing, flavored with salt, white pepper, and fresh dill, is fresh and cool with or after the curries.

Pineapple is a particularly good fruit after curry: A platter of unpeeled wedges and unhulled strawberries makes a handsome sight—and the fruit can be eaten with the fingers.

White wine, a Riesling or Sylvaner from Germany or California, would be good to drink with the chicken.

1 two-and-one-half to three-pound chicken, cut up	1 large tart apple, peeled, cored, cut in ½-inch dice
2 tablespoons cooking oil Salt and freshly ground black pepper	2 medium carrots, cut in thin slices
1 large onion, chopped	½ teaspoon thyme
2 garlic cloves, finely chopped	2 tablespoons tomato paste
3 tablespoons curry powder	1½ cups chicken broth
1 teaspoon grated fresh ginger, or ½ teaspoon dried	1 bay leaf
1 teaspoon brown sugar	⅓ cup half-and-half
	¼ cup finely chopped parsley

Pat chicken pieces dry with paper towel. They won't brown if they are wet.

Heat the oil in a heavy skillet, and when a light haze appears, brown the chicken, a few pieces at a time. Start with skin sides down. Sprinkle with salt and pepper as they brown.

As the chicken is browned, transfer to a wide heavy saucepan or flameproof casserole with a good lid. Turn heat on low under the casserole. Add the onion and garlic. Stir and cook for 2–3 minutes.

Add curry powder, ginger, and sugar. Stir to blend. Add apple, carrots, and thyme. Make a smooth mixture of tomato paste and chicken broth, and add, stirring, to mix all and clear the bottom of the pot. Tuck in the bay leaf.

Bring to a simmer. Cover and cook on low heat for 30–40 minutes, or until chicken is tender.

Remove chicken from the sauce, and pick out and discard bay leaf. Tip the pot and skim off fat. Purée the sauce until smooth in the blender or food processor. Put through a sieve if even more smoothness is desired. Add the half-and-half and check for salt and pepper. Combine sauce and chicken.

❈ At this point stew can be refrigerated or frozen after cooling.

Serve sprinkled with parsley.   *4 servings*

SPANISH-STYLE CHICKEN

Red wine is used in this delectable chicken dish, instead of the more customary white wine. A little hotness and olives in the sauce give a Spanish flavor. Two chickens, quartered, are used. Not only do they look attractive, but breast, thighs, legs, and wings are as easy to distinguish as on a roast, and there is plenty of each part for everybody.

Serve the chicken with rice and a salad of sliced tomatoes, green peppers, red onions, with just a squeeze of lemon, salt and pepper, a sprinkle of oregano, and a few Italian or Greek olives.

For dessert, sprinkle slices of pound cake with medium (Amontillado) or sweet (Oloroso or Cream) Sherry, and top with whipped cream.

Serve with a red wine, a Rioja, or a Côtes du Rhône.

3 tablespoons olive oil	1 teaspoon oregano
1 green pepper, chopped	Several drops of Tabasco, to
2 medium onions, finely chopped	taste
1 garlic clove, minced	2 frying chickens, quartered
1½ cups chicken broth	Salt and freshly ground black
1 eight-ounce can tomato sauce	pepper
½ cup dry red wine	½ cup small pitted green olives
1 tablespoon chopped fresh basil,	1 lemon, thinly sliced
or ½ teaspoon dried	

In a heavy, lidded flameproof pot, heat 1 tablespoon of the oil and slowly cook the green pepper, onions, and garlic until the onion is soft but not brown. Add broth, tomato sauce, wine, basil, oregano, and Tabasco. Cook, uncovered, over medium heat for 30–40 minutes, or until sauce is reduced by half. Turn down to a simmer.

In a large, heavy skillet, heat the remaining 2 tablespoons of oil and brown the chicken pieces lightly, sprinkling with salt and pepper. Do a few pieces at a time. Add the pieces, as they are browned, to the simmering sauce, skin side down, spooning sauce over them.

Cover and gently simmer for 30–45 minutes, or until chicken is tender. Turn the chicken pieces during cooking, skin side up, and baste with sauce. Test for doneness by pricking at the joints—juices should be clear, not pink. Distribute olives over chicken, cover and cook 5 minutes.

❈ Stew can be refrigerated or frozen after cooling. Garnish with olives and lemon after reheating.

Serve garnished with lemon slices placed in a row.   *6–8 servings*

LAPIN AU PRUNES

This wonderful rabbit stew has been called a little Belgian masterpiece, and with good reason. The rabbit is marinated for 24 hours in well-seasoned red wine with a lacing of vinegar, cooked in wine with dried fruits, and finished with its sautéed liver and some currant jelly. The marinade, if it is used in the cooking, supplies a gamey taste, but it can be replaced by fresh wine if you prefer.

Serve with rice or parsley potatoes and, if it is the season, endive in a salad or braised as a vegetable. Lacking endive, a salad of mixed greens with some lemon in the dressing would be good. Ice cream with a topping of grated candied ginger makes a fine dessert.

St. Émilion with fur, Médoc with feathers, say the English about clarets to serve with game. Gastronomes of Bordeaux are apt to use minor château bottlings from either district for cooking and a finer bottle, at least 10 years old, for drinking with this dish.

MARINADE

Tops of 2 celery stalks	1 teaspoon salt
2 sprigs parsley	8 whole peppercorns
½ teaspoon thyme	½ cup wine vinegar
1 bay leaf	2 tablespoons olive oil
1 clove garlic, unpeeled, smashed	1 cup dry red wine
2 medium onions, quartered	

Place all ingredients in a non-metallic bowl large enough to hold meat.

1 three- to four-pound rabbit, cut up	⅓ cup finely chopped parsley
3 tablespoons butter	1 clove garlic, minced
2 tablespoons olive oil	½ teaspoon thyme
¼ cup chopped shallots	1 teaspoon salt
3 tablespoons flour	1 cup pitted prunes
1 tablespoon wine vinegar	½ cup dried apples
3-4 cups dry red wine, including strained marinade if used	½ cup seedless raisins
	Liver of the rabbit
	2 tablespoons currant jelly

Wipe the rabbit pieces with damp paper towel. Trim the liver and reserve. Put the rabbit pieces into the marinade, cover and refrigerate for 24 hours. Stir occasionally.

Continued

Turn on oven to 325°.

Drain the rabbit and discard the marinade, unless you want to use it, in which case strain it and set aside. Dry the rabbit pieces thoroughly with paper towel.

Heat 2 tablespoons of the butter and the oil in a heavy skillet.

Brown the rabbit pieces, a few at a time, removing them to a lidded flameproof casserole as they are done. With the heat turned on low under the casserole, add the shallots and cook and stir for 2–3 minutes, until the shallots soften slightly.

Sprinkle in the flour, a little at a time, stirring and turning until flour disappears.

Add the vinegar, and gradually add the wine, including the strained marinade wine if you are using it, to barely cover, stirring to incorporate the flour and to detach any bits stuck to the bottom.

Add 2 tablespoons of the parsley, the garlic, thyme, and salt. Stir in the fruit. Bring to a simmer, cover and place in the oven. Check in 10 minutes and adjust temperature to just maintain the simmer. Cook 1 to 1½ hours or until rabbit is tender.

Tip the pot and skim off fat.

Sauté the liver briefly in remaining tablespoon of butter, then mash it, discarding any fibers that won't mash. Stir into the stew; Stir in the jelly.

❊ Stew can be refrigerated or frozen after cooling.

Serve sprinkled with the remaining parsley.   *4–6 servings*

HUNGARIAN RABBIT STEW

Plenty of onions, tomato paste, and paprika make the sauce for this delectable, good-looking rabbit stew. Green peppers added at the end give extra flavor and make a beautiful garnish.

Serve with noodles, potatoes, or rice, and bread, pumpernickel, rye, or white and crusty. Sour cream is optional, although it is always good with dishes that contain paprika. As a first course or salad serve broccoli flowerets, at room temperature, dressed with thinned mayonnaise (thin mayonnaise with water).

For dessert—offer something satisfying but not too heavy, like cookies and stewed or fresh fruit, or a light Lemon-Walnut Cake (page 83).

To drink with the stew, try a Cabernet Sauvignon from Rumania or Hungary.

1 three-pound rabbit, cut up	2 teaspoons marjoram
3 tablespoons butter	1 tablespoon flour
2 tablespoons cooking oil	6 tablespoons tomato paste
4 medium onions, chopped	1 to 1½ cups water
3 tablespoons Hungarian paprika	Grated rind of 1 lemon
2 teaspoons salt	2 medium green peppers, chopped
¼ teaspoon freshly ground black pepper	

Cut off and discard any chunks of fat from the rabbit, and dry the pieces for browning. They don't brown well if they are wet.

Heat 2 tablespoons of the butter and the oil in a heavy skillet and when a light haze appears, brown the rabbit pieces, a few at a time. Transfer the pieces as they are browned to a heavy, lidded saucepan or flame-proof casserole. Add the onions to the rabbit in the saucepan or casserole. Cook over moderate heat, stirring, until onions soften slightly. Stir in the paprika, salt, pepper, and marjoram. Sprinkle in the flour and stir it in.

Mix the tomato paste with 1 cup of the water and stir the mixture into the stew. Add enough water to cover the bottom of the pan by about ½ inch. Bring to a boil, cover and simmer for 1½ to 2 hours or until tender. Check periodically to see if water is needed. Add a little hot water if stew is sticking.

❁ Stew can be refrigerated or frozen after cooling.

To serve, sprinkle with lemon rind; lightly sauté the peppers in the remaining tablespoon of butter and scatter over the stew.   *3–4 servings*

DUCK WITH YELLOW TURNIP

Duck and yellow turnip have a surprising affinity for each other. Combined here to cook in white wine and chicken broth, they make a handsome sight—and taste very good.

Serve with potatoes—parslied or mashed—and a green vegetable, like snow peas or Purée of Broccoli (recipe follows). A salad with some fruit in it would complement the duck. Seedless green grapes cut in half, with scallions, endive, and Boston lettuce, is a happy combination.

Orange Rice Dessert (page 317) goes well with this duck recipe.

White or red wine goes with the dish—a Chardonnay for white, and a Côtes du Rhône for red.

<table>
<tr><td>1 two-pound yellow turnip (rutabaga)</td><td>1 teaspoon thyme</td></tr>
<tr><td></td><td>½ cup finely chopped parsley</td></tr>
<tr><td>1 four-pound duckling, cut in serving pieces</td><td>1 small bay leaf</td></tr>
<tr><td></td><td>½ cup dry white wine</td></tr>
<tr><td>2 tablespoons cooking oil</td><td>2½ cups chicken broth</td></tr>
<tr><td>½ cup finely chopped shallots</td><td>1 tablespoon flour</td></tr>
<tr><td>1 teaspoon salt</td><td>¼ cup milk</td></tr>
<tr><td>¼ teaspoon white pepper</td><td></td></tr>
</table>

Peel and cut turnip into ¾-inch cubes. Put the cubes into cold, well-salted water. Bring to a boil and boil for just 5 minutes. Drain and set aside. This is to get a little salt into the turnip before cooking with the duck.

Remove any large obvious pieces of fat from the duck pieces and prick the skin here and there. Dry the pieces with paper towel for easier browning.

In a large, heavy skillet heat the oil until a haze appears. Put in the duck, a few pieces at a time, and brown them well, particularly the skin sides, to render their fat. As they are browned, transfer them to paper towel to drain. This process can take 20 minutes or longer. There will be a lot of fat in the pan from the skin. Keep it hot until all duck is browned.

Blot the duck pieces and place them in a heavy lidded pot or casserole that will accommodate the duck and turnip to be added later. Add the shallots and stir over medium heat until shallots soften. Sprinkle in the salt, pepper, thyme, and ¼ cup of the parsley. Tuck in the bay leaf.

Add the wine and cook for 2 minutes. Add 2 cups of the chicken broth, reserving the rest. Bring to a boil, reduce heat, cover and simmer for

1 to 1½ hours, or until duck is barely tender. Add the parboiled turnip. Baste with a bulb baster to flavor the turnip with pan juices. Cover and cook another ½ hour, or until duck and turnip are tender.

With a slotted spoon, transfer the duck and turnip to a warm serving or baking dish, with the duck in the middle. Keep warm while the sauce is finished. Skim off fat from the surface of the liquid in the cooking vessel. Reduce by boiling if there is more than 1 cup of liquid. If there is less, add the remaining chicken broth. Make a smooth mixture of flour and milk. Stir into the sauce and cook for 1–2 minutes, until sauce thickens. Pour over the duck, and serve sprinkled with the remaining parsley.

❈ This dish does not lend itself to freezing, but it can be prepared earlier in the day and reheated at serving time. Reheat, loosely covered with foil, in a preheated 325° oven for 15–35 minutes, depending on how cool it has become. *4 servings*

PURÉE OF BROCCOLI

Broccoli, when puréed with a little sour cream, is a beautiful pale green. It is easy to make in the food processor, but do not over-process—there should be some texture left.

1 large bunch broccoli (2 pounds or slightly over)	**¼ cup sour cream**
3 tablespoons butter	**Salt and freshly ground black pepper**

Wash broccoli, trim off ends of stalks, and leaves. Separate tops into uniform size flowerets. Pare stems and cut into ¼-inch slices. Cook in rapidly boiling salted water for about 5 minutes, until the broccoli is just tender and bright green.

Drain and place half in the food processor with 1 tablespoon of the butter and 2 tablespoons of the sour cream. Using the metal blade, process until no large pieces remain, but there is still some texture. Add salt and pepper to taste. Do the same with the rest of the broccoli.

The purée can be served at room temperature. To heat, place the remaining tablespoon of butter in a lidded saucepan and add the purée. Cook for 5 minutes, stirring occasionally. *4–6 servings*

DUCK AND RED CABBAGE

Dark purple and slightly sweet, this classic combination may be a happy surprise for those who have not encountered it before. The cabbage cooks for ½ hour before the well-browned duck pieces are added, and then they cook together for 1 hour more. The cabbage in this dish is not crisp but well done, tender, and juicy, a pleasant foil for the duck.

Serve with boiled or mashed potatoes, and dark bread. Another vegetable is hardly needed, but a cool salad to follow of sliced tomatoes, red onion rings, and thin rounds of green peppers, with an oil and vinegar dressing, is good.

In keeping with the Dutch flavor, a first course might be Edam or Gouda cheese with those thin crisp rye crackers and apple slices. A delightful dessert for this is Orange Rice (recipe follows).

Serve with beer or a Riesling Kabinett or Sauvignon Blanc—white wines with a little sweetness.

1 four- to four-and-one-half-pound duckling, cut in serving pieces	1 teaspoon salt
1 two-pound red cabbage	¼ teaspoon freshly ground pepper
2 tablespoons butter	⅛ teaspoon ground cloves
2 medium onions, chopped	⅛ teaspoon cayenne
2 tart apples, peeled, cored, sliced	2 tablespoons cooking oil
2 tablespoons brown sugar	Salt and pepper
½ cup dry red wine	½ cup finely chopped parsley
¼ cup cider vinegar	

Discard large chunks of fat from the duck and dry the pieces on paper towel; they brown better if dry. Set aside.

Trim off the end of the cabbage, remove any bad outside leaves. Cut in 4 wedges and remove cores. Cut across in ¾-inch slices.

Melt the butter in a large, heavy pot or kettle or flameproof casserole equipped with a lid. Add the onions and apples. Cook slowly until onions are limp and transparent. Add the sugar and continue cooking until apples are soft and glazed.

Add wine, vinegar, salt, pepper, cloves, and cayenne. Stir in the cabbage, mixing everything well. Bring to a simmer. Cover and cook on low heat for 30 minutes.

Heat the oil in a large, heavy skillet until a light haze appears. Brown the duck pieces well, particularly the skin, to render its fat. Sprinkle liberally with salt and pepper as you go. The oil is just to get the browning started; there will be plenty later. Keep it hot until all the duck is browned. Put the pieces on paper towel to drain as they are browned. This browning can take 20 minutes or longer.

Press the duck pieces down into the cabbage. Return to a simmer. Cover and cook on low heat for 1 to 1½ hours, or until duck is tender.

With a slotted spoon, transfer the duck and cabbage to a warm serving dish, leaving the juices in the pan. With tongs, turn up the duck pieces to expose the skin. Cover loosely with foil. Skim off fat from the liquid, and cook down until liquid is almost syrupy. Pour over the duck and cabbage.

❀ Stew can be prepared in advance to this point. Do not freeze. Cooled, loosely covered, and then well covered, it can be refrigerated for 1–2 days.

Cover loosely with foil. Place in the upper third of a preheated 350° oven for 20–40 minutes, depending on how cool the food has become. When it is warmed through, remove the foil and turn on the broiler. Broil for 2–3 minutes just to crisp the skin slightly.

Serve sprinkled with parsley. The parsley is important to brighten up the beautiful, but dark dish.   *4 servings*

ORANGE RICE DESSERT

The Florida orange people have developed this delightfully fresh orange dessert, easy to make and lighter than you might think for a rice dish.

2½ cups water	¾ cup long-grain rice (do not use
2 cups orange juice	converted rice)
½ cup sugar	2 oranges

In a large lidded saucepan combine water, orange juice, and sugar; bring to a boil. Stir in rice and cover. Cook on low heat 40–45 minutes, until almost all liquid is absorbed. Stir occasionally to avoid sticking. Remove from heat and cool to room temperature. Turn into a serving dish. Chill or serve at room temperature. Before serving, peel the oranges, leaving no white, and with a sharp knife, cut out the sections from between the membranes and place on the rice.   *6–8 servings*

12

Vegetable Stews

RATATOUILLE I

Ratatouille enthusiasts divide into two camps, some preferring a dry version, others a wet one. Here is a wet version; a dry one follows. Both are excellent. Try the dry one with a stew, the moist one with a roast.

You need big pots for this redolent Mediterranean delight of eggplant and zucchini, green pepper and tomatoes, onion and garlic and herbs. Although it is not a main course, it could be used as a sauce for pasta, with salad, Italian bread and fresh fruit to round out the meal. It is hard to make just a little, since the best blend of flavors comes from making a lot. Fortunately, it keeps for a week in the refrigerator. Ratatouille is marvelous with roasts and grilled meats, particularly lamb, and delicious as a cold first course with crusty bread.

Eggplants should be shiny, firm, unspotted, flat rather than dimpled on the bottom, and long rather than squat, if possible.

6 tablespoons olive oil, more as needed
2 large yellow onions, coarsely chopped
2 medium green peppers, coarsely chopped
2 cloves garlic, minced
1 medium eggplant
2 medium zucchini
4 cups tomatoes, peeled, crushed, or 1 two-pound can tomatoes, crushed

1½ teaspoons salt
¼ teaspoon freshly ground black pepper
1 teaspoon oregano
1 tablespoon chopped fresh basil, or 1 teaspoon dried
1 bay leaf
¾ cup finely chopped parsley
¼ teaspoon crushed red pepper flakes (optional)

In a large heavy, lidded skillet or flameproof casserole, preferably enameled ironware, heat half the olive oil and put in the onions, green peppers, and garlic. Cook until they are tender but not brown. Turn off the heat while the other vegetables are being prepared.

Wash the eggplant, cut off the stem, cut into 1-inch cubes. Peeling is not necessary.

Wash and lightly scrape the zucchini, cut off ends and cut into ½-inch slices.

In another skillet, heat the rest of the oil. On high heat, quickly sauté the eggplant and zucchini, a few pieces at a time, about 1 minute on each side. More oil may be needed for this. As each batch is done, transfer it to the vessel with the onions, peppers, and garlic. Add the tomatoes to the rest of the vegetables.

Stir in the salt, pepper, oregano, basil, and bay leaf. Stir in ½ cup of parsley and the red pepper flakes, if used. Bring to a simmer. Cover and cook on very low heat for 45–60 minutes, or until eggplant and zucchini are tender but not too soft.

Check and correct seasonings, adding more salt, pepper, herbs, or red pepper flakes in small quantities to taste.

❋ Stew can be prepared in advance to this point.

Serve sprinkled with the rest of the parsley.

The ratatouille can be served hot, cold, or room temperature.

8–10 servings

Note: The eggplant and zucchini can be cooked with no preliminary cooking in oil, for those who worry about using all that oil. The dish will not have the rich Mediterranean taste and seasonings may have to be strengthened to compensate.

RATATOUILLE II

This dry, or drier, version of ratatouille is particularly delicious served cold. It is a refreshing first course when eaten by itself or spread on bread or served with slices of Polish or other garlic sausage. Hot, it is a good accompaniment for a pork roast or chops, for a simply cooked chicken dish, for veal. It is excellent for a buffet—as relish, vegetable, or salad—hot or cold.

Small eggplants, called for in this recipe, should weigh less than 1 pound each. Large eggplants, if that is all you can find, will have more moisture. To extract it, place the slices in a bowl, or on a platter, sprinkle them with salt, and allow them to stand for 30–60 minutes. Drain, wash, and dry each piece. Cut into pieces to match the zucchini slices.

2 or 3 small eggplants	2 tablespoons tomato paste
3 or 4 small zucchini	1 teaspoon salt
6 tablespoons olive oil, more as needed	¼ teaspoon freshly ground black pepper
2 large onions, sliced	1 teaspoon oregano
2 medium green peppers, sliced	1 tablespoon chopped fresh basil, or 1 teaspoon dried basil
3 cloves garlic, minced	1 bay leaf, crumbled
4 cups tomatoes, peeled, seeded, chopped, or 2 one-pound cans tomatoes, drained	¾ cup finely chopped parsley
	Salt and pepper

Wash the eggplants, remove ends, and cut in ½-inch slices. If slices are very unequal in size, cut the larger ones in half. Peeling is not necessary. Wash and lightly scrape the zucchini, remove ends and cut in ½-inch slices.

In heavy skillet, heat half the oil and quickly sauté the eggplant and zucchini slices, 1 minute on each side, removing them as they are done to a bowl or plate. In the same skillet, heat the rest of the oil (or add more if the other is used up), and slowly cook the onions, peppers, and garlic until they are tender but not brown. Add the tomatoes mixed with the tomato paste.

Stir in the salt, pepper, oregano, basil, bay leaf, and ½ cup of the parsley.

Turn on oven to 325°.

Put ⅓ of the tomato mixture into the bottom of a heavy, lidded casserole. Next add a layer of ½ the eggplant and zucchini. Sprinkle lightly with salt and pepper. Put half of the remaining tomato mixture on top, then the rest of the eggplant and zucchini. Sprinkle lightly with salt and pepper and finish with the last of the tomato mixture.

Cover and place in the oven for 45–60 minutes, or until vegetables are tender. Check occasionally. Tip pot and baste with the juices. If it appears too moist, leave cover off for a while.

❋ Stew can be prepared in advance to this point.

Serve sprinkled with ¼ cup finely chopped parsley.   *8–10 servings*

CALABACITAS

A few additions turn this popular side dish of vegetables into a meatless main course. Made of zucchini, onions and corn mostly, with green chilies, it is probably Mexican in origin and is found wherever the combination of corn and squash is enjoyed. An unexpected addition, which works very well, is cottage cheese; then the whole dish is topped with sharp Cheddar cheese and buttery crumbs and crisped under the broiler.

A salad to go with the Calabacitas might contain fruit—orange or grapefruit sections for instance, with Boston lettuce and scallions. Crusty bread goes with it. Corn chips and strips of red and green peppers make good nibbles to start the meal, and chocolate cake wouldn't be too much for dessert.

Serve with beer, or a red or white jug wine.

2 tablespoons cooking oil, more if needed	chilies (not jalapeño), chopped
1 medium onion, chopped	Salt and pepper
1 garlic clove, minced	8 ounces creamed cottage cheese
3 medium zucchini (about 1½ pounds) coarsely chopped	4 ounces sharp Cheddar cheese, coarsely grated
4 green chili peppers (see note) or 1 four-ounce can peeled green	½ cup soda cracker crumbs
	2 tablespoons melted butter

Heat the oil in a wide, shallow casserole that can be used on top of the stove and in the oven and brought to the table. Put in the onion and garlic, stir and cook for a few seconds and add the zucchini and the chilies. Cook until onions have softened and zucchini is brown in spots and tender but not overdone and soft. Add salt and freshly ground pepper to taste.

Stir in the cottage cheese, sprinkle with the Cheddar cheese. Mix the cracker crumbs with the melted butter, and scatter over the cheese. Put under the broiler to lightly brown on top.   *4 servings*

Note: The chilies are about 1 inch in diameter at the top, tapering to a point, about 6 inches long. It is essential to wear rubber gloves to handle the chilies and to keep hands away from the face. Cut off the stem end and split down one side. Remove seeds and cut into ½-inch pieces.

CAPONATA

This Sicilian dish is related to the French ratatouille (on page 318). Although this version has no zucchini or green pepper as is often found in it, it does have the obligatory eggplant and the characteristic sweet-sour taste.

A magical eggplant mélange, *la caponata* is a versatile concoction, served cold or at room temperature. It can be a first course alone or part of an antipasto with bread; instead of salad or vegetables with some stews and broiled meats; for a buffet, as a sort of relish, and with slices of cold roasts, chicken, or ham.

¼ cup olive oil, or more
2 medium eggplants, unpeeled, cut in 1-inch cubes
2 medium onions, finely chopped
1 large garlic clove, minced
2 stalks celery, chopped
Salt and freshly ground black pepper
2 cups peeled tomatoes, chopped, or 1 one-pound can tomatoes, undrained, chopped

½ teaspoon dried basil, or 1 tablespoon chopped fresh basil
½ teaspoon oregano
4 flat anchovies, chopped
10 black olives, pitted, chopped
2 tablespoons pine nuts or chopped walnuts
2 tablespoons capers, drained
¼ cup vinegar
1 tablespoon sugar

Heat the olive oil, 2 tablespoons at a time, in a heavy skillet and quickly sauté the eggplant in batches until lightly browned in spots. Use more oil if necessary. As the pieces are browned, transfer them to a flameproof casserole.

In the skillet, heat more oil and cook the onions, garlic, and celery until the onions are soft but not brown. Sprinkle with salt and pepper. Add the tomatoes, basil, and oregano and cook for 15 minutes. Transfer to the casserole. Stir in the anchovies, olives, nuts, and capers.

In a small saucepan, heat the vinegar and melt the sugar in it. Stir into the casserole. Cook, stirring, for 15–20 minutes. Caponata should be thick but not dry. Add a little water if it is too dry, and cook a little more if it is wet.

Taste the mixture and adjust to your liking with salt, pepper, sugar and vinegar.

Serve chilled or at room temperature.   *6–8 servings as a course*

EGGPLANT AND BULGUR

This completely meatless dish is surprisingly satisfying, due to the meaty quality of eggplant and the delightfully chewy quality of the bulgur—and the good flavor. The final green topping is important too, and among all the suggestions, there will be one that you can have fresh, certainly parsley.

With this dish serve one of those fabulous salads, with sprouts and tofu, once hard to come by but now widely available. The accompanying bread could be an assortment, including some pita bread.

Homemade applesauce with cake or cookies would make a wholesome dessert.

For those who wish to include meat, this can be a side dish. It would be good with sausages, roast chicken, cold meats, or even another stew.

Beer or a dry white jug wine would be good to drink with the stew.

2 medium eggplants, about 1 pound each	1 one-pound twelve-ounce can tomatoes, drained, juice reserved
2 tablespoons butter	¼ cup slivered almonds
2 tablespoons olive oil	Freshly ground black pepper
1 medium onion, chopped	½ cup fresh chopped basil, chives,
2 garlic cloves, minced	scallions, or parsley or a
1 cup bulgur	mixture
½ teaspoon oregano	1 cup yogurt
½ teaspoon salt	Juice of ½ lemon

Slice ends off eggplants, cut into ¾-inch slices, then into cubes. Drop the cubes into boiling salted water and cook for 2 minutes. Drain thoroughly.

In a heavy, lidded saucepan or flameproof casserole, heat the butter and oil, and put in the onions and garlic. Stir and cook over low heat until the onions are transparent, but not brown.

Mix the dry bulgur with the oregano and salt and add to the pot. Stir to coat the grains, add the eggplant cubes and stir.

Add half the liquid from the tomatoes, bring to a simmer, cover and cook 5 minutes. Stir in the rest of the tomato liquid. Cover and simmer another 10 minutes, or until most of the liquid has been absorbed. Stir occasionally.

Add the almonds and a few grindings of the pepper mill. Add the tomatoes, broken up by hand. Cover and simmer 15–20 minutes more, or until bulgur is cooked but still bitey, liquid has been absorbed, and tomatoes are heated. Taste and add salt and pepper if needed. If bulgur gets too dry, add a small amount of water.

Serve sprinkled with chopped fresh basil or any of the alternatives or a mixture. Offer yogurt in a small bowl, and sprinkle lemon juice over the stew.

This may be served hot or at room temperature. *6 servings*

VEGETABLE STEW WITH FENNEL SEED

This flavorful pot of vegetables, with the interesting, slightly licorice taste of fennel seeds, can be a meal in itself, with good crusty bread, a leafy salad, and a couple of strong cheeses—a Canadian Cheddar and a Provolone for instance. Apples and pears go well with the cheese, and a big bowl of nuts in their shells provides some entertaining busy-ness over coffee, as well as a nourishing finish to a meatless dinner.

Served with Italian sausages or ham steaks, this makes a hearty vegetable accompaniment, even eliminating the need for a salad, unless it is tomato time, in which case a platter of them would be very good. When it is fresh corn time the meal, whether it is meatless or not, could begin with a feast of corn on the cob.

The taste of the stew can be subtly varied by using oregano instead of thyme in the seasoning, and yellow turnip (3 cups, cut in ½-inch dice), instead of carrots as one of the vegetables. Serve with beer or a dry white jug wine.

1½ teaspoons fennel seeds, crushed
1 teaspoon thyme
1½ teaspoons salt
¼ teaspoon freshly ground black pepper
¼ cup olive oil
2 medium onions, thinly sliced
4 medium carrots, cut in ¼-inch slices on the diagonal

5–6 medium potatoes, cut in ¾-inch slices
4 small zucchini, cut in 1-inch pieces
2 medium green peppers, cut in ½-inch strips
1 to 1½ cups beef broth, or vegetable stock

Mix together the fennel, thyme, salt, and pepper.

Heat 2 tablespoons of the olive oil in a casserole large enough to hold all the vegetables and equipped with a lid. Add the onions and cook on low heat for 2–3 minutes, until onions are soft but not brown.

Stir in the carrots and sprinkle with some of the seasoning mixture. Layer the rest of the vegetables, ending with green peppers, sprinkling each layer with seasoning. Dribble the rest of the olive oil over the top.

Pour the broth down the side of the casserole to a depth of about 1 inch. Bring to a boil, reduce heat, cover, and simmer for 15–20 minutes, or until vegetables are just tender. Test by inserting a fork with 2 long prongs, or a long skewer.

6 servings

CURRIED VEGETABLES

Snowy white cauliflower is covered with a golden curry sauce made of vegetables and served surrounded by rice. This dish makes a wonderful accompaniment to a roasted chicken, or sautéed chicken breasts.

With or without the chicken, a salad is called for. The fruit in the curry—dried apricots and raisins—do not make the dish sweet, so a salad of orange or grapefruit sections, with Boston lettuce and scallions in an oil and vinegar dressing, would be a good choice. Another is diced apples or pears, sprinkled with lemon juice to prevent browning, diced Swiss cheese, sliced cucumbers, and chopped walnuts on lettuce with an oil and vinegar dressing. This might be a time for one of the fruit vinegars.

Dessert is hardly needed if the salad is fruity, just good bread, French or Italian, or thin and dark.

Serve with beer, Soave, or iced tea.

3 tablespoons butter	⅓ cup raisins
1 small onion, finely chopped	2 cups chicken or vegetable broth
2 garlic cloves, minced	4 medium carrots, cut in ¼-inch
3 celery stalks, chopped	slices
¼ teaspoon salt	1 small cauliflower
1 tablespoon flour	1½ cups raw rice, cooked
2 tablespoons curry powder	Juice of ½ lime
¼ cup chopped dried apricots	

Heat the butter in a heavy saucepan and add the onion, garlic, and celery. Cook and stir until onions are golden but not brown. Sprinkle with salt.

Stir in the flour and curry powder. Add the apricots and raisins. Pour in the broth, a little at a time, clearing the bottom of the pan and making a smooth mixture. Cook at a simmer, uncovered, for about 10 minutes. Add the carrots, cover and simmer for 15–20 minutes, until carrots are just tender.

The cauliflower is to be cooked separately. Cut it into flowerets, uniform in size. Cook in well-salted boiling water for 4–5 minutes, until they are just tender but not soft. They are done almost as soon as the water comes back to a boil.

Drain the cauliflower and place in a serving dish with rice at each end, or around the edges. Pour the curried sauce over the cauliflower, and sprinkle with the lime juice.

3–4 servings

Index